WORLD PEACE

ALEX J. BELLAMY

WORLD PEACE

(AND HOW WE CAN ACHIEVE IT)

OXFORD
UNIVERSITY PRESS

OXFORD

UNIVERSITY PRESS

Great Clarendon Street, Oxford, OX2 6DP,
United Kingdom

Oxford University Press is a department of the University of Oxford.
It furthers the University's objective of excellence in research, scholarship,
and education by publishing worldwide. Oxford is a registered trade mark of
Oxford University Press in the UK and in certain other countries

Published in the United States of America by Oxford University Press
198 Madison Avenue, New York, NY 10016, United States of America

British Library Cataloguing in Publication Data
Data available

Library of Congress Control Number: 2019936313

ISBN 978–0–19–883352–9

Printed and bound in Great Britain by
Clays Ltd, Elcograf S.p.A.

For Isaac

PREFACE

It isn't enough to talk about peace. One must believe in it. And it isn't enough to believe in it. One must work at it.

—Eleanor Roosevelt, *Voice of America broadcast*, November 11, 1951

For as long as humans have fought wars, we have been beguiled and frustrated by the prospect of world peace. Like alchemists, we have searched in vain to unlock the secrets of peace. We have dreamed up extraordinary ways of cracking the code. In Ozgur Mumcu's 2016 novel, *The Peace Machine*, the protagonist Calal Bey becomes embroiled in a shadowy plot at the turn of the twentieth century to build a machine that employs electromagnetism to manipulate human souls and turn all of humanity peaceful. The enigmatic Sahir, apparently the plan's mastermind, tells Calal that electromagnetism 'is perhaps the most democratic force in the world. It exists everywhere in every single moment. It has the power to influence every single person's soul'. But there's a problem. The conspirators can't generate enough electrical energy to give all humanity the peace treatment. So Sahir tells Calal and his allies that they must first free peoples from despotic and authoritarian rule. Only when people have liberty will the democracy of electromagnetism bring world peace, he tells them. Not until the adventure's climax, where our protagonists find themselves at the palace gates disguised as circus performers during a coup in Belgrade, does anyone mention the obvious problem: to achieve world peace, they must eradicate free will. Yet even when Sahir points this out, our heroes barely think twice about switching on the peace machine. Sahir tries to stop them. The machine doesn't work. It doesn't bring peace; it sends people mad by stripping away their freedom. The only way we can have world peace, Sahir tells Calal, is if people decide that they want it. For that they must be free to make up their own minds.

Mumcu wasn't the first to dream up a peace machine. In Bob Shaw's *Ground Zero Man*, first published in the 1970s and then republished in 2011 with the title *The Peace Machine*, the technology had a quite different orientation. An unlikely hero, Lucas Hutchman, designs a device that can explode all the world's nuclear warheads simultaneously. He writes to world leaders threatening to detonate the global nuclear arsenal unless they put an end to war. They refuse. With the world's intelligence agencies on his heels, Hutchman gradually descends into a paranoia-driven madness.

Peace machines aren't confined to the literary world. In 2018, school pupils visiting MOD, a 'future-focused' museum in Adelaide, Australia, were invited to design their own peace machine. Drones, the museum suggested, were a technology of war that could be converted into a peace machine. Pupils were invited to create others. Meanwhile, researchers at the University of Helsinki claimed that they were getting close to perfecting a peace machine: a machine learning tool to analyse speech that would help people build common meaning and avoid misunderstandings. Used this way, artificial intelligence could help us resolve our disputes peacefully. There is even a blues rock album called *Peace Machine*. Performed by Phillip Sayce, the musical peace machine seems no more promising than Calal's electromagnetism. The album opens inauspiciously with 'One Foot in the Grave', and includes songs called 'Sweet Misery' and 'Blood on Your Hands'. Perhaps Australia's young inventors will fare better, but I doubt it.

For in truth there is no machine that can deliver peace. No equation to unravel. No hidden secret to uncover. It may be this realization that makes us so sceptical about the very possibility of peace, so cynical about attempts to think about what world peace might look like and how it might be achieved. In his book on *War and Conflict in Africa*, Paul D. Williams suggested that understanding war was much like understanding cooking. Wars have different ingredients that are 'cooked' in different ways to produce different effects. Peace is the same. I think we know what most of the ingredients are. I think we are getting better at understanding the recipes that give us the most satisfying results—though there is still some way to go. But we remain unsure about whether we want to buy the ingredients and dedicate time to cooking. Other things seem more important, interesting, or alluring. Sometimes violence appears to offer quicker and easier ways of getting what we want. Sometimes violence in other parts of the world seems less important than the seemingly pressing issues right under our noses. As Sahir reminds us, 'people have to decide whether they want peace or not'.

For more than a decade, I have dedicated my professional life to supporting the implementation of an international principle called the 'responsibility to protect'. 'R2P', as it has become known, demands the protection of populations from the very worst of abuses—genocide and other atrocity crimes.

I came to realize that as important as this work is, we cannot hope for lasting and permanent change without a deeper transformation in how we organize things—a transformation towards greater peacefulness. I also came to realize that we were not moving in the right direction; that unless things changed, the world my son would inherit would be one possibly even more violent than the one I had grown up in.

Last year, I took a train from London to Brussels. The trainline goes right through the battlegrounds of the First World War, where so many lives were lost. I crossed international borders once ferociously disputed without anyone even checking my passport. Looking out on the fields of Flanders, I was struck by what can be achieved when we put our hearts and minds to the cause of peace. But as my mind turned to Brexit, I was reminded that such achievements are always temporary, always contested. Peace is something for which every generation will have to struggle.

The urgent moral imperative to find solutions to the problem of war lay behind the endowment of the first academic Chair of International Relations, at what was then the University of Wales in Aberystwyth. It was for the express purpose of improving our understanding of war so that it might be prevented that David Davies endowed the Woodrow Wilson Chair in Aberystwyth in 1919. I had the privilege of spending three formative years there in the late 1990s studying for my doctoral degree. The first Professor appointed to the Woodrow Wilson Chair was Alfred Zimmern. Zimmern believed in the moral imperative of peace and in its possibility. So often nowadays unfairly cast as a naïve utopian, Zimmern was anything but. He understood that peace would have to be organized; that it would be achieved only if governments committed themselves to it. He was also painfully aware in the 1930s that most of the world's most powerful governments were working against peace. Concerned by growing international discord, in 1934 Zimmern published 'Organize the Peace World!', an essay that challenged governments to build a better peace. It was a powerful essay that levelled strong moral arguments about why peace matters and why governments should care about it with practical points about how that might be done. 'War must be so effectively prevented as to eliminate it from the calamities to be reckoned with in the modern world', he wrote. 'That is to say, not only must war itself disappear, but the fear of war, and all that fear carries with it, must be eliminated also'.[1] To do that, he argued, governments must be prepared to prioritize the common good, establish a collective system for the maintenance of peace, be clear in their purpose of preventing war and wholehearted in their support for collective measures, reflect their commitment to peace through domestic policies that promote the welfare of their peoples (Zimmern coined the term 'welfare state'), and foster bonds of international cooperation in peacetime (Zimmern lobbied for the establishment of UNESCO and served as its first Secretary-General).

Both the moral urgency that Zimmern expressed in 1934 and the approach to peace he set out remain relevant today. So, I have taken a step back from the details of atrocity prevention policies to set out some thoughts about the larger questions of world peace. This book is the result. In the pages that follow, I will try to persuade you that world peace is possible and to encourage you to think about it more carefully, debate it more keenly, and pursue it more actively. We need to recover both the moral imperative for peace and the sober approach to its organization that Zimmern—and many other figures that we will meet in the following pages—embodied.

In setting out this case, I have been guided by G.K. Chesterton's quip that 'if something is worth doing, it is worth doing badly'. Striving for world peace, I think, is worth doing. I don't pretend to have all the answers, or to be comprehensive, hence the 'doing it badly'. What follows is simply my best effort to untangle some very difficult problems. Nor do I pretend to know what the destination—if there is one—looks like. What I hope, though, is that this book will encourage conversations and arguments about the possibility of world peace and how we might achieve it.

This book was conceived at the home of my friend and colleague, Roland Bleiker, in Thalwil, Switzerland. The inspiration for it came from Roland's excellent and diverse collection of books about peace, war, art, and other things—and for that and much else, I am very grateful to Roland. Most of it was written in Brisbane, Australia, but the final chapter, outlining an agenda for world peace, was drafted in the Bodleian Library, Oxford. I am grateful to the Department of Politics and International Relations at Oxford for granting me a visiting fellowship in 2017–18 that allowed me the time and space to write about pathways to world peace. Aspects of the argument have been presented at the Australian National University, the University of Oxford (more than once), St Andrews University, and Uppsala University. I'm grateful to all those who organized and attended these sessions. I am especially grateful to all in the OxPeace network at Oxford, as well as to Tony Lang, Richard Caplan, Hugo Slim, Annette Idler, Jonathan Leader Maynard, Lisa Hultman, and Peter Wallensteen. The late Nicholas Rengger warmly and generously engaged with the arguments I am offering here. The book is much improved and the arguments better refined as a result, though I doubt he would have been wholly convinced by them. As ever, I owe a debt of gratitude to my dear friend Paul D. Williams, whose influence can be seen on every page. His understanding of how wars are caused guides my own, as well as my thinking about how peace is caused.

Particular gratitude is owed to a heroic few who not only helped and engaged with me on the arguments and ideas throughout the lifespan of this book, but who also read and commented on the whole manuscript. I learned so much from this hardy and inspiring group and the book is so much richer as a result of their engagement, though it still does not do their insights justice. My deepest gratitude goes to Rev. Liz Carmichael, John Gledhill, Peter Freeman, Luke Glanville, and Stephen Mcloughlin.

It is always a great pleasure to write for Oxford University Press, and as so many times in the past I am grateful to my editor, Dominic Byatt, for his advice, support, and fortitude, and to Olivia Wells for all her help and support.

My greatest debt, as ever, is to my long-suffering but ever-supportive family, and especially my wife, Sara Davies. A remarkable scholar, Sara has read multiple drafts of this book and engaged with the arguments from their earliest conception. I have learned a great deal as a result. She was always steadfast in her encouragement to write on the crazy topic of world peace. But she is so much more than that. I simply could not be, without Sara. This book is dedicated to our son, Isaac, in the hope that his generation does a better job than mine at building peace. In fact, whenever I'm with Isaac, I am filled with hope for the future and a strong belief that they will indeed succeed where we have so often failed.

BRISBANE
November 2018

Publisher's acknowledgements

We are grateful to the following rights holders for permission to use quotations as epigraphs:

Chapter 2: Alva Myrdal, Nobel lecture. Copyright © 1982, The Nobel Foundation.

Chapter 3: World excl. US & Canada: Friedrich Hayek, *The Fatal Conceit*, p. 12. © 1990, Routledge. US & Canada: Friedrich Hayek, *The Fatal Conceit*, University of Chicago Press © 1988, The Collected Works of F. A. Hayek.

CONTENTS

CHAPTER I

THE ELUSIVE QUEST

Perpetual peace…is no empty idea but a task that, gradually solved, comes steadily closer to its goal.

—Immanuel Kant, *Perpetual Peace*, 1795

The quest for world peace has excited, and eluded, political leaders, philosophers, religious elders, activists, and artists for millennia. For as long as there has been war, there have been those who have schemed and campaigned for its elimination. Yet today we rarely reflect on what world peace might look like; much less on how it might be achieved.[1] This needs to change.

Renowned British military historian John Keegan concluded his *History of Warfare* with a hopeful salute to peace. 'There are grounds for believing', he wrote, 'that at last, after five thousand years of recorded warmaking, cultural and material changes may be working to inhibit man's proclivity to take up arms'. 'War', he continued, 'may well be ceasing to commend itself to human beings as a desirable or productive, let alone rational, means of reconciling their discontents'.[2] This book is an enquiry into that tantalizing proposition: that world peace is possible.

World peace was once an important subject of debate and discussion. Some of our most prominent leaders, activists, philosophers, economists, psychologists, and even mathematicians and physicists turned their attention to the question of peace at some time in their careers. Yet nowadays, it has been largely consigned to the realm of intellectual history, commonly treated as intellectual fantasy. Undaunted, I will argue that world peace is possible. I will also suggest some ways in which our world might be nudged towards greater peacefulness. My hope is that by doing so I can help restore world peace to its rightful place at the forefront of our intellectual and political endeavours. I want to persuade you that world peace is a serious question that merits attention, research, thought, debate, activism, and action.

The challenges are immense. Our daily newsfeeds are consumed by war and violence. That is why most of us believe that war is a permanent and common feature of human life. But the long arc of history bears out Keegan's claim that war is actually going out of fashion. Just a few years ago, at the turn of this century, the tally of global war reached its lowest recorded ebb.[3] Still today, amidst all the chaos and devastation of war in the Middle East, sub-Saharan Africa, and elsewhere, many regions enjoy a degree of peacefulness not experienced in generations—if at all. War in East Asia is at its lowest point in recorded history and has been for nearly three decades.[4] For all the talk of new geostrategic competition in that region, there has still been no interstate war there since the late 1970s. And the number of civil wars is lower than at any point since decolonization. War is all but extinct in the Americas, the Caribbean, and Western Europe. It is now uncommon in Eastern Europe, Southern Africa, and increasingly so in coastal West Africa—though peace is more recent here and easily reversible. However we count, and whatever explanations and implications we read into it, the simple fact is that humans lucky enough to be alive in the first decades of the twenty-first century are less likely to die as a result of wars, genocide, or other mass atrocities than their parents and grandparents were in the twentieth century. What is more, despite all the horrors that visited the twentieth century, our immediate forebears were less likely to die violent deaths than their forebears.[5]

It is true, though, that since around 2010 war has staged something of a revival, mainly due to conflicts in the Middle East, North Africa, and the Horn of Africa (the war in Ukraine adds to the global tally). After declining some 72 per cent during the 1990s, the number of major civil wars grew from four to eleven between 2011 and 2016. In 2014 and 2015, the global cumulative number of battle-related deaths reached levels not seen since the end of the Cold War. Conflicts described by the statisticians of war as 'minor' civil wars (consuming fewer than twenty-five battle-related deaths each year) also increased, by 2016 reaching levels not seen since the mid-1990s.[6] These increases were mainly caused by new armed conflicts in the Middle East, in particular in Syria but also in Iraq and Yemen, and by the rise of Islamist non-state armed groups such as Islamic State, al-Qaeda and its affiliates, Boko Haram, and al-Shabaab.[7] The frequency and scale of atrocity crimes—violence targeted not at soldiers but at ordinary civilians—have also increased. Since 2011, civilian populations in the Central African Republic (CAR), Democratic Republic of Congo (DRC), Myanmar, Iraq, Libya, South Sudan, Sudan, Syria, and Yemen have been subjected to mass violence, whether by their own government or by non-state armed groups. As a result, global trends showed an increase in 'one-sided' violence against civilians, beginning in 2013.[8]

This increased incidence of war has fed our sense of crisis. Foreign affairs experts in the West are today preoccupied by what they see as the decline of the 'liberal' or 'rules-based' international order established in 1945.[9] In the global battle of ideas, what Martin Ceadel described as 'warism' appears to be in the ascendancy.[10] The forces that give rise to war—authoritarianism, nationalism, racism, populism, and protectionism—are on the march across much of the world as Russia, China, and Iran look to challenge the existing order and bend it to their will.[11] The ascendancy of Donald Trump with his 'America first' slogans and disdain for shared morals, laws, or institutions further fuels these worries. Soon after stepping down as a Special Adviser to the United Nations Secretary-General, Jennifer Welsh wrote eloquently of the 'return of history' to world politics, as barbarism (warfare unregulated by international humanitarian law), mass migration, a renewed Cold War, and increasing inequality challenged the 'liberal order' from within.[12] Having come so close to world peace—and having accomplished relative peace in so much of the world—we appear to be in danger of letting it slip out of reach.

This comes as no surprise to most people. We tend to believe that war is eternal and the very idea of world peace hopelessly naïve and utopian. In 2009, US President Barack Obama used his Nobel Lecture to paint a picture of a world at war in which our only hope was to mitigate—not terminate—organized violence. 'War, in one form or other, appeared with the first man', he told his audience at the Oslo City Hall. 'At the dawn of history, its morality was not questioned; it was simply a fact, like drought or disease—the manner in which tribes and then civilizations sought power and settled their differences'.[13] In other words, war is innate and ancient; peace a more modern human invention. We should not be sanguine about the human potential for peace. 'World peace', such as it is, sits squarely within the domain of dreamers and beauty pageants, not of serious thinkers and certainly not of the architects of world order.

Obama's fatalism well reflects contemporary attitudes towards world peace. Today, we tend to see the world as Maurice Davie did in 1929 when he wrote that 'War…is universal. It has affected every part of the earth's surface where man has come into contact or collision'.[14] 'All civilizations', Keegan reminds us, 'owe their origins to the warrior'.[15] Our entire human past, Steven Pinker argues in his best-selling account of the historical decline of violence, 'is a shockingly violent one', a past plagued by incessant raiding, feuding, and violence.[16] 'Not one major power, empire or culture decided not to go into the war business and not one so far has gone out of it', opines British philosopher of war Christopher Coker.[17]

The idea that we humans are inherently violent, selfish, and warlike is deeply ingrained in Western cultural and religious traditions. It is an article of faith that we are aggressive, flawed, and sinful; our souls in need of a redemptive deity and our bodies of regulation by strong rulers. The book of Genesis records that 'the inclination of man's heart is evil from childhood'. In his famous 1910 essay on the 'Moral Equivalent of War', American philosopher William James, himself a pacifist, expressed the point in equally blunt fashion. 'The earlier men were hunting men, and to hunt a neighbouring tribe, kill the males, loot the village and possess the females, was the most profitable, as well as the most exciting, way of living. Thus were the more martial tribes selected, and in chiefs and peoples a pure pugnacity and love of glory came to mingle with the more fundamental appetite for plunder...Modern man inherits all the innate pugnacity and all the love of glory of his ancestors'.[18] War, in other words, is a part of the human condition. The very notion of peace is at best a recent and temporary invention.[19] It is peace, not war, that is the anomaly requiring special explanation.[20]

Little wonder, then, that only a very few of us today believe that world peace is actually possible. Indeed, the very mention of the term 'world peace' raises incredulity. Not even pacifists believe in it nowadays.[21] It is not difficult to understand why. The grim persistence of war and the abysses of violence that characterized the twentieth century bequeathed a legacy of deep-seated scepticism towards peace. It is a scepticism reinforced by the way that war and peace are fed to us.

News channels and websites, the way most of us now access information about the world, feed us a steady stream of stories about human avarice, aggression, insecurity, and conflict whilst tending to downplay the everyday stories of cooperation, altruism, and innovation that have helped improve the overall human condition on virtually every measurable front over the past century. War itself is fed to us and sustained in a way that peace is not. It is warmakers (typically, but not exclusively the successful ones), not peacemakers, who are honoured by national monuments. Even 'glorious defeats' tend to receive more accolades than the individuals and groups that stopped, prevented, or opposed wars. History too favours war over peace. We know far more about the disputes that ended in violence than we do about those resolved peacefully. More than 50,000 books have been written about the US Civil War alone; yet there are fewer than three dozen recent treatises on world peace. More than one writer has succumbed to the view that war is simply more exciting than peace.[22]

Scepticism about world peace is a problem because it helps sustain war as a self-fulfilling prophecy. War can become an end in itself. *Si vis pacem, para bellum*—if you want peace, prepare for war—wrote the Roman author Flavius Vegetius in his treatise on 'military matters'. But as the theory of the 'security dilemma' teaches us, by preparing for war, we create fear in the minds of our neighbours who are driven, in turn, to prepare for their own defence by arming themselves. These preparations make us feel less secure, creating a vicious cycle of insecurity that can lead to violence. It is precisely because we expect war that we retain a readiness to fight it. That readiness to fight implants radical uncertainty about our intentions in the minds of others. This makes war a permanent possibility. In fact, the uncertainty itself can cause it. In 1914, the great powers sleepwalked into a war none of them really wanted because of their deep mistrust of each other's intentions.[23] Sometimes, our assumptions about the world define its reality.

Why, in the face of all this, do I think nonetheless that world peace is possible? Partly because peace is more common than we tend to think, partly because our contemporary sense of crisis is born out of a Pollyannaish vision of recent history and an overly despondent sense of our present, and partly—and most fundamentally—because of our immense capacity for adaptation and change. Let's look at each of these in turn.

First, *peace is more common than we think*. There is immense variety in the human story and numerous examples of societies and civilizations enjoying long periods of peace. Overall, most societies have enjoyed peace most of the time. Those that have not have typically not prospered.

For example, the Ancient Minoan civilization (*c.* 3,000–1,500 BC) on the Greek island of Crete was amongst the most advanced and wealthy of its time, yet as far as historians and archaeologists can tell, they were not much—if at all—in the business of war. The Minoans had fortifications and weapons, yet there is no evidence that they fought battles or annexed territories. Their neighbours, the Egyptians and Hittites, kept extensive records, especially of wars. Neither documented any armed struggle involving the Minoans.[24] And the Minoans were not alone in this.

At around the same time (3,300–1,700 BC), in the Indus Valley in present-day India, the sophisticated Harappan civilization flourished.[25] Here, evidence of peacefulness is even stronger than it is for the Minoans. Harappan settlements had no effective fortifications; they did not have weapons suitable for warfare; there is no artwork depicting war; there are no other sources of evidence or fossil remains pointing to war. Here, then, are two major and advanced civilizations. They had towns, large buildings, and roadways. They had flushing toilets and writing. They endured for more than a millennium and, from what we can tell, they never got into the business of war.

Neither the Minoans nor the Harappans owed their existence to warriors. Neither did the ancient Phoenicians—the civilization credited with creating the alphabet. With the exception of the colony established at Carthage, theirs was a society based on commerce, not war, a society that thrived for more than a thousand years in arguably the most violent and war-ridden region on the planet at that time. And they did so without ever having an armed force.

Powerful rulers have sometimes put themselves out of the war business. Ashoka ruled the Mauryan empire from 268–232 BCE, an empire that stretched from the Hindu Kush in Afghanistan to what is today Bangladesh in the east. Around 260 BCE, he led an invasion of Kalinga (modern-day Odisha). Ashoka prevailed after a bloody struggle that reputedly left some 200,000 people dead. Aghast at the devastation and suffering he had wrought, the King confessed that 'the slaughter, death, and deportation is extremely grievous'.[26] Influenced by his Buddhist beliefs, Ashoka feared that the glories of battle and conquest would be short-lived but the damage inflicted on the soul permanent. If armies had to fight, they must do so humanely, with humility and the least amount of violence necessary. He instituted a reign based on fairness, compassion, and human dignity; an order based on moral force and legitimacy rather than military power.[27]

Whatever we might think of the world today, it is nearly forty years since the last interstate war in East Asia. Western Europe, a cauldron of violence for much of the past few centuries, has been at peace since 1945. South America has been free of major war since the end of the Cold War. In many parts of the world, war between states has been almost eliminated and wars within them greatly reduced.

Sustained peace has been achieved in many different times and places. Most people alive today have never experienced war and do not live in fear of it. If we stop to think of the generations of people past, in different parts of the world from ancient Crete to Gaul, the Indus Valley and Egypt, who experienced lives of peace, the possibility of its attainment starts to feel vaguely possible.

Second, *we are not living through the decline of a peaceful liberal rules-based order*. Stepping outside the bubble of largely American commentators on world order and security affairs that lament the decline of the 'peaceful liberal rules-based order' established in 1945, it becomes painfully obvious that the 1945 order was neither 'liberal' (human rights did not triumph over state sovereignty or great power interest) nor 'rules-based' (the superpowers routinely violated international law, including the law prohibiting armed aggression, when it suited them to do so). And in Asia, Africa, and Latin America, it was not very 'orderly' either. International wars, proxy wars, civil wars, and violent coups—many of them aided and abetted by the great powers—were much more common in the heyday of the so-called 'rules-based order' than they are today. To give just one example, during the 1970s, the 'rules-based order' saw the US government drop more tonnage of munitions on Laos and Cambodia than it had employed during the entirety of the Second World War to support campaigns that not only violated international law but were waged without the knowledge and approval of the legislative arms of the US government itself. In Cambodia, US bombing caused utter devastation, helping propel the radical Khmer Rouge to power. More than a quarter of Cambodia's entire population died as a result of US bombing and Khmer Rouge genocide. The 'rules-based order' stood for nothing. Amidst all this violence, over the course of close to a decade, the United Nations Security Council—the body primarily responsible for managing that order—did not meet even once to discuss the carnage in Cambodia.

When asked what he thought of Western civilization, Gandhi reputedly replied, 'I think it is a good idea'. The same might be said of the 'rules-based international order'. We kid ourselves if we think there was a halcyon time of benign superpower hegemony where action was guided by shared rules, a time that is now passing. The truth is that a rules-based order remains 'a good idea'.

To understand the contemporary situation, we need to see it in its proper context. That partly involves getting a proper sense of just how bad things used to be and being careful not to romanticize the recent past as being more peaceful than it actually was. But it also means having a clear and accurate picture of where things are today. We need to put our sense of crisis into perspective. There are already signs that the escalatory trends that emerged after 2010 have begun to taper off. In 2017 and 2018, the overall number of wars started to decline again. So too did the number of fatalities caused by wars and by 'one-sided' violence, despite the wave of genocidal violence unleashed against the Rohingya people by Myanmar's army in 2017. In broader perspective, for all our gloominess and sense of crisis, civilian killing in 2017 was about where it was in 2005—a time when we had little sense of a global crisis. It also bears remembering that wars in the 2010s peaked at a level far lower—in terms of incidence and lethality—than their average for the whole of the 1990s.

Third, and most importantly, *war and peace are human creations*. That is, neither war nor peace is embedded in our nature. Humanity has the potential for both.

Wars happen, ultimately, because some people choose to make them happen. Those that make war can also call a halt.[28] War and peace can be made and unmade. If that is true, then world peace is possible. And if peace is possible in some times and places, there is no inherent reason why peace cannot be possible in all places. Peace is neither inevitable nor irreversible, of course—it is something that every generation must strive for because the forces that make war possible are likely to remain with us.[29] Yet greater peacefulness in human relations is revealed through our striving for it.

What may at first appear to be a ridiculously utopian claim—that world peace is possible—is actually deeply pragmatic. It rests on the fact that human nature is not immutable, that what it means to be human changes in response to social and environmental pressures. Whole societies—including our deepest social structures—change and evolve over time. In 1922, the American philosopher John Dewey, a leader in what is now called the 'pragmatic' school, wrote in *Human Nature and Conduct* that it was 'foolish' to believe that change was impossible. Dewey argued that history and experience furnish us with all manner of examples of how humanity has changed over time; how practices once considered normal have been eradicated and other practices, once thought impossible or contrary to nature, have become normal. Human nature is adaptable. Societies are not doomed to follow a predestined path characterized by repeated war. How we live and adjust and evolve will be determined by our own choices and actions. Future societies can *choose* to work towards world peace or they can opt for permanent war. They can also opt for everything in between these two poles.[30]

It is our capacity for adaptation and change that makes world peace possible. There are grounds for optimism because the motives, rationales, and impulses that gave rise to war and sustained it—the quest for survival, enrichment, solidarity, and glory—are now better satisfied by peaceful means. War—both international and civil—is not inevitable. It is an increasingly anachronistic practice, more likely to impoverish and harm than satisfy. What we experience today are largely the 'remnants'—to borrow John Mueller's apt phrase—of an historical institution that has exhausted its potential.[31]

Central to my argument, then, is the view that whatever goods that may once have been achieved by war are now better achieved through peace, and that this is a calculus we can tilt ever more decisively in peace's favour. For example, legitimate and effective modern states have largely resolved questions of how to protect individuals and communities from armed conflict. Thanks to international law, institutions such as the United Nations (UN), and diplomatic practice, modern states have also come close to perfecting the art of managing relations between them without the need for war. Some states have even managed to build regional 'security communities' in which war is not only unlikely, but unthinkable. Territorial conquest and empire-building—among the principal causes of war throughout our history—have been outlawed. States may physically invade and occupy land belonging to other states, as Russia did in Crimea in 2014, but they can no longer translate these gains into lawful, and thus profitable, ownership. Conquest pays well only if others recognize it as legitimate. If they do not, conquest can become very expensive very quickly. The greatest leaps in human progress have come in peacetime, not war. Martin Van Creveld shows that even those scientific developments most associated with war—computer technology and anaesthesia, for example—would have undoubtedly emerged in peacetime too and within a very similar span of time.[32]

Changes in the nature of war are making it costlier to fight and less rewarding to win. As the Americans discovered in Iraq and Vietnam, and the Soviets found in Afghanistan, societies bound together by nationalism or other common identities and ideologies tend to resist foreign occupation to the last. To the extent that decisive battles ever delivered decisive political results, their capacity to do so today is much diminished.[33] Nowadays, as NATO's more recent experience in Afghanistan shows only too well, even overwhelming military force tends to produce marginal and uncertain outcomes. War delivers quick and decisive victories *only* if opponents accept the results of battle. If they do not—as is increasingly the case today—war tends to devolve into bitter, protracted, bloody, and invariably expensive insurgency struggles whose outcomes are anything but decisive and durable. Meanwhile, increasing economic interdependence propelled by globalization has helped societies achieve unprecedented levels of wealth through peaceful trade, whilst the opportunity costs to wealth imposed by war have soared. Multinational production chains mean that national wealth is literally dependent on others in a way never seen before. Because of this, where war once held out the allure of enrichment, now it is more appropriately dubbed economic 'development in reverse': a burden that inhibits wealth, wellbeing, and security.[34]

But although social and political change is making war more costly and peace more profitable, schemes for world peace continue to flounder, their advocates denounced as naïve utopians. Unfortunately, sceptics have plenty of material to work with. All too often, even peace enthusiasts successful in other fields of endeavour have failed to carry their acumen with them into the pursuit of peace. For example, the pioneer of the modern production line, Henry Ford, singularly failed to translate his remarkable business skills to the field of peace. Horrified at the terrible losses inflicted by the First World War and feeling increasingly sympathetic towards the anti-war movement, in 1915 Ford chartered a ship and filled it with peace activists charged with sailing to Europe and negotiating peace. The effort achieved nothing but a large bill and public ridicule. Before the 'Peace Ship' even reached Europe, the activists on board began bickering amongst themselves and divided into factions. There was an outbreak of influenza that killed one passenger and affected Ford himself. Ford slipped off the ship quietly at the first opportunity and the whole effort fell into ignominy. 'In uselessness and absurdity, it will stand without equal', commented the Democrat's 1904 Presidential Candidate, Alton Parker.[35]

All too often, peace activists have tended to think of war as stemming from some misplaced pathology born of psychological illness, capriciousness, or ignorance. For example, in a letter written to Sigmund Freud in 1932, Albert Einstein commented that war was driven by 'strong psychological factors' including the selfish will to power of a 'small clique' and a 'collective psychosis' that propelled people to sacrifice their own lives with 'wild enthusiasm'.[36] But there are, and always have been, rational reasons why people choose to fight.

That is why a new approach is needed. If world peace is to be taken seriously, it has to be pursued and debated in a hard-headed, practical, and realistic fashion. Nearly fifty years before President Obama's Nobel Prize speech, another US President, John F. Kennedy, painted a very different picture of humanity's past, and its potential. Just five months before his assassination in 1963, Kennedy delivered a commencement address at the American University in Washington, DC. His subject was peace—'peace for all time'—a goal he described as 'the natural, rational end' of 'rational men'. Kennedy urged his audience to reject the 'dangerous, defeatist belief' that 'war is inevitable, that mankind is doomed, that we are gripped by forces we cannot control'. In sharp contrast to Obama's fatalism, Kennedy stressed the possibility of peace: '[o]ur problems are manmade, therefore, they can be solved by man', he told his audience.[37]

Not only is peace a 'natural end', it is also our preferred end. One of the towering figures of the eighteenth-century Enlightenment movement, Charles-Louis de Secondat, Baron de La Brède et de Montesquieu, wrote that in the state of nature—a theoretically hypothesized time before organized societies—'peace' was the first law. This may have been taking things too far, but there is evidence that we humans have a 'universal preference for peace'.[38] Time and again anthropologists have recorded that no matter how violent a society actually is, its members express a preference for peace. The Jalemo warriors of New Guinea, people who regularly boast about their violent exploits and enjoy occasional cannibalism, repeatedly commented that war was a 'bad thing' that depleted food stocks, increased debt, and inhibited travel and trade. The 'fierce head-hunting Jivaro' of South America saw war as a curse. More recent studies attest that most soldiers prefer not to kill their enemies and that societies value peace more highly than war.[39] True, some people find excitement and fulfil-ment in war, but these are a minority.[40] Throughout history, people have gone to extraordinary lengths to avoid participating in war. Military history is replete with complaints about the average soldier's lack of what British Generals in the First World War called 'aggressive spirit'.[41] More than a million soldiers already lay dead when, in Christmas 1914, soldiers on both sides of that war left their trenches to celebrate with their erstwhile enemies (see Chapter 7).

To stand any chance as a political enterprise, the starting point for world peace has to be blunt recognition of why wars happen. There are, I think, three principal underlying reasons deeply embedded in the way we organize our-selves. We must face them head on.

First is the basic fact that *humans are divided into different political groups that have contending interests and values.* We have always been social animals. Cooperation within groups is absolutely necessary for the survival and flourishing of indi-viduals. The more coherent a group is—the more closely tied together it is—the more effectively its members cooperate. The more a group cooperates, the better off its individual members become. Groups—be they political, social, ethnic, or religious; co-located with a state, spread across several, or a minority in somebody else's state—came to use force against one another because organized violence at times proved necessary for their defence, bare survival, the protection of their core values and ways of life, the maintenance and extension of their living space, the acquisition of resources, and much else. Over time, many of the most successful groups developed organizations or classes of individuals specialized in the art of war. Early principles of citizenship even tied the rights of citizens to their service in war. Democracy too was in part driven by this social bargain of rights in return for war service.[42] Many, if not most, groups developed the art of coercing their members into military service, sometimes on pain of death. In this context, war became the *ultima ratio*—the final arbiter of conflicts between groups.[43] In a world lacking a single government capable of enforcing the law, covenants not backed by physical force, explained the English philosopher Thomas Hobbes in the seventeenth century, were merely words.

Second, *war has proven itself to be useful or profitable* to some of those willing and able to use it. War has opened the door to immense wealth and privilege for some. Many empires, for example, were founded on war or violent conquest. Empire delivered great riches to the imperial centres and their peoples. But material gain is not the only way war can be productive. War is sometimes necessary to restore or sustain peace (e.g. the Second World War was a necessary response to German and Japanese expansionism). War may also be thought necessary to protect cherished social goods or moral values such as group survival, justice, and self-determination—things for which some people are prepared to kill and die.

Third, *war is contagious*—warless societies can, and often do, have war imposed upon them from outside. It is also a self-fulfilling prophecy that contains within it the seeds for its own escalation. No matter how peaceful a single society, war cannot be eliminated until *all* societies become peaceful. Indeed, it takes only one society prepared to use violence to get its way to infect the whole. Once one society arms, all others confront an unenviable choice between arming to defend themselves or bending to the will of those that have. Given that choice, most societies have opted to arm themselves.

War's contagiousness explains why pacifism (understood here as the moral renunciation of all war) cannot work as a doctrine of world peace, for the renunciation of arms would deliver the desired effect only if everyone did it at the same time. What is more, just as domestic order has to be policed and laws enforced, so too does world peace demand that some rights be defended and enforced, by violence if necessary. Yet, I will show, there are steps that can be taken to limit war's contagiousness. Indeed, we already have many of the laws and institutions we need. Our task is to make them work.

Any account of world peace needs to pay careful attention to these forces that sustain war (difference, productivity, and contagion). We must also deal with the other institutions, forces, and social phenomena which, whilst not necessarily causing war itself, help push societies in that direction. These include patriarchy, authoritarian government, and economic inequality.

To sustain the case that world peace is possible, I will first show that peace itself has a history as long and varied as that of war. Then, I will turn to claims about war's omnipotence and ubiquity to show that these ideas are drawn largely from myth and not historical reality. The book then moves on to three important sets of questions: about how we organize ourselves, about the costs and payoffs of war and peace, and about our emotional relationship to them. How we address these, I will argue, shapes how peaceful or warlike a society or epoch is likely to be. At the end, I will set out an agenda of practical steps that can be taken to strengthen peace and further weaken the forces that sustain war's remnants, broadly following the structure of Immanuel Kant's landmark treatise for *Perpetual Peace* (1795).

As well as understanding the forces that give rise to war, we also need to recognize the building blocks of peace. Peace is not merely the absence of war; it is the presence of norms, institutions, and practices that enable the peaceful management of societies. But part of the problem is that we lack a shared understanding of 'peace'. According to the *Oxford English Dictionary*, 'peace' means 'freedom from war'—a definition that most of us would recognize. Yet to some of the earliest thinkers on the subject, peace meant more than this. For the Romans, and for early Christian writers such as Augustine, Dante, and Marsilius (on whom more in Chapter 2), peace meant not so much the absence of war as the presence of a just civic order. Peace, in other words, meant having a well-ordered society—something for which it was occasionally necessary to wage war. These three writers, I should add, disagreed on what constituted a just civil order.[44]

In the late nineteenth and early twentieth centuries, peace activists began to flesh this out. One of the pioneers of modern peace thought and activism, Jane Addams (1860–1935), argued that peace demanded social justice and poverty alleviation, ideas that she brought to the fore in practice both in the Chicago migrant communities where she worked and as the first President of the Women's International League for Peace and Freedom—an organization that still leads the charge for world peace today. These ideas were further developed from the 1960s, to the point we arrive at today where many who think and write about such things insist that 'peace' means a great deal more than the absence of war or presence of social order. Indeed, Johan Galtung, anointed by some as the 'father' of 'Peace Studies', gave the notion of peace as the absence of war a pejorative label: 'negative peace'—a form of peace 'which would be a good description of the failed peace treaty after World War I', wrote another.[45] Instead of negative peace, Galtung argued, 'positive peace' (a term first coined by Addams) fully understood must include harmonious relations between genders, races, classes, and families. It must also entail the absence of non-physical forms of violence. This includes freedom from the 'structural violence' caused by poverty, what Galtung called the 'nonintended slow, massive suffering caused by economic and political structures of exploitation and repression'. And it must include freedom from 'cultural violence', discriminatory practices such as racism that elevate some groups over others.[46] In similar vein, Martin Luther King famously argued that peace was not the absence of violence but the presence of justice.

Today, the high-profile Global Peace Index defines positive peace as the 'attitudes, structures and institutions which create and sustain peaceful societies'.[47] These include a 'sound business environment', 'high levels of human capital', low levels of corruption, the free flow of information, good relations with neighbours, acceptance of the rights of others, well-functioning government, and the equitable distribution of resources. In other words, peace can be defined as those things most valued by social democratic societies.

Of course, eradicating poverty, ending discrimination, and achieving justice are good things in and of themselves. They may also make states and societies more inclined towards peacefulness. As Jane Addams understood, the 'abolition of degrading poverty, disease and ignorance' may be essential for peacebuilding.[48] But it is important to distinguish between what we think peace *is* and those factors that make states, societies, and individuals more inclined towards it. Not least because peace demands harmonious relations between individuals and groups that have *different* views about how societies and states ought to be organized. Those social goods are the sorts of things that contribute to peace and that we may expect to flow from peace. But they are not synonyms for peace. Ralph Bunche, one of America's great internationalists, explained this point when he observed in his Nobel Lecture of 1950 that 'Peace, to have meaning for many who have known only suffering in both peace and war, must be translated into bread or rice, shelter, health, and education, as well as freedom and human dignity—a steadily better life. If peace is to be secure, long-suffering and long-starved, forgotten peoples of the world, the underprivileged and the undernourished, must begin to realize without delay the promise of a new day and a new life'. What Bunche was saying here was that prosperity and justice create and flow from peace, not that they are synonymous with it.

An expansive understanding of 'positive peace' was also not what the Romans had in mind when they uttered the word *pax*. What they envisaged was something narrower, more precise, but no less valuable. For them, *pax* was a condition of social harmony or tranquillity; more precisely, a 'pact' designed to achieve these conditions. The absence of violence and disorder—primarily at home, the civic order mentioned earlier, but also internationally—was central to their understanding. As it was for Bunche, *pax* was both a product of and necessary prerequisite for prosperity and justice. True, without *pax* there could be no justice, no wellbeing, no art. But *pax* itself was distinct from these other social and political goods.

Several things recommend a narrower approach to defining what peace actually is (as distinct from the factors that contribute to, and flow from, it). If we define peace so broadly as to include virtually every aspect of human wellbeing, the problem of organized violence slips from view. If 'peace' is defined as everything, then it simultaneously becomes nothing or, rather, nothing specific. If we accept Galtung's proposition, we leave ourselves with the conundrum of explaining what 'peace' adds to terms like 'justice', 'development', 'fairness', or 'security'. Conceptually, it becomes all but impossible to distinguish peace from these other social goods. A broad understanding of peace thus comes to rely on circular thinking that confuses factors that we think cause or flow from peace with the meaning of peace itself. The fundamental question of ending large-scale organized violence becomes just one of a series of 'mega-sized' problems to address, its fate tied to that of other political agendas.

The broad definition of peace also erodes important normative, legal, and political distinctions between peace and war. This way of thinking has a troubling colonial heritage in two senses. First, some apologists of empire justified the subjugation of non-Europeans by reference to their sense of having a 'civilizing mission'. Europe, they argued, had achieved peaceful and civilized societies. It was now the mission of Europeans to compel others to civilize and find peace just as they had, the logic went. Second, a corollary, in their conduct towards their colonies European powers acted as if there was no meaningful distinction between war and peace in places they judged to be uncivilized. Colonial powers used terror bombing, for instance, as a means of policing.[49]

Embedded within the concept of 'positive peace' are political commitments derived from twentieth-century European political ideologies with a distinctly leftist orientation. This discounts experiences of peace in societies that live according to different sets of values. What we have, in effect, are the values of some masquerading as a great universal vision of peace. But throughout history, different types of society have enjoyed protracted periods of peace— sometimes spanning many hundreds of years—in the absence of factors now widely considered fundamental to positive peace. The Roman provinces had no concepts of human equality or social justice, yet many generations lived without fear of major war. We ought to recognize that societies have different ideas about what constitutes a legitimate civic order.

To elide (positive) peace with justice is also to miss the point of most wars entirely. Most wars have justice disputes at their heart. Only mercenaries and psychopaths volunteer to fight wars they know to be unjust—though of course many people have been compelled to fight in such wars. Most warriors—and most of the leaders that have sent or led them into battle—seemed to have genuinely believed theirs to be a justifiable cause. Saying that peace must include 'justice' implies we can all agree on what justice is and on what justice demands in any particular case. The reality is that individuals and societies have different concepts of justice and can disagree radically about what justice demands. These are often genuine disagreements based on the deeply held beliefs of rational, ordinary (i.e. not criminal, not psychopathic) human beings.

Take, for example, the Syrian civil war. Members of the Alawite community that supported President Bashar al-Assad genuinely feared that should the rebels prevail, they would lose their livelihood and probably their lives. For them, justice demanded that the government's sovereign authority be respected. Members of the Kurdish community, meanwhile, believed that justice— through the principle of national self-determination—demanded that they be granted national autonomy. The Free Syrian Army, meanwhile, argued that justice required that the government be held accountable to the people under the democratic principle. Islamic State believed that justice demanded fidelity to its radical interpretation of *Sharia* law and that apostates, infidels, and those that stood in its way opposed God's will and therefore deserved death.

Obviously, some of these arguments are more compelling than others. My point here is that it is precisely because Syrians have different ideas about what justice is and what it demands that their country was wracked by civil war. One cannot therefore simply elide peace with justice, because it is disputes over justice that make peace so difficult to achieve and sustain. To ignore this funda-mental point is to hold a mistaken view about the nature of human conflict, seeing it as somehow pathological, and to elide peace with a particular concep-tion of justice. This is precisely the sort of thing that could be used to justify untold violence and imperialism—a great war for a great (positive) peace. But, although they may be related, peace and justice are not the same thing. We can have just peace or unjust peace; just war or unjust war.

Broader conceptions of positive peace as social harmony or social justice, or both, are therefore problematic, as Michael Banks pointed out in an important essay published in 1987. Whilst 'peace as harmony' ignores (or worse, represses) the fact that humans have different interests and values to argue over, 'peace as justice' assumes agreement on what justice is and how it should be achieved—neither of which exists. This is not to argue that human rights, justice, and development are not important social goods, but merely that they should not be treated as synonymous with peace.

To be a distinct and identifiable social condition, peace should be primarily understood as the absence of war—that is, the absence of organized group-level violence. But by itself, peace as the absence of war is too narrow, not least because of the often-fuzzy distinction between war and peace in practice and the fact that such an approach could lead us to designate societies experiencing genocides and other one-sided atrocities as peaceful. It is better, Michael Banks argues, to think of peace as a process of managing conflict without violence.[50] This implies a condition of civic order within states and societies as well as non-violent relations between them. Or, as Peter Wallensteen argues, we might think of 'quality peace': societies having the necessary conditions for the prevention of war. Precisely what those qualities are, Wallensteen explains, are difficult to identify in the abstract but include attributes such as safety and dignity.[51] What both Banks and Wallensteen are alluding to are perhaps the qualities of legitimate civic order that Augustine, Dante, and Marsilius wrote of. These are qualities best worked out in specific times and places.

By 'peace', therefore, I mean the absence and prevention of war (international and civil) and the management of conflict through peaceful means, implying some form of legitimate civic order. By 'world' peace I mean the extension of these things globally. But this is not without its problems.

We need to think just as carefully about what we mean by 'world' peace because grand visions of peace can be dangerous. A great moral good, world peace can—and has—been used to justify untold horrors. For if peace is an ultimate good, there is almost no limit to what can be done to achieve it. As British historian A.J.P. Taylor famously put it, the Prussian chancellor Otto Von Bismarck (1815–90) 'fought "necessary" wars and killed thousands, the idealists of the twentieth century fought "just" wars and killed millions'.[52] He had a point. The novelist H.G. Wells, best known for his futurist accounts of war, believed the First World War was one such situation where the noble goal of peace justified immense violence. The war would propel the world to peace, he believed. It should therefore be waged with every fibre of being until the bitter end. It would be, he wrote, 'the war that will end war'. It was 'a war not of nations but of mankind. It is a war to exorcise world-madness and end an age…For this is now a war for peace…Every soldier who fights Germany now is a crusader against war. This, the greatest of all wars, is not just another war—it is the last war!'[53] More than ten million people were killed in this 'war to end war'. With so much blood spilt in the name of such noble a goal as peace, the warring sides found they could not negotiate an early truce. Compromise is difficult when goals are cast as absolute and universal moral goods. But the First World War did not end war. It set the stage for an even greater catastrophe. Unless we are careful, peace talk can contribute to great harm.

In fact, the most radical utopian projects of the twentieth century caused immense violence and suffering. The pursuit of Stalin's new order, Hitler's *lebensraum*, and Mao's great leap forward and cultural revolution were all prefaced on claims that new and more perfect, just, and peaceful orders could be fashioned through willpower and brute force. But each of these grand utopian visions had to be sustained by immense violence. Great extirpating violence justified by the immense virtue of the goal—peace and justice without end. The obvious lesson, philosopher Jonathan Glover reminds us, 'is the importance of avoiding grandiose utopian social projects'.[54] Many such attempts have failed altogether or succeeded only in forging fascist, communist, imperial, racist, or nationalist dystopias that have cost tens of millions of lives.[55] George Orwell's *1984* and Aldous Huxley's *Brave New World* remind us only too well that utopias tend to collapse into dystopia.[56]

The problem arises from the fact that, as mentioned earlier, from the earliest civilizations, humans have developed different ideas not only about what is just and unjust, but about the standard of justice itself. We do not have a universally accepted account of justice. Different groups believe that justice requires different things. They also tend to believe that their own vision of justice ought to be privileged over those of others.[57] To make matters more complex, even agreed principles can sometimes contradict one another. Most obviously, we occasionally agonize over whether peace is always compatible with justice and whether one should sometimes be sacrificed to achieve the other.[58] There can therefore be no singular vision of peace beyond a politics that embraces the non-violent resolution of conflicts between groups and the idea that states and societies ought to be organized in ways that make them more peaceful and seem orderly and legitimate to those within them.[59]

Taking a more definitive view about the sorts of justice that ought to inspire peace runs into the problem, as Susan Sontag pointed out, that what we understand by 'peace' is really just 'victory'—the triumph of our own moral vision over those of others.[60] Lassa Oppenheim's classic legal definition of war described it as an armed confrontation between states 'for the purpose of overpowering each other and *imposing such conditions of peace as the victor pleases*'.[61] But a victor's peace is only ever a temporary peace, one resisted by the vanquished. By contrast, 'world peace' must involve living with a degree of moral plurality. It must be about peaceful coexistence despite differences of interests and values. Even when we argue that some goods are necessary to achieve world peace—for example, effective and legitimate states, or gender equality— we must recognize the plurality of ways in which these things might be achieved and sustained in different times and places.

We should therefore think of world peace not as a singular grand project but rather as the cumulative effect of multiple 'minor utopias'. These, historian Jay Winter tells us, are imaginings and practices of peace, liberation, and wellbeing rooted in specific times and places and shorn of the 'grandiose pretensions' and 'unimaginable hubris' of major utopian projects such as communism, fascism, and empire.[62] Minor utopian projects include efforts to ban war and limit its conduct through law; to establish and sustain global institutions to manage world order and support peace; to mediate between disputants to help them resolve their differences without violence; to support peace-building in the aftermath of war; to promote and protect human rights and dignity; to reduce inequalities between genders; to lift the poorest out of poverty; to carefully manage the deadliest weapons and ban those that cannot be used discriminately; to monitor and police ceasefires; to provide humanitarian aid and places of asylum to civilians imperilled by war; to understand and mitigate the unique threats faced by women and girls in war; and much more besides. Each of these is a 'minor utopia'—a limited, rooted vision of how war itself, or a single specific war, might be prevented, limited, or ended. They help build more just societies and maintain a *modus vivendi* between them. Most of what I argue for in Chapter 8, where I outline some paths to peace, draws upon these minor utopias—blueprints drawn up not by me, but negotiated already by the world's governments and societies. These are visions and practices based in the here and now, not on abstract dreams of a different world. They are compromises between different value sets, identities, histories, and interests based on over-lapping points of consensus between different communities. Unlike the 'major utopians' of the twentieth century, minor utopians do not want to do away with our world of sovereign states and diverse peoples. They want to build on the progress already made and rethink it in order to make it more peaceful. They aim to protect the fundamentals of life and manage differences peacefully. World peace is best thought of and pursued as the combined product of lots of different minor utopias, not as something legislated from the top.

We should also mention those for whom world peace—even when conceived in non-grandiose terms—is not just a chimera, but a menace. Nationalists and Romantics have long lamented that peace can erode moral discipline and fighting spirit. Proving that at least some things never change, in 1912 a commentator in the *Daily Mail* complained that 'Peace may and has ruined many a nationality with its surfeit of everything except those tonics of privation and sacrifice' whereas even 'the severest war wreaks little practical injury'.[63] One cannot get much further from the *Daily Mail* than the German philosopher Friedrich Nietzsche, and yet on this subject at least they agreed. Nietzsche rejected the idea of a common morality rooted in religion or natural law and instead embraced the (sometimes violent) struggle for survival as the engine room of artistic beauty and social achievement. Nietzsche's Zarathustra teaches, 'you should love peace as a means to new wars. And the short peace more than the long'. He continues, 'You say it is the good cause that hallows even war? I tell you: it is the good war that hallows every war'.[64] In perpetual peace, Nietzsche wrote, humankind would be left scratching around like animals, devoid of the higher culture and emotions aroused by war. The 'beginning of everything great on earth', he wrote in *Genealogy of Morals* (1887), is 'soaked in blood thoroughly and for a long time'.[65] Without war, he reckoned, humanity is lost. This love of war stands squarely opposed to the pursuit of peace.

Finally, some caveats are in order. I am arguing that world peace is *possible*, not that it is imminent or likely. As we sit right now, we are in danger of letting slip some of the hard-fought gains of the past and losing precious ground in the 'war against war'.[66] The history of our present, one filled with growing prejudice, discrimination, authoritarianism, and conflict, must be set against the broader global history of violence. Viewed that way, we see that whole regions once plagued by incessant war—such as Western Europe—can achieve stable peace and that despite its current chaos, the world is still relatively peaceful in historical terms. The assumption underlying all this is that if peace can be achieved in *some* places, there is no logical reason why it cannot be achieved in *all* places. Humanity is capable of striking adaptation and profound change.[67]

The recent upturn in armed conflict may be quite modest in historical terms—the global burden of war is similar to that in 1995, and still lower than at any point since around 1960—but it has created a deep sense of foreboding about the future. This foreboding has given rise to 'fear and loathing' in world politics as societies turn inwards and the politics of xenophobia, nationalism, authoritarianism, and mercantilism come to the fore.[68] This is a politics epitomized by President Putin in Russia (an aggressive nationalist authoritarian whose forces have invaded and annexed foreign territory and enabled untold atrocities in Syria), President Trump in the US (a nationalist with authoritarian tendencies who promises to withdraw support from international institutions, build up the US military, and aggressively pursue the country's material interests), President Xi Jinping in China (an authoritarian who made himself president for life, cracked down on civil liberties, and adopted a bellicose position on the South China Sea), Brexit in the UK (an act that divides Europe and jeopardizes one of the most successful experiments in regional peace-building), and a range of minor authoritarians such as Duterte (in the Philippines) and Orban (in Hungary). A product of our fear and foreboding, these political forces are possible portents of a more violent world to come. Little wonder, then, that some see striking parallels between our current situation and the world in 1914, on the eve of the First World War.

Margaret MacMillan, author of an acclaimed book on the causes of the First World War, wrote on the centenary of the First World War that some of the forces that propelled the world to war in 1914 are evident today.[69] These include 'national rivalries, imperialism, the arms race…as well as ideologies and assumptions such as Social Darwinism and militarism'. Underlying these was a power transition as emergent Germany challenged a declining British empire. MacMillan also observed that far from guaranteeing peace, the relatively high levels of trade between European powers in the early twentieth century intensified the rivalries between them. The recent spread of democracy, while beneficial overall, also had negative effects in that public opinion began to matter to decision-makers. Not all of that opinion was 'on the side of calm and reason'. All this was compounded by an air of complacency.

We seem, then, to be at a turning point. State consolidation, trade, democracy, the diminution of ideological struggles, and sustained efforts in peace-making and peacekeeping have made the world a more peaceful place than it once was. This progress, brought about by minor utopias in different times and places, nudged humanity towards world peace. But the ideas and social forces that give rise to war now seem to be in the ascendancy. Unless they are met with countervailing activism for peace, our future may become more violent than our immediate past. That is why we need to talk about world peace. That is also why we need to act.

CHAPTER 2

DREAMS OF PEACE

The longing for peace is rooted in the hearts of all men.
But the striving which at present has become so insistent
cannot lay claim to such an ambition as leading the way to
eternal peace...The economic and political roots of the conflicts
are too strong.

—Alva Myrdal, Nobel Lecture, 1982

'War appears to be as old as mankind, but peace is a modern invention', wrote Sir Henry Maine in the mid-nineteenth century. It was only after the Enlightenment, historian Michael Howard tells us, that political leaders came to see peace as a desirable or practicable goal. Before that, 'war was recognized as an intrinsic part of the social and political order'.[1] War certainly has a history. But so too does peace. Indeed, thoughts, dreams, and *practices* of world peace have a history as long as that of war.[2] For as long as there has been war, there have been efforts to prevent, limit, and resolve it. Indeed, war's emergence was accompanied by proposals for its elimination. That the history of peace is less well known than the history of war should not be taken as meaning that peace has less of a history or that its history is limited to the idealistic dreams of a handful of visionaries. The theory and practice of world peace has a history just as long, varied, and contested as that of war. To shake the myth of war's ubiquity in thought and deed, we need to recognize and understand our long struggle for peace.

This chapter opens a window on this past by offering the briefest of snapshots of peace's history. I want to show that humanity's failure to build world peace is not for the want of trying or the shortage of ideas and proposals.

Dreams and practices of peace can be found everywhere. Indeed, even within the heroic visions of war presented by the ancient Greeks. Homer's epic tales of the Trojan War and its aftermath may have depicted war as a worthy and glorious undertaking, but not far beneath the surface lay aspirations for peace and recognition of its value. Battles are portrayed in vivid and brutal detail, revealing them to be anything but glorious. Zeus describes Ares, the god of war, as the 'most hateful' of all gods.[3] Homer's careful description of the shield forged by the god Hephaestus for the Greek hero Achilles before his battle with Hector reveals a work of art that celebrates peaceful life—not war.[4] Where *The Iliad* ends with a truce between the warring parties, the epilogue to its sequel, *The Odyssey*, concludes with an invitation to peace: 'let the mutual goodwill of the days of old be restored, and let peace and plenty prevail'.[5]

Reacting to the incessant internecine wars of their time, which pitted city-states against one another, later Greeks applied the full range of their intellectual and artistic talents to the advancement of peace. Better known for his contribution to geometry, Pythagoras advanced a 'scientific' theory of universal harmony as a guide to effective government.[6] The follies of war were a recurrent theme in the tragedies of Euripides and Sophocles, hubris often the undoing of their heroes. Aristophanes used comedy to expose war's absurdity. In *Peace*, a farmer effects a miraculous end to the Peloponnesian War by rescuing the character 'Peace' from the cave where she had been imprisoned by 'War' and prevented from returning by unscrupulous politicians. Peace's return brings an abundant harvest and much merry-making. In *Lysistrata*, the women of Athens and Sparta try to compel the men to end the war by refusing them sex. After much frivolity involving actors with comedic erections, sexual frustration drives the men of Athens and Sparta to negotiate peace. Even the historian Herodotus gave himself license to comment on the virtues of peace and follies of war. Peace, he suggested, was a universal way of life that improved the human condition; war an aberration. 'In peace, sons bury their fathers. In war, fathers bury their sons'. The other great historian of the period, Thucydides, rarely spoke for himself through the pages of his epic history of the *Peloponnesian War*. Yet on the occasions that he did, he left little doubt that he saw his tale as a cautionary one about the destruction of Athens by its own imperial hubris. The Athenian commanders who led the infamous negotiation with the islanders of Melos in which they argued that it was the prerogative of the powerful to determine what was just—the epitome of imperial hubris—were the very same generals who later led the disastrous attack on Syracuse (in Sicily) that marked the beginning of the end for the Athenian empire.[7]

Some Greeks focused on building political instruments to prevent or limit war. The Delphic peace tradition, from 1100 BCE, established a truce during the Olympic Games. Homer reveals other examples, such as in the protection of heralds, the use of negotiations and treaties to resolve disputes, and the practice of duelling as replacements for battles. All were attempts to limit war and temper its violence. Sometimes Greek city-states used arbitration and legal means to settle their disputes. Before its war with Athens, Sparta—a city with few imperial ambitions of its own—often played the role of arbiter between squabbling polities.

The Greeks also pioneered thinking about how relations between political communities could be organized to better sustain peace. Various empires and 'peace leagues' were established to this end, some quite complex in form. The Second Athenian League, for example, built a multilayered decision-making structure comprising a decision-making assembly, the *synedrion*, and the Athenian assembly—entities which acted independently of one another. Renowned mathematician, Thales of Miletus, took this logic one step further and proposed a Hellenic union of city-states that would be guided by an assembly composed of representatives of all its members. Binding city-states into a single political unit, the union would reduce the possibility of war between them, he argued. The idea was never adopted, but the proposition that peace between communities required the establishment of a union or league of states became a mainstay of later proposals. It lies at the heart of contemporary projects such as the United Nations and European Union.[8]

It was in India, though, where the first comprehensive peace doctrines we know of emerged, doctrines built on the principle of non-violence. The most ancient Indian traditions of thought broadly sanctioned war and violence, viewing them as necessary for social order. Beneath the surface, though, lay a preference for peace, a sense that however heroic, the warrior's virtue was corrupted by violence. By the eighth century BCE this strain of thinking had evolved into creeds that renounced war and violence altogether. One school, known as Jainism, was partly inspired by the teachings of Mahavira, who called on his followers to turn their backs on mainstream society and establish a new life of non-violence and the renunciation of harm. He taught that only by cultivating the sentiments of friendship, empathy, and compassion towards all living things could the soul be truly awakened. Jainism forbade all forms of violence and harm, as well as any intent or desire to harm other living beings. Violence was deemed wrong because all living things were sacred and should be left to live to their full potential. Causing harm to others damaged one's own soul. A second school to emerge from India became better known: Buddhism. Not long after Mahavira, the Buddha taught that the path to an enlightened and peaceful state—which he called *nirvana*—lay through non-violence. Buddhist teachings on violence resembled those of Jainism but the Buddha was more of a pragmatist. He called for his followers to go out into the world to help others and spread Buddhist teachings. Rather than simply rejecting violence, the Buddha called on his followers to instil the values that would help prevent it.[9]

Like the Greeks, the emergence of early Chinese thinking about war and peace came in response to internecine war: that of the 'warring states' period that accompanied the terminal decline of the Zhou dynasty after around 480 BCE. The Confucian school recognized that war was unlikely to be abandoned, but lamented its costs. It emphasized the role of good government in establishing peace and social harmony. Virtuous rule aimed not at the enrichment of the leader but at the maintenance of order, balance, harmony, and the eradication of evils such as poverty. Governing with wisdom would establish order and stability at home and harmony between states. These themes underscored the ideas of later Confucians who, like the Roman and Christian thinkers that emerged afterwards, emphasized the importance of civil order to the establishment of peace. Mencius taught that rulers were responsible for the wellbeing of their people and that this should be their first concern. China's troubles could be ended only by a king with power enough to impose order and peace over the whole country.[10] Xunxi too emphasized that the unity of people and ruler was the key to harmony and prosperity, noting that this would be achieved by humane and just rule.

Among the alternatives to the Confucian school in early Chinese thinking, the Daoists turned within the self in their search for peace. They taught that individuals should pursue their own peace and avoid harm. War, in this view, was always a potential source of harm, for even if waged for justifiable reasons, it caused unforeseen consequences and great suffering. Even ancient China's foremost strategist of war, Sun Tzu, taught that the very best way to prevail over an enemy was without fighting at all since war was so costly and unpredictable. 'To subdue the enemy without fighting is the acme of skill'. And, just like the Greeks, the Chinese developed a school of thought on peace between states. But whereas Thales focused on the imperative of political union, the Mohist school looked beyond Chinese civilization, insisting that all rulers had a shared interest in peace and a role in instantiating it through the practice of peaceful coexistence and renunciation of aggression.

Back in Europe, the Romans bequeathed a concept of peace that remains with us today, and that stands out for its capacity to reach out across religious and cultural difference: peace as the absence of war and presence of a just civil order. For those fortunate enough to live in the imperial provinces, the much-professed *Pax Romana* was a really existing phenomenon—one of considerable duration. At the empire's peak, Roman provinces experienced roughly three centuries without war, whilst in the imperial borderlands Rome's legions fought relentless wars against raiders and foreign powers. Of course, the establishment of Rome's empire—like that of most empires before and since—was immensely violent. But once conquest was achieved and initial revolts suppressed, the provinces enjoyed sustained periods of peace in which trade, prosperity, the rule of law, civil engineering, and the arts flourished. Provincial life benefitted materially. The key to this was the Roman strategy of coopting local elites, sharing material benefits, the fungibility of Roman identity, and opportunities for violence, enrichment, and glory beyond the empire's borders. Roman citizenship—with its special rights and responsibilities—was defined in political, not ethnic, terms. Colonized elites could aspire to becoming Roman citizens. Indeed, citizens from across the empire could rise to the very top of the imperial government. Three of Rome's most renowned leaders—Trajan, Hadrian, and Marcus Aurelius—came not from Italy, but from the province of Hispania (Spain). Rome allowed conquered regions to largely govern themselves so long as they paid their dues in return for which they received the protection of Rome's laws and legions. And, by and large, the Romans tolerated diversity of belief to a greater extent than most other empires of the time, though Roman tolerance was limited to those belief systems that posed no threat to the empire itself or the supremacy of its belief system.[11]

It was enrichment and glory that inspired Roman conquest, not *pax*, yet once the imperial peace was achieved, Roman thinkers and leaders started to rationalize it and develop concepts and ideals to sustain it. Some of these have stood the test of time. Some Roman thinkers drew sharp moral and legal distinctions between what could be done to protect the *Pax Romana* and the violent attacks made by others upon it. Perhaps the most significant of these was the philosopher Cicero (108–48 BCE), who argued that wars could be justified only if they were directed towards the defence of the (Roman) state or the exacting of revenge for harms done to it. Acts of aggression against the state were crimes and their perpetrators criminals. Once started, though, wars must be waged justly without undue cruelty. Particularly important was Cicero's explanation of *why* the Roman Empire was justified in waging wars to uphold justice or defend itself, for this goes to the heart of how the Romans understood peace itself. Sadly, the original text has been lost, but we do have St Augustine's (on whom more later) summary. According to Augustine, Cicero had observed that:

> It is unjust that men should be under the domination of men, and yet unless the imperial state indulges in this injustice…it cannot rule the provinces. On the part of justice the reply is made that it is just because for such men subjection is advantageous, and the rule is carried on for their good, when it is properly carried on, that is, when license to do wrong is taken from the bad; and (under this rule) the subdued will be in better condition, for they were in a bad condition when unsubdued. And finally the question is raised (Do we not see that by nature herself mastery has been granted to all the best men to the very great advantage of the weak?), 'why does God rule man, the mind rule the body, and reason rule lust and all other vicious qualities of the mind?'[12]

The key point being made here was that Roman rule, and the empire's right to wage war, was justified by the benefits it bestowed on its conquered subjects.[13] Civil order underwritten by imperial power allowed people to live happier, more rewarding, and prosperous lives. Peace is rooted in this civil order. But because of that, peace cannot mean the total renunciation of war for it may sometimes be necessary to wage war in order to protect the peace, such as when civil order is challenged by external threats or internal agitation.

These themes were picked up by other prominent Romans. The poet Ovid (43–17 BCE) wrote that that soldiers may bear arms only to quell aggression.[14] Emperor Augustus (ruled 27–14 BCE) decreed that the principal purpose of the state was the guaranteeing of peace and maintenance of the rule of law. But it was the Christian theologian, St Augustine of Hippo (354–430), who developed these ideas into a coherent theory. The earliest Christians largely rejected war. For example, Tertullian taught (writing c. 198–202) that because Jesus had rejected violence, it was wrong for Christians to raise a sword in war.[15] But by the time that Augustine came to consider these matters, these were practical as well as theological issues for he lived in a time of imperial decline and mounting disorder. In 410, Alaric's Visigoths sacked Rome for three days, traumatizing its people and striking fear into the provinces. When Augustine died, his home city of Hippo, in North Africa, was under siege by the Vandals. Achieving Christian salvation was difficult in such trying circumstances. Prayer and contemplation require peace and order. The question of whether Christians should fight to defend the Christian empire against non-Christians was now more acute.

Augustine developed a moral doctrine that permitted Christians to participate in war. As such, he is commonly known today as the father of the 'just war tradition'. But it is his concept of peace that interests us here. In his opus, *City of God*, Augustine maintained that all people long for peace. They wage war not because they desire it, but because they wish the peace 'changed into a peace that suits them better'. Wars happen, in other words, because people want a more perfect peace. But this peace is only ever the earthly peace of the city of man—a point Augustine underscored with his reference to peace that is more or less preferable to individual tastes. This peace Augustine contrasted with the heavenly and eternal tranquillity of the peace achieved in the city of God. The question, therefore, was how to connect the earthly peace with the heavenly. The answer lay in civic order or *concordia*. This Augustine described as the 'well-ordered concord of civil obedience and civic rule'.[16] By establishing civil peace, the city of man could create the conditions needed for people to reach the city of God through prayer, contemplation, and obeying God's will. Augustine explained:

> The earthly city, which does not live by faith, seeks an earthly peace, and the end it proposes, in the well-ordered concourse of civic obedience and rule, is the combination of men's wills to attain the things which are helpful to this life. The heavenly city, or rather the part of it which sojourns on earth and lives by faith, makes use of this peace only because it must, until this mortal condition which necessitates it shall pass away...Even the heavenly city, therefore, while in the state of its pilgrimage, avails itself of the peace of earth, and...desires and maintains a common agreement among men regarding the acquisition of the necessities of life, and makes this earthly peace bear upon the peace of heaven.[17]

Peace meant not so much the absence of war as the presence of civil order characterized by order and justice. Only when the earthly city guaranteed these goods could the city of man be connected to the heavenly city of God. And Augustine was telling us something else important too, something alluded to but not systematically developed by Cicero: not all earthly cities were equally valuable. Only particular types of polity—those that promoted theologically sound order and justice—were valuable. Only these polities could be justly defended by war, since in those cases war was waged to protect peace and through it, justice. Those cities that did not have these attributes, had no such rights.

Ultimately, *Pax Romana* broke down not primarily because of its own flaws—though the increasing costs associated with maintaining the legions were a problem—but because the empire that nurtured it was weakened from within by misrule, division, and civil war. As *concordia* went, so went the empire. Its ideal of peace, however, lived on.

The collapse of the Roman Empire plunged Europe and the Middle East into the 'Dark Ages'. The light of world peace dimmed but was not fully extinguished. Sometime between 1309 and 1314, Dante, the renowned Florentine humanist best known for *The Divine Comedy*, penned an essay entitled *De Monarchia* (sometimes translated, not entirely accurately, as *On World Government*. The problem with this translation is that Dante's vision was imperial, in the image of the emperor Charlemagne). The essay was not published until the sixteenth century and so had no discernible impact on the tumults of its own time. But it is of interest to us as an expression of the continuation of Roman/Augustinian thought about peace. Dante drew a less sharp distinction than had Augustine between heavenly and earthly peace but argued—much as Augustine had—that peace was achievable through a well-ordered society governed by law. That law, he argued, should be administered by a monarch. Writing at a time of intense conflict between the Holy Roman Empire (a legacy of Charlemagne) and the Papacy over the nature of true law and authority, Dante was unabashedly pro-empire. He argued that the Papal law covered only spiritual matters and that temporal authority lay with the emperor alone. The rule of law required a single authority to sit in judgement, and Dante argued that this could be achieved only through a universal (understood as European at the time) empire governed by similarly universal temporal law.[18] The supreme ruler on earth must have a monopoly of power, Dante argued, to enforce the law and preserve the peace. His was a vision of peace as civil order writ large.

A few years later (1324), Marsilius of Padua, a one-time soldier of Paris who became known for his exploits in negotiating peace treaties between Italy's fractious states, wrote *Defensor Pacis* (*Defender of the Peace*). His was a more secular account of civil peace, stripped of both divine purpose and imperial ambition, one where peace itself became the state's purpose. In Marsilius, peace—still understood as civil order—becomes an end in itself, not—as it was for Augustine and Dante—a means to a more spiritual end. Peace, meaning 'civil peace or tranquillity', was necessary, Marsilius argued, for the flourishing of virtue and prosperity. For a state to be at peace, it had to be functioning properly, its parts moving in harmony.[19] Secular states were best placed to achieve this goal, Marsilius insisted, because of their superior capacity to sustain order (owing to their dependence on the consent of the governed) and resolve disputes peacefully. Peace, then, involved a properly functioning society governed by laws enforced by the state.

In the late fifteenth and early sixteenth centuries, the rejection of war returned to the fore in some Christian thinking. The Dutch reformist Erasmus (born 1466) is best known today for his humanist theology which called for a return to scripture and rejection of ecclesiastical laws not consistent with the teachings of Christ. War was uppermost in his mind as one of those issues on which scripture and Church seemed to profoundly disagree. For whilst Christ had repeatedly emphasized the sinfulness of violence and virtue of peace, the Church had become complicit in the business of war and its moral justification through the 'just war' tradition. Erasmus penned tracts denouncing the sinfulness of war. It should be avoided at all costs, he insisted. There was nothing more wicked or destructive. To Erasmus, war was a corruptor of humanity, a blatant violation of Christ's teachings. Nature dictated that humans must strive for peace, since they are inherently social and equipped with few natural attributes for violence (like horns, claws, etc.).

Whilst he may not have developed a systematic theory of peace, Erasmus did offer three important insights into how it might be achieved. First, he appealed to self-interest. War, he pointed out, is expensive and self-defeating; it is contrary to reason. It was probably premature to say that in the sixteenth century, since kings and princes continued to reap the material benefits of conquest through war, but in the twenty-first century the costliness and indecisiveness of war have become key drivers of peace. Second, Erasmus argued—much in the spirit of Thales before him—that 'humanity', by which he meant Christendom (where Thales had meant only Greeks), was a single entity united by shared faith. It should therefore be organized as such. In particular, the Church should be called upon to arbitrate disputes between princes. Interestingly, although his prescriptions related only to Christendom, Erasmus did not sanction unlimited war against the Ottoman Turks, who in 1529 had besieged Vienna. War against the Turks was permissible, but only in self-defence and only when all other avenues had been exhausted.[20] Third, Erasmus argued that people were bestowed with natural attributes and capacities for speech, reason, and friendship which, if properly nurtured, equipped them to resolve conflicts without war.

Meanwhile, in the Swiss city of Zurich in the early 1520s, the Anabaptists led by the charismatic reformer Ulrich Zwingli taught that Christians should not participate in war and should follow Christ's teachings about non-resistance. Their teachings spread rapidly, and Anabaptists rose to prominent positions not just in Zurich but across Switzerland and southern Germany. But their teachings posed a threat to the state and it was not long before the Holy Roman Emperor, Charles V, issued a raft of laws to suppress them.[21]

Gradually more systematic thinking about world peace began to emerge, further crystallizing ideas such as the importance of political union, collective decision-making, and shared rules, first articulated by the ancients. In 1623, Emeric Cruce proposed an association of independent states governed by a permanent council of diplomats based in Venice. Decisions would be taken by majority vote and each member would contribute the resources needed to deal with common problems and execute the council's decisions. The association would use arbitration to resolve disputes between its members but could also use force to impose its will if necessary. Cruce's community was not limited to Christendom but, drawing on a sense of common humanity, extended beyond Europe to include the other major world powers: Persia, China, India, and Ethiopia. '[A]ll nations are bound together by a natural and consequently indestructible tie which ensures a man cannot consider another a stranger', he wrote.[22]

Fifteen years later, in 1638, a proposal for peace issued in the name of King Henri IV of France (who had been assassinated in 1610) was published. Written by one of the King's former ministers, the Duke of Sully, the tract proposed a 'Grand Design' for peace centred on the establishment of a Christian republic comprising fifteen European states. The republic would be managed by a council of representatives from the member states and would have a common army. The council could arbitrate disputes between its members and impose binding resolutions backed by force if necessary. Force might also be used to prevent members leaving the union. William Penn's schema, published in 1693, combined a withering critique of war drawn from Erasmus with a proposal for world peace that involved a supra-national parliament (extending beyond Europe) with a monopoly on the right to use force.

Some of these ideas found their way into a plan devised by the polymath Abbe Saint-Pierre, published in 1712. Saint-Pierre's plan involved a broader union that included Muscovy (Russia) and Ottoman Turkey, though he later dropped Turkey on the grounds (not unfamiliar to modern ears) that Europe's common (Christian) identity made political union more feasible and that this unity would be undermined by the inclusion of predominantly Muslim Turkey. Saint-Pierre's plan included a decision-making council along with an important innovation: an international court to adjudicate disputes between its members. But the scheme contained most, if not all, of the weaknesses of its predecessors. These flaws were exposed by one of the pre-eminent thinkers of the time—Jean-Jacques Rousseau.

Ironically, Rousseau's interest in peace was piqued when Saint-Pierre commissioned him to organize and write up the latter's chaotic papers on the subject. 'Never did the mind of man conceive a scheme nobler, more beautiful or more useful than that of a lasting peace between all the peoples of Europe', observed Rousseau. Yet the plans could never be realized, Rousseau reasoned, because people were inherently self-interested and irrational. Peace was impossible 'not because it is Utopian', Rousseau acknowledged, 'but because men are crazy'. We should distinguish between apparent (short-term, selfish) and real (long-term, enlightened) rationality. Since princes always privileged the former over the latter, they would never accept the limits on their freedom of action proposed by Saint-Pierre. Without a confederative government able to wield preponderant force, which Rousseau thought highly unlikely, the scheme was doomed to fail.[23]

Many of the ideas that inform the pursuit of peace today—international organization, political union, law, arbitration, and collective security—can trace their intellectual heritage to this fertile period. In their own time, however, the schemes suffered from at least three crippling weaknesses that consigned them to obscurity.

The first problem was practical. These schemes failed to secure political support. Kings, queens, and princes simply refused to contemplate setting aside their own self-interest in favour of a broader conception of the good. Royal houses that enjoyed the privileges of sovereignty were loath to consider forgoing their hard-won rights. 'You have forgotten, sir', the Cardinal Fleury is reputed to have told Saint-Pierre, 'a preliminary condition on which your five articles must depend. You must begin by sending out a troop of missionaries to prepare the hearts and minds of the contracting sovereigns'. Frederick the Great made the same point in a letter to Voltaire: 'the thing is most practicable; for its success all that is lacking is the consent of Europe and a few similar trifles'.[24]

The second problem was more theoretical. Critics pointed out that these schemes for peace suffered a contradiction at their very core: their dependence on brute force. Rousseau explained that because different polities had different conceptions of political rights, disputes could arise between equally legitimate claims. In this context, a union or association of states could secure compliance with its collective will only if it enjoyed a preponderance of force sufficient to impose its will if necessary. Leaving aside the question of why a sovereign prince would ever voluntarily accept this imposition (Rousseau was convinced they would not), this reality made peace ultimately reliant on the very thing it was trying to eliminate: war.

A third problem was political. Understood within their own contexts, the different schemes were not impartial models for building peace but political agendas designed to support particular interests. Though sold as such, peace was not necessarily their ultimate objective. The principal concern for Sully and Saint-Pierre (and we might add Dante here too) was not peace but rather the restoration of a united (Catholic) Europe being torn apart by the forces unleashed by the Protestant Reformation. At the time, Sully's 'Grand Design' was seen as little more than a vehicle for instituting the regional hegemony of his former patron: the King of France. Leibniz made the point caustically: the plan 'may be suspected of having had in view more the overthrow of the House of Austria than the establishment of a Society of Sovereigns'. Rousseau agreed, detecting that the plan was aimed more at 'humbling a formidable enemy' (the Habsburgs) than solving the problem of war.[25]

These three problems were tied together by a common theme: that without prior changes to the nature, attitudes, and behaviour of states, schemes for world peace were doomed to fail. This is a problem that remains with us today.

Without doubt, the most famous of the philosophers' peace plans, Immanuel Kant's 'perpetual peace' (1795), was also one of the most realistic. Kant, who lived in the East Prussian outpost of Konigsburg (today, the Russian outpost of Kaliningrad), was a prodigious writer best known for his moral theories and contribution to idealism. *Perpetual Peace*, written towards the end of his career, was a rare intervention into political life, one inspired by the political events of the time. At first enamoured by the French revolution of 1789, Kant was horri-fied by Prussia's decision to wage war against the new French republic. But he was also too much of a patriot to criticize his own state or even to wish it ill in war. He was therefore delighted when—having discovered that the French republic would be no pushover—Prussia withdrew from the war in late 1794, a decision ratified by the Treaty of Bale early the following year. Filled with optimism about the potential for a law-based peace to supplant war, Kant decided to publish a pamphlet showing how this could lay the foundations for a more perpetual peace. The pamphlet was a best-seller in its own time, and continues to influence our thinking today. Yet it is also one of the most misunderstood tracts on peace.

Often taken to be a defence of cosmopolitanism or world government, *Perpetual Peace* is anything but. In fact, Kant keenly understood that states could not be simply swept away and replaced by world governments or confederations. Nations, he realized, wanted to live in states of their own. Peace could be achieved only by better ordering relations between them. But Kant also understood that unless their own internal constitutions were changed, states would be unlikely to change their capricious, power-seeking, and self-interested ways. Peace could be achieved only if there were prior changes to the nature, attitudes, and actions of states. Kant's was therefore an account of how sovereign states might establish a law-governed and peaceful community amongst themselves. It was underpinned by the idea that the rule of law established within states could be extended to governing relations between them.

Kant understood that the basic fact of international anarchy—in other words, the absence of a world government—dictated that world politics be characterized by war and the pursuit of self-interest rather than by peace and a natural harmony of interests. Polities had different interests and values and no authority was set above them to arbitrate their disputes. In that context, war had become the principal means of settling disputes—an 'unanswerable test of strength', as George Orwell later put it. But it could not be a *legitimate* arbiter of disputes, Kant argued, since war was a contest purely of strength and not of rights. Its outcomes told us nothing about what law and reason had to say about the relative merits of the disputants' positions. From this condition of international anarchy, peace would have to be established; it would not emerge naturally. But neither could it be imposed from the top, since that would arouse suspicion and opposition from below. Kant thought the idea that sovereigns could have perpetual peace imposed upon them utterly absurd—a 'sheer political delusion', according to W.B. Gallie.[26]

Perpetual peace could be achieved only if states themselves embraced it as their goal. That must be the first step. Without a political commitment to peace, political union or some other 'grand design' could not be sustained in practice. Even if one were established, its member states would continue to have different values and interests to compete over and therefore could not be relied upon to support the union's decisions, abide by its judgements, or commit sufficient resources to the common good. Only if their values and interests were harmonized first—through shared recognition of the goal of peace—and states moved to freely commit themselves to a law-governed order would political association or union become a practical possibility. Until then, world government—no matter how necessary for world peace—would remain unachievable.

So, instead of a world republic, Kant proposed something much more modest: a 'federation of free states'. This would be a voluntary international organization to promote peace. But even this modest proposal could be achieved only if some basic conditions of civilized and harmonious relations between states were realized first—Kant's 'preliminary articles for perpetual peace among states'. These were: (1) treaties that contain seeds of future war are not valid; (2) no independent state shall come under the dominion of another; (3) standing armies shall—in time—be abolished; (4) national debts that could create friction should be avoided; (5) no state shall interfere by force in the domestic constitution of any other; and (6) no state shall use a form of war-making that makes future peace impossible. These preliminary articles would establish peace, or rather they would abolish war, by establishing an international order based on the rule of law. Achieved first within a community of the like-minded, others would be pulled towards peace by its apparent benefits. But by themselves these conditions would not establish a permanent peace. That would need something more.

Often dubbed a 'cosmopolitan', 'utopian', or 'idealist', Kant was actually among the more conservative of the schemers for world peace. Better than almost anyone else up to this point, he understood that peace had to be built from the ground up. His was a gradualist approach to peace *between* states, whose ambition would be realized only in the long-term and only if it survived the setbacks and challenges set before it—something he was at pains to emphasize again and again. Kant recognized that without fundamental changes to how states functioned and acted, international organizations for peace would remain built upon pillars of sand, liable to dissolve. Only once the six preliminary articles—designed to limit, and hopefully end, war between states—were firmly established in practice could the final three, much larger, leaps towards perpetual peace be attempted: the establishment of republican constitutions in all states, a law of nations founded on a federation of free states, and a concept of world citizenship based on rights of hospitality. Once all this was achieved, peace would be preserved not by the coercive power of the central confederation but by the willing acceptance of independent states and their preparedness to do their share of the work needed to achieve and maintain it.

This overall logic is perhaps best exemplified by the third of the definitive articles: the right to enjoy hospitability. Kant argued that beyond their own states, individuals had but one right—that of hospitality. In other words, the right to the free movement of people and goods between states. Once in another state, however, individuals were subjected to the laws of that state. A state could not use force on another to enforce its own law there, for instance. Nor could a supra-national federation. Later formalized by political scientists as 'convergence theory', the free movement of people could help transmit ideas, practices, habits of cooperation, and shared understandings of justice across borders as governments recognized their mutual obligations towards one another's citizens. This offered a bottom-up pathway for establishing bonds of community that extended beyond political borders.[27]

Unlike many of those that came before him, Kant understood that the degree of peacefulness within an international system rested, ultimately, on the nature of that system's main actors—sovereign states. He also recognized that human diversity produced a plurality of communities with different values and interests that could not be forced by a higher power to live together peacefully. States can be constrained by a supra-national authority only if they voluntarily choose to be so. This is a path they would be unlikely to take unless they had already changed how they thought and acted internationally (the six preliminary articles) and changed their internal constitutions to align both their interests and their values with the common interests and values of the world community as a whole. There could be no law of nations or federation amongst them except through the voluntary acceptance of these things by states, however long that might take to achieve. Such a union would be directed not towards the attainment of some higher value (of an empire, state, or common religion) but towards the peaceful coexistence of its members. Peace would become an end in itself founded, ultimately, on the mutual interests and shared values of enlightened (and republican) states. Where Rousseau believed that the irrationality of human passions made this a hopeless cause, Kant trusted that if sufficient attention was paid to establishing solid foundations, constitutional governance and with it peace could be extended beyond individual states and into the international realm. This would take time, and the attainment of many 'minor utopias' both at home and abroad, to achieve but eventually, Kant believed, the aggressive passions and selfish interests of rulers could be tamed by the application of law.

Republican government, the rule of law, and mutual hospitality became canons of an emerging liberal peace. To these, eighteenth- and nineteenth-century liberals added commerce.[28] Trade figured large in Adam Smith's *Wealth of Nations*, still one of the cornerstones of economic theory, first published in 1776. Smith argued that free trade was not only essential for prosperity (and hence domestic harmony) but that it could also help establish international peace. The republican publicist and agitator, Thomas Paine, agreed, writing that 'if commerce were permitted to act to the extent it is capable, it would extirpate the system of war'—and inspire liberal revolutions.[29] Another liberal reformist of the period, Richard Cobden, maintained that trade and peace went hand in hand: trade required peace for its flourishing but in turn contributed to the peace by making societies dependent on one another for their prosperity. Cobden believed that it was not only war, but also preparation for war, that ruined wealth.[30] He campaigned against mercantilism and in support of the control and limitation of armaments and the compulsory arbitration of disputes.

Trade coupled with law also featured prominently in Jeremy Bentham's (1748–1832) proposal for a rule-governed international order. Commonly attributed with coining the term 'international law', Bentham saw law and trade as the cornerstones of world peace. He argued that rights and other social goods could not exist naturally but only when prescribed by law. Evoking the utilitarianism for which he is best known, Bentham argued that the lawmaker's primary duty was to ensure the maximum happiness of the greatest number of people. In the international realm, this would be best achieved through a law-based order that aligned interests and permitted the peaceful resolution of disputes. Bentham argued that colonies should be abolished because they represented the triumph of might over right, running roughshod over the right to self-government in particular, the sale of weapons should be controlled by law (since expenditure on armaments reduced national wealth), and disputes between states should be subjected to arbitration and settled on their legal merits.[31]

Free trade—'the invisible hand of peace'—became an article of faith for many nineteenth-century liberals, and with seemingly good reason.[32] Not only did trade contribute to unprecedented improvements in wealth and social wellbeing, its acceleration seemed to be connected to the greater peacefulness experienced by post-Napoleonic Europe. Some liberals, however, preferred imperial expansion over free trade. They argued that the path to world peace was paved by empire, since—much as Cicero had claimed—empires 'civilized' and tamed colonized non-European peoples to the general improvement of all. This would be a new imperial peace on a global scale fifteen centuries after the demise of *Pax Romana*. Bentham and Cobden, though, repudiated imperialism. Bentham's utilitarianism rested on the equal value of all humans—men and women, white and black—an egalitarianism rejected by the imperialists. Cobden, meanwhile, understood that imperial trade was anything but free. Only *free* trade produced peace, he insisted. Unequal and coercive economic relations lay the foundations for war.[33] Cobden was a particularly outspoken critic of one such war, the British empire's war to compel China to accept the import of opium.

The second of Bentham's keen interests, international law, also rose to greater prominence. In the twentieth century, as law came to be used to both regulate and prohibit war there was sometimes a tension between the two goals. Progressives in the nineteenth century, however, hoped that one would lead inevitably to the other: that the creation of international law would bind peoples together into a common humanity and that from this would spring world peace. Early efforts to regulate the conduct of war were not, as some contemporary critics suggest, aimed at justifying and supporting war but at limiting it in the hope of moving the world towards its elimination—an early form of what nowadays we call 'nudge politics'.[34] One of the founding lights of the Red Cross movement, Gustave Moynier, made exactly this point at a lecture he gave in Geneva in the winter of 1890. Reflecting on the first Geneva Convention of 1864, which had mandated the provision of medical care for war-wounded soldiers, Moynier observed that the Convention 'has furnished an argument in favour of the brotherhood of men'. By adopting it, 'the several factions of civilized mankind have—never before with so much unity—placed themselves under a common rule, formulated entirely in the light of moral considerations…Recognizing that after all they belong to the same family, men have concluded that they ought to begin by showing some regard for one another's suffering'.[35] If those sentiments could be nurtured, Moynier explained, it could lead to yet more limitations on war, first moderating the suffering caused, then eradicating unjustified war, and then abolishing war itself.

Endowed with its own internal debates and contradictions, nineteenth-century liberalism bequeathed both a defence of European empire and the idea of individual human rights based on the equality of humans that would undermine it. The principle of humans' equal worth gave rise to notions of democratic government and the concept of the democratic peace, belief in the power of reason to resolve disputes peacefully, and the idea that humanity could have common values and interests. These were extensions of ideas developed earlier by champions of the Enlightenment.[36] If trade could harmonize interests, they wondered, could reason, empathy, and humanity harmonize our values sufficiently to achieve world peace?

Europeans of this time were not idle thinkers; they were great 'doers' imbued with a self-confident belief that innovation, technology, and hard work could solve the world's problems. The problem of war was no exception. They turned an idea of world peace into a mass international political movement. Agitation for a better world, based on natural rights, emerged as a political force in the late eighteenth century, driven among other things by William Wilberforce's long and ultimately successful campaign to abolish the international slave trade. Peace activism, meanwhile, had its roots in the moral renunciation of war advanced by non-conformist Christians such as the Mennonites and Quakers. The first European peace movements, such as the London Peace Society established in 1819, were initially Christian, middle-class, and quite conservative.[37] Peace was understood as a religious not political concern, one that should be pursued through personal disavowal of war and the charitable donation of humanitarian aid to its victims. In the decades that followed, peace societies spread across Europe and North America. In 1843, some 2,000 delegates attended the first International Peace Congress in London. Subsequent congresses were held in Brussels, Paris, Frankfurt, and Manchester. The 1849 conference in Paris was chaired by renowned novelist Victor Hugo. Hugo proposed a 'United States of Europe'—an idea that harked back to earlier times but that also looked forward to the future European Union.

Towards the century's end, Alfred Nobel instated the Peace Prize that bears his name and American industrialist Andrew Carnegie threw his weight—and financial resources—behind the peace movement. There was an urgent need, Carnegie argued, to 'hasten the abolition of international war, the foulest blot upon our civilization. Although we no longer eat our fellowmen, nor torture prisoners, nor sack cities killing their inhabitants, we still kill each other in war like barbarians. Only wild beasts are excusable for doing that'.[38] All this created a self-confident belief that the world was progressing towards peace, even if there was still no shared understanding of what that would entail or obvious signs of political commitment to the ideal. Undeterred, organizations for peace continued to be established, some of which, including the International Parliamentary Union and International Peace Bureau, endure today.

The peace movement reached its zenith at the turn of the century. In 1899, Tsar Nicholas II of Russia—one of Europe's last absolutist monarchs—summoned an international conference to end war and limit armaments. Most European governments were sceptical, seeing the Tsar's peace overture as a thinly veiled attempt to buy Russia time in an international arms and technology race that it was losing. Nonetheless, the Tsar's call transformed the international peace movement into an apparently viable political force. The 1899 Hague Conference was a major international spectacle, its proceedings covered daily in the popular press across Europe and followed with interest. Peace advocates campaigned for two innovations above all: the compulsory arbitration of disputes between states and an agreement to limit armaments. Europe's rulers were, as we might expect, reticent. None wanted to limit their right to wage war wherever and whenever they saw fit. Moreover, the powers profiting from the new arms race—Germany especially, but also France and Britain—were adamantly opposed to restrictions on their armaments. The opposition of the great powers, and their deep scepticism towards the conference's objectives, ensured that the peace activists' hopes were never likely to be satisfied.

Today, history books tend to recall the conference as a monumental failure; a testimony to the peace movement's folly. But that is not how it was seen at the time, for it produced a series of Conventions—including one providing for the voluntary arbitration of disputes, and another limiting the use of certain types of weapons (such as dum-dum bullets and aerial projectiles)—that enshrined ideas central to peace into international law for the first time. What is more, the delegates agreed to return to The Hague to continue their deliberations. Thus, the 1899 conference set in train a process—interrupted but also pushed along by two world wars—that culminated in the outlawing of aggressive war and establishment of a system of collective security in the United Nations Charter, adopted in San Francisco on 26 June 1945.

Whatever disappointment there might have been at this first attempt to organize world peace, activism continued in the face of the gathering storm clouds of war. As Michael Howard explained, the abolition of war 'seemed almost within reach' through 'the civilized intercourse of rational men, representing the aspirations of the broad, peace loving masses of the world'.[39] But in reality these hopes were fading fast thanks to the rising tide of nationalism and great power competition. At the 1907 Hague Conference, states agreed to create a permanent tribunal to adjudicate disputes—an institution we know today as the International Court of Justice. Six years later, Andrew Carnegie's pantheon to peace in The Hague—the Peace Palace—was opened. Just twelve months after that, the world was plunged into the Great War.

It is one of the ironies of the history of peace that the First World War erupted at precisely the moment when peace activism seemed at its height. At the turn of the twentieth century, hundreds of peace societies existed across Europe; parliaments were regularly presented with proposals and petitions for peace; states had even, as we have seen, accepted limitations on their right to wage war and restrictions on how it must be fought. They had also agreed to consider more limitations. Yet none of this prevented or even delayed Europe's slide into war.

Why? The march to war in the thirty-six days following the assassination of Austria's Archduke Franz Ferdinand exposed the fact that the peace movement was neither as influential nor as international as it had appeared. Peace activists had grossly overestimated the capacity of reason to leash the passions of war. In particular, they had badly misjudged the power of nationalism to mobilize populations to war—something that later generations of peace activists would do too. Once the dogs of war began to bark in the wake of the assassination in Sarajevo, Europe's peace activists could do little to arrest the 'return of warrior society'.[40] Sometimes, it must be said, it took physical force to silence the voices of peace. On the eve of war, the enigmatic French socialist peace activist, Jean Jaures, was gunned down at a Montmartre cafe by a nationalist agitator determined to silence his campaign for peace. But, in truth, the peace movement put up little resistance to the march of war. Nationalism did not just trump peace, it ripped it apart as peace societies rallied behind their own national cause, each claiming that its side had the cause of peace and justice behind it. Ultimately, the passions that drove societies to war in 1914 were simply too strong for the peace movement to counter. 'Every German friend of peace', President of the German Peace Society, Ludwig Quidde, wrote in a pamphlet shortly after war was declared, 'must fulfill his duty to the fatherland'. Peace activists would not be 'outdone in patriotic devotion'.[41] Quidde went on to win the Nobel Prize for Peace in 1927.

Why did Europe's supposedly civilized and rational leaders lead their peoples into such a disastrous war, one that destroyed or massively weakened every one of the states that joined it in 1914? Dozens of books have sought to answer that question, revealing the many factors at play: nationalism, fear, mistrust, the cult of the offensive, but also a series of tragic misunderstandings. Ultimately, though, as Christopher Clark shows well, Europe's leaders sleepwalked into war. Confident in their own abilities and unaware of the dangers that lurked ahead, only at the very last minute, when it was too late, did they realize what they had unleashed. On the eve of war, Sir Edward Grey, Britain's foreign secretary, looked out of his window across Horse Guards Parade: 'The lamps are going out all over Europe', he said, 'we shall not see them lit again in our lifetime'. Only then, at the very brink, did the grim reality of a general European war become apparent.

The Allies dubbed the First World War the 'great war for peace'.[42] The immense sacrifices made by their populations could not be repaid by anything less than a new world order that would prevent future aggression and establish sustained peace. In the decades that followed, and despite the fact that the global peace movement never again reached the heights of popularity seen prior to the First World War, genuine progress was made on the further legal restriction of the right of states to wage war.

Alfred Zimmern was one of those who argued that the great war should be succeeded by a great peace, guaranteed by a new kind of international political order. Sceptical of arguments for world government put forward by John Hobson and H.G. Wells, among others, on the grounds that such concentration of power would lead to tyranny and more practical grounds that the great powers would never agree to it, Zimmern argued for a commonwealth of nations that would promote cooperation and collective action. During the First World War, he was brought into the British government to advise on how that might be done.

After the war, the great powers agreed to establish an international organization for peace. The new League of Nations would arbitrate disputes between states and could recommend collective measures against those judged guilty of launching aggressive wars. Whilst states retained their basic right to wage war, this was for the first time limited. States were now required by law to accept arbitration before committing their forces to battle, though they were not obliged to accept the results and retained their right to use force should peaceful means prove unsatisfactory. The League's Council, which took decisions by consensus, could recommend (but not compel) measures up to and including war to address threats to the peace. But although the League enjoyed some early successes, it was crippled from the outset by the American decision not to join, which left it with the authority but not the material power to impose its will. The League was further hampered by a legal framework that relied on the goodwill of states themselves (to accept arbitration and implement the League's recommendations) and their capacity to find common ground. The League's failure to respond effectively to the Japanese invasion of Manchuria in 1931 and Italian invasion of Abyssinia four years later exposed these limitations brutally.

Aware that the League's Covenant imposed only limited restrictions on the rights of states to wage war, Chicago attorney and peace activist, Samuel Levinson, began to agitate for a complete legal ban. The idea was taken up by James Shotwell, an adviser to Woodrow Wilson's administration, who found an enthusiastic supporter in the form of Aristide Briand, the French Foreign Minister. Briand proposed the renunciation of war to his American counterpart, Frank Kellogg, who found the idea appealing because it seemed to insulate America from involvement in future European conflicts. The 'Kellogg–Briand' pact was signed in 1928. Its signatories, which included the US, France, and a dozen others (and eventually nearly fifty states), agreed to renounce war as an instrument of policy. Written off by many modern historians as an act of naïve utopianism at a time of rising fascism and communism, the pact established in the minds of some the radical notion that states ought to be stripped of their right to wage war altogether.[43]

Another, yet more devastating, world war pushed governments to actually take this ultimate legal step. The horrors of the Second World War and the dawning of the nuclear age reinforced the view that more must be done to fashion a peaceful world order. Indeed, even the hardened realists of the Cold War period opined for peace. Thus, Hans Morgenthau told readers of his 1948 book *Politics Among Nations* that 'the abolition of war is obviously the fundamental problem confronting international thought'.[44] In his 1946 book on atomic weapons, Bernard Brodie observed that: 'Thus far, the chief purpose of our military establishment has been to win wars. From now on its chief purpose must be to avert them'.[45]

The Charter of the United Nations, agreed in 1945, prohibited the threat or use of force in international affairs (Article 2(4)). At the stroke of a pen, the presumption that states have an inherent right to wage war was replaced by the presumption that no such right existed. Wars to expand territory or build empires were outlawed. In place of a right to wage war, states were given a right to enjoy the non-interference of outsiders in their domestic affairs. In their international dealings at least, force could be used lawfully only to defend themselves and others from attack (Article 51) or when specifically authorized by the UN's Security Council (Article 39). The Security Council, composed of five permanent (China, France, the UK, the US, the Soviet Union/Russia) and (ultimately) ten elected members, was vested with primary responsibility for international peace and security and granted the legal authority to authorize the use of force and other coercive measures to that end.

The new legal order established at San Francisco in 1945 severely limited the rights and capacities of states to wage war. Once a defining right enjoyed by states, aggressive war and territorial conquest were now forbidden. This diminished the allure of war in two ways. Now rendered illegal, it would be much more likely that acts of aggression would be treated as violations of the law and subjected to censure, punishment, and possibly even a forceful collective response—as the North Koreans and Iraqis discovered in 1951 and 1991 respectively. The chances of coming out on top of an overt war of aggression were now much reduced. What is more, the outlawing of aggressive war and territorial conquest meant that even if a state could prevail on the battlefield, it would find it impossible to translate its gains into the legitimate and lawful acquisition of territory. As Indonesia (with respect to East Timor), Israel (Occupied Palestinian Territories), and more recently Iraq (Kuwait) and Russia (Crimea) have discovered, it is one thing to seize territory from another state, but quite another to have their right to rule it recognized by others.

War between states fell sharply. Overtly aggressive international wars, such as North Korea's invasion of the south in 1950 and Iraq's invasion of Kuwait forty years later, were repelled by large, multinational interventions authorized by the UN. Countless others were no doubt inhibited by the sizable costs that would now likely be imposed. But there were gaps in the system. Enforcement of the new legal order rested chiefly on the great powers, who were expected to exercise responsibility for international peace and security. But, as one of the leading authorities on world politics during the Cold War, Hedley Bull, famously explained, these powers acted more often like the 'great irresponsibles', pursuing their own interests at the expense of their global responsibilities and therefore 'forfeiting the claims they had begun to build up...to be regarded by others as responsible managers of international society as a whole'.[46] The great powers themselves continued to defy the law—the Soviet Union in Afghanistan, the US in Iraq, for example—and found themselves deadlocked in cases involving allies or clients.

Another gap in the post-1945 system, one brutally exposed by the end of the Cold War, was that whilst it prohibited war *between* states, it said nothing about war *within* states. As interstate war declined, so intrastate wars rose to take their place.

Determined leaders could always find exploitable gaps in the law. To close these gaps, some international lawyers advanced the idea of individual criminal responsibility for war. That is, rulers who violate Article 2(4) of the UN Charter should be judged to have committed a crime of aggression and should be punished as such. The crime of aggression was included in the statutes of the Nuremberg and Tokyo Tribunals which prosecuted leading Nazi and Japanese perpetrators for crimes committed during the Second World War. The crime of aggression formed a significant part of the prosecution's case and featured in the final judgements too. After a lengthy hiatus, the crime appeared once again during the negotiations on the Rome Statute of the International Criminal Court (ICC) in 1998. Considered too controversial to reach a consensus upon, delegates nevertheless agreed to revisit the concept at a later stage. At the 2010 Kampala conference of ICC state parties, a definition of the crime of aggression was agreed and ratified by twenty-eight states. The crime of aggression means the 'planning, preparation, initiation or execution, by a person effectively in a position to exercise control over or to direct the political action of a state, of an act of aggression which, by its character, gravity, and scale, constitutes a manifest violation of the Charter of the United Nations' (Articles 8 (1 and 2) of the Rome Statute of the International Criminal Court). This means the use of force against the territorial integrity or political independence of another state and can include invasion, occupation, annexation, and blockade. By the time it came into force, in July 2018, thirty-five states had committed themselves to the law. Whilst uptake remains limited, not least because rulers are wary about placing themselves in potential legal peril, aggression is now formally prohibited as an international crime. Leaders who commit such acts can now (albeit only sometimes) be held individually responsible by law. What was once a fundamental right of states is now a punishable crime.

Another strand of activism that reached new heights after the Second World War focused on the alleviation of suffering in war. Driven by a determination to ensure that never again would the world see atrocities such as those of the Holocaust, international human rights and humanitarian law were further developed and codified through a series of international treaties. On 9 December 1948, the newly established UN General Assembly approved a Convention prohibiting the crime of genocide and establishing a legal duty to prevent it and punish the perpetrators. The very next day, the Universal Declaration of Human Rights was proclaimed. The laws of war were further codified in the four Geneva Conventions (1949), two additional protocols (1977), and in a range of other treaties and protocols covering the use of Certain Conventional Weapons (1980, 1995, 1996, 2008). Of particular importance in all this were Common Article 3 of the 1949 Geneva Conventions, which committed parties to respect the human rights of all those placed *hors de combat*, and the Convention on the Protection of Civilian Persons (Convention IV), which offered legal protection to non-combatants in occupied territories. The Geneva Protocols (1977) extended the legal protection afforded to non-combatants to situations of non-international armed conflict. International humanitarian law thus established a normative standard of civilian protection that not only prohibited attacks on non-combatants and restricted the use of certain weapons but that also called for the prevention of atrocity crimes (genocide) and punishment of perpetrators.

This legalist approach received the political backing of the UN's Security Council, enabling the extension of practical action for peace into civil wars, which, since the end of the Cold War, had become the most common form of warfare. Since 1998, the Security Council has adopted a relatively broad civilian protection agenda that encompasses demands for compliance with International Humanitarian Law, operational issues connected to peacekeeping operations and humanitarian access, international responses to humanitarian emergencies, disarmament issues, and peace-building. The Security Council has also established that the protection of civilians from mass violence is a matter of international peace and security that falls within its purview. In 1999, it unanimously adopted Resolution 1265, expressing its 'willingness' to consider 'appropriate measures' in response 'to situations of armed conflict where civilians are being targeted or where humanitarian assistance to civilians is being deliberately obstructed'. It also promised to explore how peacekeeping mandates might be reframed to afford better protection to endangered civilians. In 2006, the Security Council adopted Resolution 1674, which demanded that parties to armed conflict grant unfettered humanitarian access to civilians, restated the Council's willingness to take action in cases where civilians were deliberately targeted, and affirmed the 'responsibility to protect' principle.

The most obvious way in which the UN has lent practical support to this civilian protection agenda is through its peacekeeping operations, an approach that has again focused primarily on limiting civil wars and supporting peace processes afterwards. Starting in 1999 with the UN mission in Sierra Leone (UNAMSIL), the Security Council has increasingly authorized peacekeepers to use all means necessary to protect civilians. In the 2010s, the Council became gradually more proactive in its civilian protection actions during (some) civil wars. Missions in the Central African Republic (MINUSCA), Mali (MINUSMA), and South Sudan (UNMISS) took on this role as their primary function. In the Democratic Republic of Congo (DRC), the Security Council went even further by tasking a 'Force Intervention Brigade' composed of African soldiers to 'eradicate' non-state armed groups that attacked civilians.

Meanwhile, legal regimes and international institutions were established to protect those made especially vulnerable by war, including refugees, displaced persons, women, and children. Of these, the best developed is the international refugee regime governed by the 1951 Refugee Convention and subsequent 1967 Protocol and overseen by the UN High Commissioner for Refugees (UNHCR). This system grants people facing persecution the right to claim asylum and receive resettlement in third countries and mandates the UNHCR to ensure that refugees have access to protection and durable solutions to their displacement.[47] During the 1990s, it became apparent that this system was unable to cope with a new displacement crisis—that of *internal* displacement: people forced from their homes by mass violence and other ills but remaining within their host country. Seen as a largely 'domestic' issue, there was little appetite for an international convention governing the displaced, so instead the UNHCR extended its mandate to cover the protection of all displaced persons and UN officials developed 'guiding principles' for their treatment based on the human rights they already enjoyed.[48]

One longstanding aspect of war that gained political prominence only in the 1990s was sexual and gender-based violence. The use of rape as a weapon of war or genocide in Bosnia, Rwanda, and elsewhere helped shine light on crimes that had until then been hidden or seen as inevitable consequences of war. This pushed the UN Security Council to establish the protection of women and girls as one of the principal elements of its 'Women, Peace and Security' agenda adopted in Resolution 1325 (2001). Since then, the UN has established a number of mandates focused on the prevention of sexual and gender-based violence, and the prosecution of perpetrators. It has instituted a series of annual reports that identify where these crimes are committed and advocate for steps to be taken in response. These developments paralleled initiatives focused on protecting children in armed conflict.

Beyond this, the principle of individual criminal responsibility for crimes committed during war, raised in the Nuremberg statute, has become well established, as has the principle (though not yet the practice) of universal jurisdiction for these crimes.[49] The Rome Statute, which established the International Criminal Court (ICC) in 1998, held that the court's jurisdiction could be invoked when a state party proved unwilling or unable to investigate allegations or widespread and systematic war crimes, crimes against humanity, and genocide. The ICC prosecutor's office could initiate proceedings in cases where it was able to persuade a panel of judges, where a complaint was made by a signatory state, or when a case was referred to the prosecutor by the Security Council. The Security Council reserved the right to postpone investigations by one year.

To date, the Security Council has referred situations in Darfur and Libya to the ICC and the governments of the DRC, Uganda, and the Central African Republic have requested that the ICC investigate and prosecute crimes committed in their countries. An investigation into atrocities committed in Kenya 2007–8 was triggered by the fact that Kenya was a party to the Rome Statute. And whilst the 'great irresponsibles'—namely, Russia and China in this case—have thus far blocked the application of International Humanitarian Law to Syria's civil war, the law's long arm is reaching there nonetheless. Frustrated by the Security Council's failure to refer the situation in Syria to the ICC, the UN's General Assembly—which includes all states—voted overwhelmingly in 2016 to establish its own mechanism to gather the evidence of atrocity crimes needed to support future prosecutions. But although legal accountability delayed is not necessarily accountability denied, the ICC has struggled to bring forward successful prosecutions as many states have refused to cooperate, choosing instead to protect themselves and their friends. The Court has also been beset by accusations of bias. Unsurprisingly, some governments that welcomed the concept of international criminal justice in theory started reacting against the Court when it actually began indicting leaders and soldiers for their crimes.

A separate line of effort that emerged from the ashes of the Second World War focused on harmonizing the interests of states as a way of increasing the payoffs of peace. In the 1930s, Romanian-born academic David Mitrany began developing what would later be known as the 'functionalist' theory of world politics. In fact, 'functionalism' ought to be reckoned among the most compelling theories of world peace. It is disarmingly simple. Like Kant, Mitrany believed that peace could only be built on the solid foundation of mutual interest. Without mutual interest, peace was doomed to fail. However elegant in their design, pacts between states were always unresponsive to demands for social change, and for that reason would always be disregarded by those pursuing change. What was needed was an approach that harnessed rather than resisted these social forces. 'Community itself will acquire a living body not through a written act of faith but through active organic development', wrote Mitrany.[50] Peace could not be inscribed from the top down. It must be built 'branch by branch'.

Mitrany argued that states and societies should focus on matters of practical cooperation with one another, beginning with those things that were least controversial such as postal services, telecommunications, and transport. Cooperation would yield practical rewards and establish the bonds of trust needed to support deeper cooperation. Meanwhile, war would become costlier and less rewarding. Eventually, states and societies would become so enmeshed and interdependent that war between them would become unthinkable—an idea later popularized as the 'Golden Arches theory of conflict prevention' by Thomas Friedman.[51] These were ideas put to work through European integration after the Second World War. They proved spectacularly successful, helping make the world's most violent continent become its most peaceful in the space of a single generation.

But it was not only in Europe that functional interdependence helped the pursuit of peace. In East Asia, and to an extent Latin America too, the demise of interstate war was propelled by burgeoning interdependence. As Mitrany knew well, economic interdependence makes war and the threat of war costlier whilst increasing the payoffs of peace. War, and threatened war, disrupt cross-border trade, significantly weakening economies that are heavily dependent on trade. Militarized tensions also damage confidence, reducing investment flows and increasing the costs of borrowing. International stability is a prerequisite for confident economic planning and management and for the direction of national efforts towards the civilian economy. Trade requires stability to ensure the safe and timely passage of physical goods, to create confidence in contracts and protect the stability of currency. Partners must also have confidence that stability can be maintained in the long-term, or at least over the term of an investment cycle. Reciprocity is vital too—trade requires buyers, sellers, and a marketplace that both have confidence in. It requires rules for transferring goods, mutually satisfying taxation and tariff regimes, and—usually—some understanding that the relationship is positive-sum, in that both parties extract value from it. Governments that choose a path to economic betterment through trade and cooperation acquire an interest in protecting stability and reciprocity. They also gain an interest in limiting those forces that might challenge stability and reciprocity, including armed conflict, mercantilism, and atavistic nationalism. These forces reduce confidence and trust, and discourage investment in production and consumption by increasing the chances of loss or low-return, dampening trade and therefore domestic growth prospects. Governments may, of course, still choose to ferment military instability but economic interdependence makes such courses of action more expensive than they once were.

To become successful traders, states in Western Europe, East Asia, and elsewhere adopted an *internationalist* approach to their foreign relations that emphasized freedom of trade and privileged the maintenance of order and stability. In the political field, the adoption of internationalist mindsets encouraged the development of habits of multilateralism and the proliferation of international and regional organizations governing every aspect of a state's foreign relations and embedding them within dense functional networks of cooperation. This encouraged some governments to prioritize goals that could be achieved through cooperation over territorial disputes or other aspects of foreign rivalry. Elite coalitions across government and the economic sector 'locked in' national commitments to internationalism: 'there is a virtual built-in guarantee that like-minded internationalizing coalitions will be...reluctant to defect through militarized strategies or to exacerbate territorial or ethno-religious disputes. The potential for armed conflict and extensive military buildups threatens the economic and political fundamentals—fiscal conserva-tism, macroeconomic, political and regional stability; global access—that an internationalizing strategy requires'.[52] In regions where interdependence took off, regional elite networks locked themselves into self-binding commitments in support of regional peace and stability. As Mitrany foresaw, it was these commitments and not formal institutions or security alliances that bound states and societies together.[53] They provided reassurance and built confidence through informal yet tangible—and often highly personal—networks and delivered wider social and economic benefits. And those regions where cooper-ation took off performed much better than those where it did not.

The natural corollary of cooperation is that predation becomes less rewarding. As national economies become more reliant on international trade, so the costs and benefits associated with predatory military behaviour shift. The threat or use of violence becomes prohibitively expensive because of its disruptive effects, pushing governments away from belligerent or expansionist foreign policy postures towards more cooperative stances that support the prevailing status quo. Game theorists, for example, have long shown how mutually beneficial trade relations make even states in conflict less willing to fight. The 'initiating' state is inhibited from fighting because of the expected losses to trade, whilst the 'target' is more likely to make concessions to the initiator for precisely the same reasons.

The weakening of predatory military politics, brought about in some parts of the world by the conscious adoption of 'functionalist' approaches to peace, was reinforced by the outlawing of aggressive war, the rise of humanitarian-ism, and the emergence of individual criminal responsibility described earlier. These changes to the nature of state power made predatory behaviour much less rewarding than it once was. Technology, information, and productivity replaced land and labour as the principal sources of economic wealth, mak-ing trade and investment a better pathway to prosperity than armed aggres-sion and territorial acquisition.[54] War, quite literally, stopped paying.[55] Meanwhile, the security system established by the UN Charter, underpinned by rules of non-interference, non-use of force, and collective security, was more hostile to the aggressive use of force than any that had gone before.[56]

After centuries of thought and activism in pursuit of peace, war was finally forced into decline by international law, collective action, functional interdependence, trade, and human rights. War's elimination is now foretold by some military historians and moral philosophers alike. But despite all the undoubted progress, war has proven resilient. It has even staged a comeback. World peace, meanwhile, has proven elusive. That it remains so is clearly not for the lack of thought or activism. Perhaps the problem lies in human nature itself. What if war is an innate part of the human condition; our inner demons given outward expression? What if it is an 'enhancer' of our culture, as Christopher Coker suggests?[57] Were that true, world peace would face an unbeatable opponent: nature itself.

CHAPTER 3

HARD-WIRED FOR WAR?

The condition of Man ... is a condition of warre of every one against everyone.

—Thomas Hobbes (1651)

The primitive individualism described by Hobbes is hence a myth. The savage is not solitary, and his instinct is collectivist. There was never a 'war of all against all'.

—Friedrich Hayek (1988)

A re we innately warlike? It is not difficult to find arguments saying that we are. American anthropologist and ecologist, Michael Ghiglieri, for example, maintains that war predates humanity itself, that it is natural, and that it vies with sex for the distinction of being the most significant driver of human evolution.[1] Mike Martin, too, argues that war is caused by subconscious desires formed over millennia by evolution.[2] These are views of humanity's natural condition widely associated with a description of the 'state of nature'—the human condition before states and societies—penned by one of England's foremost philosophers, Thomas Hobbes (1588–1679). Hobbes suggested that in the state of nature, all humans were essentially equal. None had the intellect or strength to protect themselves sufficiently from others and neither was it possible to trust others, for without laws and states there was nothing to inhibit human rapaciousness. Humans could, and would, attack one another for their food, their shelter, and their mates. An indomitable fear of being attacked would force individuals to attack others first, to pre-empt the inevitable assaults on themselves. In this situation, 'every man is enemy to every man' since none could assuredly trust or defend himself from the others.

In such condition, there is no place for industry; because the fruit thereof is uncertain: and consequently no culture of the earth; no navigation, nor use of the commodities that may be imported by sea; no commodious building; no instruments of moving, and removing, such things as require much force; no knowledge of the face of the earth; no account of time; no arts; no letters; no society; and which is worst of all, continual fear, and danger of violent death; and the life of man, solitary, poor, nasty, brutish, and short.[3]

Before the state, the human condition was a perpetual 'warre' of all against all—*bellum omnium contra omnes*—a daily struggle for bare survival in a kill-or-be-killed world. In such conditions, American polymath William Sumner explained in 1906, 'the first task of life is to live'.[4]

Hobbes' portrayal of life before civilization has come to be seen in some quarters as a more or less accurate historical description, though whether he intended it as such is open to debate. Thomas Henry Huxley, a zoologist made famous by his 1860 Oxford debate with Samuel Wilberforce on the subject of evolution, wrote nearly thirty years later that the struggle of all against all was the normal and natural condition of existence.[5] Then, in the early twentieth century, a series of remarkable finds by Raymond Dart appeared to prove the point—that early humans were violent, aggressive, and lived in a perpetual state of 'warre'.

In 1924, whilst working as Professor of Anatomy in South Africa, Dart, who was born above a shop in the Brisbane suburb of Toowong, made a startling discovery in a limestone quarry at Taung: the fossil of an *Australopithecus*, an extinct hominid that lived 2–3 million years ago and was closely related to humans. The fossils he found included fractured skulls and shattered bones. Evidence, Dart concluded, that the specimens had died violent deaths at the hands of conspecifics. From this relatively scant evidence, Dart enthusiastically deduced that our distant ancestors were murderous, cannibalistic 'killer apes' who waged perpetual war on one other as well as on other species. 'The blood-bespattered, slaughter-gutted archives of human history', he colourfully explained, 'accord with early universal cannibalism, with animal and human sacrificial practices...and with the world-wide scalping, head-hunting, body-mutilating and necrophilic practices of mankind in proclaiming this common bloodlust differentiator, this predaceous habit, this mark of Cain that separates man dietetically from his anthropoidal relatives and allies him rather with the deadly Carnivora'.[6] 'The loathsome cruelty of man', he continued, 'forms one of his inescapable, characteristic and differentiative features'.[7] *Australopithecines*, Dart insisted, 'were murderers and flesh eaters; their favourite tool was a bludgeon of bone'.[8]

The idea that humans evolved from murderous killer apes proved popular. It has featured in Hollywood epics. The opening scenes of Stanley Kubrick's *2001: A Space Odyssey* feature a primitive 'monkey-man' who discovers a conveniently shaped animal bone and promptly bashes in the skull of the nearest conspecific. 'Man is a predator whose natural instinct is to kill with a weapon', wrote Robert Ardrey in 1961.[9] Austrian zoologist Konrad Lorenz—whose work on animal aggression helped establish the field of ethology and earn him the Nobel Prize in Physiology in 1973—argued that patterns observed in animals could explain innate human aggression.[10] Through the savage process of their evolution, humans, Lorenz argued, had acquired an instinct for aggression that had served them well. But because early humans were not endowed with natural faculties for finding and killing prey, they had developed none of the inhibitory mechanisms against conspecific killing evident in other predators (such as tigers, for example).[11] Once they had learned to fashion weapons, humans gave themselves the capacity to kill each other with ease but had none of the natural inhibitions to stop them. 'There cannot be the slightest doubt', Lorenz insisted, 'that human militant enthusiasm evolved out of a communal defence response of our pre-human ancestors'.[12]

One popular school of thought holds that violence is an inherited genetic predisposition, with war the logical outgrowth. This view rests on observed patterns of group violence among male great apes and some of our closest relatives, chimpanzees. In the 1970s, primatologist Jane Goodall stunned the world when she wrote up her observations of chimpanzees in Gombe, Tanzania. Before Goodall's account, chimpanzees had been regarded as peaceful animals. In 1974, however, she observed six males from one group (Kasekela) attack and kill a male from another (Kahama). Over the next four years, the Kasekela group killed six more Kahama members until the latter was virtually wiped out, allowing the aggressors to seize Kahama territory.[13] If our closest relatives, the chimpanzees, engaged in warfare and coalitional killing, then it would seem fair to suggest that aggressiveness and a tendency to form coalitions of males to attack and kill outsiders were inherited traits. Those that were most successful in this violent competition won more mates and therefore reproduced more than those that did not. Over time, therefore, sexual selection favoured male temperaments disposed towards aggressive high-risk/high-gain ventures.[14] These tendencies accelerated when men combined into groups, explaining everything from small-group violence to imperialism. Modern humans, according to this perspective, can be thought of as the 'dazed survivors' of a five-million-year violent struggle for survival. Through evolution, competition for survival selected in favour of war and aggressiveness by 'demonic males', making a propensity for war 'deeply entrenched' in our nature.[15]

A related theory suggests an innate inclination to war stems not from conspecific conflict but from inter-specific struggles with prey and predators. According to one account, *Australopithecines* first developed the art of hunting—the use of organized violence to satisfy basic survival needs—and the weapons with which to do it. War was a natural outgrowth of this organized violence once groups began to compete for the spoils.[16] But the earliest humans were not just hunters. They were also the hunted. From this deeply repressed human experience, Barbara Ehrenreich writes, we developed the 'fight or flight' instinct and our capacity to band together to see off common enemies. These psychological building blocks for war were honed through thousands of years of evolutionary experience in coping with predators until they became an 'inborn tendency'.[17]

One of the pioneers of psychoanalysis, Sigmund Freud, expressed a similar view. Freud had always believed that civilization tempered the innate desires, or primordial drives, of man. Most famously, these included the desire for sex. Bewildered by the First World War—and especially his own enthusiasm for war during the patriotic frenzy of 1914—Freud amended his theories to include a dark human 'instinct for hatred and destruction'. He told Einstein: 'you are amazed that it is so easy to infect men with the war fever, and you surmise that man has in him an active instinct for hatred and destruction, amenable to such stimulations. I entirely agree with you. I believe in the existence of this instinct and have recently been at pains to study its manifestations... The upshot of these observations... is that there is no likelihood of our being able to suppress humanity's aggressive tendencies'.[18] Humans were plagued by a dark, destructive instinct fed by hatred, Freud maintained; an instinct that defied Eros and the will to live.[19] This way of thinking lives on today. In 1998, renowned political scientist and former White House adviser, Francis Fukuyama, wrote that the 'demonic males' thesis cautioned against the inclusion of women in foreign affairs on the grounds that they lacked the necessary aggressive spirit. Female leaders, he worried, might lack the toughness needed to deal with modern-day demons like Saddam Hussein.[20]

The 'demonic males' thesis assumes that the earliest human life evolved in conditions akin to the perpetual 'warre' described by Hobbes. To ascertain whether that was indeed the case, scholars have examined archaeological and ethnological evidence—the latter based on the rather flawed assumption that primitive hunter-gatherer groups of the modern era likely exhibit the same tendencies as their ancestors. Using both methods, Lawrence Keeley found ample evidence that early societies had engaged in warfare and that, overall, some

90 per cent of human societies had experienced war at least once a generation.[21] Based on fossil finds and anthropological studies of hunter-gatherer-type groups in the modern world, he estimated that deaths from war had accounted for between 7 and 40 per cent of all deaths in prehistoric times—figures which are, even at the lower end, much higher than modern casualty rates in war. On average, he suggested, around 25 per cent of prehistoric deaths were caused by violence—a figure similar to that offered by Steven Pinker. Others agree that around one quarter of prehistoric humans died violent deaths, mainly as a result of war.[22] Constant across time was humankind's innate propensity for war and the relative absence of peace.

But, for all that, Raymond Dart's findings were eventually disproved. Damaged skulls and bones, initially taken as evidence of conspecific violence, were shown to have been caused by natural processes of compression during fossilization. As for puncture marks in the skulls of *Australopithecus* (and, it should be added, baboons found nearby), South African palaeontologist C.K. Brain showed that these were probably caused by big cats.[23] On closer inspection much of the rest of the evidence for humanity's innate drive for war proved equally shaky.

There is no denying that our ancestors waged war on one another. Fossils display the signs of violent death and archaeological sites reveal multiple bodies buried together, suggesting they died at the same time—an indication of war. The ancient dead are often found lying with the weapons that killed them. Rock art depicts battles and other types of violence. Anthropologists report that hunter-gatherer societies engage in organized violence. But the fact that some of our ancestors were occasionally violent does not mean that humans are innately warlike, conditioned by evolutionary selection to be aggressive and violent. In fact, biology, archaeology, and anthropology all suggest that our propensity for war evolved alongside our social development. They suggest, in other words, that war is a social, not biological beast.

In our distant past, war was not ubiquitous. Indeed, there is little evidence of anything resembling true warfare prior to the emergence of sedentary, agricultural, societies around 10,000 BCE. Before that time, human communities lacked the internal cohesion necessary for war-making as well as the need to compete for territory, property, and stored resources that tends to drive organized violence. This means that humans did not evolve as war-fighters from the start. Rather, war has a definite origin, a long time *after* the beginnings of humanity itself. Indeed, taking account of the entire span of human history, that point of origin was quite recent: just 12,000 years of war out of a human history spanning some 130,000 years at least. Far from being an inherited genetic predisposition, war seems to have emerged as societies evolved and environmental conditions changed. As it did, humans also developed ways of resolving or managing disputes without, or with only minimal, violence. That is, they developed the art of peace. This art, reflecting perhaps the 'better angels' of human nature, evolved not years, centuries, or millennia after the emergence of war, but simultaneously with it. From the very earliest civilizations, wherever we see war, we can also detect dreams and practices of peace.

Looking more closely, we can identify three principal clusters of objections to the Hobbesian image of life before civilization and the biological explanations for war that have flowed from it: categorical problems with the theories themselves, a paucity of archaeological evidence of war everlasting, and evidence of relatively peaceful hunter-gatherer societies.

Let us begin with the categorical problems, the first of which is that Thomas Hobbes was not himself a Hobbesian—at least, not in the sense alluded to above. In his less famous treatise on human nature—*De Homine*—incidentally his final published work, Hobbes made it clear that he believed that humans were not, by nature, egoist and selfish. They were rational and capable of learning to be both social and moral. *Leviathan*, the book containing his famous description of life without the state, was a treatise written in defence of absolute monarchy and—at a push—other forms of strong, centralized government. In that book, Hobbes had argued that humanity could escape the condition of perpetual 'warre' by establishing social contracts with sovereigns who, in return for loyalty and the authority to impose their will by force, assumed responsibility for public order and security. With order guaranteed by the state, societies could engage in the peaceful activities of production, commerce, art, and leisure. *Bellum omnium contra omnes* stemmed from the social context (of anarchy) humans found themselves in, not innate human nature. It could be eliminated through the establishment of political institutions and absolute monarchy—the *Leviathan*. Indeed, the cooperation needed to effect the *Leviathan* required peace.

Another categorical problem was raised by seventeenth-century Italian philosopher, historian, and jurist Giambattista Vico. Vico found it implausible that the 'licentious and violent' man of Hobbes' state of nature could ever have negotiated the civil contract necessary to establish the leviathan state.[24] The seventeenth-century Dutch jurist and philosopher, Samuel von Pufendorf, also doubted the validity of Hobbes' portrait: 'A common or universal War engaging all mankind at the same time, is an impossible Supposition', he wrote.[25] Even accepting that Hobbes' own view of human nature was more complex than that of the Hobbesians that followed him, Vico and Pufendorf had a point. Absent arts, letters, and society, it is difficult to see how 'Hobbesian man' could have cooperated sufficiently to establish the Leviathan. How could a social contract be written without a common language? Without negotiation? Without trust? The historical reality, of course, is that it was not. Society was not 'invented' out of a state of nature by self-interested and reasoning men. It emerged gradually out of evolutionary biology.[26] Few animals are as dependent on one another as humans, and humans have risen to prominence precisely because of their capacity to cooperate.[27] As Dutch primatologist and ethologist Frans de Waal explained, the very notion of a Hobbesian state of nature is historically untenable. Humans evolved as group-living creatures in hierarchical—if comparatively simple—societies. They were never entirely equal or atomized. 'Humans started out…as interdependent, banded and unequal. We came from a long lineage of hierarchical animals for which life in groups is not an option but a survival strategy'.[28] Nothing even closely resembling a Hobbesian state of nature ever actually existed. We humans (and our ancestors) are, and always have been, social and political animals—*zoon politikon*—a point well understood by the ancient Greek philosopher Aristotle: 'Man is by nature a social animal; an individual who is unsocial naturally and not accidentally is either beneath our notice or more than human. Society is something that precedes the individual'. For society to exist at all, our urge to cooperate must prevail more often than not over our will to be aggressive. On this basic point there is no disagreement amongst biologists: society requires that cooperation triumph over aggression more often than not. If we must accept that there is some genetic predisposition to war and violence, we must also recognize that it is counterbalanced by an equally strong (and most likely much stronger) predisposition towards cooperation—and hence peace. Alternatively, we might simply conclude that there is no genetic predisposition either way, and that bellicosity and peacefulness arise out of social interaction.

There are also categorical problems with the biological argument that humans inherited an innate tendency towards war from our immediate ancestors. The first stems from the simple fact that even if we accept that modern chimpanzees are warlike and aggressive, that does not necessarily mean that they behaved that way 5–7 million years ago when their line diverged from the line that would lead to humans. Chimpanzees observed today have experienced millions of years of evolution from those that we are related to. What is more, whilst the sorts of organized violence witnessed by Goodall have been witnessed elsewhere, they are relatively rare and episodic, not ubiquitous. The second problem is the existence of the bonobos, an offshoot from the common ancestor of humans and chimpanzees. In contrast to the warring chimpanzees, bonobo societies are peaceful and cooperative. Relations between unrelated bonobos tend to be harmonious, underwritten by sex, which is often used as a way of defusing disputes and social tensions. As closely related to humans as are chimpanzees, bonobos fundamentally undermine the killer ape theory of the origins of war. 'Among bonobos, there's no deadly warfare, little hunting, no male dominance and enormous amounts of sex'.[29] The genetic dispositions of modern humans are shaped as much by peaceful bonobos as by warring chimpanzees.

Another categorical problem with the biological argument is that it does not fit neatly with Darwin's theory of evolution. Darwin did not think that innate human behaviour stemmed from basically selfish calculations or that natural selection always favoured aggression. It is surprising but true that the closest living relative to the mighty Tyrannosaurus Rex is the humble chicken, whose avian dinosaur ancestors survived a cataclysm that the giant Theropods from which they evolved could not. In the *Descent of Man*, Darwin observed that as species move up the evolutionary scale, cooperation becomes more prominent. As communities develop and the benefits of mutual aid became more obvious, so evolution selects for cooperation over conflict. 'Those communities which included the greatest number of the most sympathetic members would flourish best, and rear the greatest number of offspring'.[30] Ultimately, he argued, there was no reason why those sensibilities could not extend across all humanity. Darwin explained: 'The simplest reason would tell each individual that he ought to extend his social instincts and sympathies to all members of the same nation... The point being once reached, there is only an artificial barrier to prevent his sympathies to the men of all nations and races'.[31] Such tendencies have been observed in higher-order primates such as the bonobos, whose cooperative societies—and mostly harmonious relations between groups—are underpinned by morality and extend beyond the immediate group. In the great evolutionary contest, those that mastered the art of large-scale cooperation always won out over those who did not.[32]

For hard evidence of what the earliest human societies were like we need to look to the archaeological record. Although any absence of proof about war's existence in the earliest human times does not necessarily equate to proof of its absence, violence and war *do* leave discernible traces in archaeology in the form of damaged bones, weapons, and fortifications. And what is striking is that with very few exceptions, there is no archaeological evidence of warfare prior to about 9,000 BCE and scant evidence of it until the emergence of organized early civilizations in the Middle East around 7,500 BCE. A survey of the fossil record up to 10,000 BCE reveals only a small number of deaths caused by conspecifics, most attributable to cannibalism and individual violence. Clear evidence of deaths from weaponry such as spears and arrows emerges only after 10,000 BCE. There is likewise little evidence of fortified settlements—a clear sign that communities feared violent raids—before around 7,000 BCE, after which they became quite common, especially in Europe and the Middle East. From this point in history, the fossil record contains several examples of humans killed by others with weapons. As Lawrence Keeley points out, there is ample evidence of violent deaths after the transition towards more sedentary societies in Europe during the Mesolithic (10,000–5,000 BCE) and of armed conflict from the Neolithic period of the first farmers after 5,000 BCE.[33] What is missing, though, is evidence of warfare before that time that would support the notion that war is innate to humankind and was thus ubiquitous at the dawn of humanity. There is much in the archaeological record, however, to support the contention that war coevolved with society and that it is a relatively recent human behaviour, emerging only in the last 10,000 years or so. War, then, was a product of the types of societies we forged, not an innate disposition.

One of the principal ways in which the earliest humans communicate to us is through the art they left on rocks. Cave paintings dated before around 10,000 BCE reveal little evidence of conspecific violence, warfare, or weaponry. The total record of rock art for this period numbers in the several thousand. The vast majority portray animals, either living in peace or being hunted. Only around 130 paintings may include humans—and some of these may not actually be human, since the drawings are too crude and not sufficiently well preserved to determine this precisely—and most are portrayed in peaceful scenes.[34] Of all the paintings of this era, only four depict people injured by arrows and of these two may well be animals (it is unclear whether one of the appendages on the creature depicted is a limb or a tail). The picture changes, literally, after about 8,000 BCE. From that time, depictions of conspecific violence, weapons, and battle scenes proliferated. There is therefore a clear contrast: depictions of warlike fighting are all but absent from rock art until the dawn of the Mesolithic age, but become more common thereafter. Even in the Mesolithic, however, depictions of war remained a distinct minority of the whole, with most fighting scenes focused on hunting and a smaller number showing the executions of single individuals.[35] Rock art, therefore, supports the theory that warfare evolved alongside organized human societies rather than predating them.

There are two important exceptions to this picture. But, as ever, the fact that they are exceptions helps prove the general rule. At Jebel Sahaba in Sudanese Nubia, close to the Nile, fifty-nine skeletons dated 10,000–12,000 BCE were discovered. Twenty-four of these, including the skeletons of men, women, and children, showed signs of having suffered violent deaths, with stone projectiles intimately associated with or embedded within them. Several of the adult males had multiple injuries, whilst markings on the children suggested that they had been executed. The findings at Jebel Sahaba are usually taken as the first definitive archaeological evidence of war, though questions remain about whether the victims were indeed killed in battles (as opposed to executions, rituals, etc.) and whether they died at the same time.[36] But even if we set aside these doubts and assume that war was responsible for the killings at Jebel Sahaba, we still have the problem of the site's exceptional character. Fred Wendorf, who led the team that excavated Jebel Sahaba, suspected that the site was a special burial area and observed that a cemetery excavated just across the Nile, and dating from the same period, revealed no evidence of violence amongst its thirty-nine skeletons.[37] To this day, Jebel Sahaba remains a rare exception in providing evidence of mass violence before 10,000 BCE.

The same may be said of the famous walls of Jericho, which date from 8,300–7,300 BC. Among settlements of its time, Jericho was alone in erecting fortifications, suggesting that other societies did not share its fear of endemic violence. Indeed, there are no archaeological signs of warfare anywhere else in the Middle East dating within a thousand years of the early Jericho walls. Another fortified site, at Catal Huyuk (in modern Turkey), dates from 7,100–6,300 BC, well within the time of transition in which war became more common.[38]

Whether it be fossils, weapons, art, or fortifications, the archaeological record is surprisingly clear: warfare was not ubiquitous to the earliest humans but emerged as societies changed and evolved after around 8,000 BCE, though obviously these transitions occurred in different ways, at different times, in different places. Key to the emergence of war around 8,000 BCE were the profound social, economic, and environmental changes of the time. During this period, which also marks the transition from the Palaeolithic to Mesolithic, humankind was reaching the upper demographic limits for sustainable hunting and gathering. Competition for land and prey grew, especially in more densely populated regions such as the Middle East. Some societies there began transitioning from nomadic hunter-gatherer lifestyles to a more settled mode of living based on agriculture and organized into state-like forms. These societies abandoned egalitarian modes of living as aristocracies formed that demanded and extracted economic surpluses from farmers. Societies became more hierarchical. Indeed, human inequality came to be seen everywhere as the natural order of things. These first aristocrats ploughed their wealth into armaments and other means of coercion, using force to compel compliance at home, to protect their assets, and to expand their territorial reach (only later were some of these surplus resources directed towards the arts, engineering, science, and other endeavours).[39] It was in this context that war first emerged. Of course, this happened unevenly in different types and places. Some societies exhibited aspects of both styles of living.[40] But there is clear evidence that the rise of war corresponded with the rise of settled societies.

A third objection to the Hobbesian image of 'warre' amongst the earliest humans arises from ethnology and anthropology, though not as straightforwardly as it might at first appear. It is widely thought (though far from unproblematic) that one way of understanding life among the simple hunter-gatherers of early history is by looking at isolated simple hunter-gatherer societies today. Some of the earliest anthropology of this type flatly contradicted the Hobbesian image and pointed instead to societies of 'peaceful savages', simple tribes living blissful and peaceful lives in paradise. In a landmark book published in 1928, Margaret Mead—the daughter of Quaker pacifists—described Samoan society as a sexually liberal culture that had seemingly abolished war and learned how to resolve their differences peacefully.[41] A little more than a decade later, as Germany and Japan began their expansionist aggression, Mead extended her arguments about war, reasoning that the existence of other 'warless' societies, including the Eskimos and the Lepchas of the Himalayas, disproved the theory that war was caused by human nature. Like Samoa, these societies, she maintained, lacked the very 'idea of war'. This idea 'is as essential to really carrying on war as an alphabet or syllabary is to writing'.[42] But Mead's vision of the 'peaceful savage' did not hold the imagination for long. Her findings and methods were subjected to sustained popular critique—though much of the critique was itself fundamentally flawed.[43] Most troublingly, though, evidence of immensely violent hunter-gatherer societies seemed to disprove her principal message.

In 1964 Napoleon Chagnon, a young graduate student, travelled into the Amazon to study the primitive peoples that lived there. There he found the Yanomamo tribes on the border of Venezuela and Brazil. Chagnon believed that this society opened a window to the distant past.[44] In a series of studies, Chagnon painted a picture of a society in perpetual war, in which some 30 per cent of the male population died violent deaths. He showed how Yanomamo men resolved even the most minor of disputes with violence, that tribes waged multiple wars against one another, some lasting several years, and that when there was nothing to fight about, they attacked each other for sport. Here, Chagnon argued, was a society founded on violence, one where natural selection favoured the innately aggressive since successful warriors had more mates than weaker ones. Yanomamo violence was driven not by competition for territory or resources—there was an abundance of both, except when war itself limited food supplies—but by desires for revenge and women. This, he argued, was a primitive society that exhibited a condition of 'warre' similar to that described by Hobbes. Yet, even here a preference for peace lingered beneath the violence. Chagnon reported that many Yanomamo warriors confessed to him their loathing for war and hope that it could be abolished from their culture.

Beyond the Yanomamo, studies of indigenous life in North America and Australia revealed other hunter-gatherer-type societies that experienced war, sometimes extensively. Anthropologists reported that groups in both continents experienced raiding or battles at least once a generation.[45]

But there are limits to what the Yanomamo and other like groups can tell us about our ancient past. One particular problem is that the Yanomamo are sedentary peoples, inhabiting around 250 villages. They are not, like most humans of the Palaeolithic, nomadic hunter-gatherers. What is more, Yanomamo tribes have hierarchy. The same may be said for some indigenous groups in North America and Australia—some were more complex, sedentary, and hierarchical than others and their experiences were, therefore, different. Any insights that might be gained about our ancient past from studying these societies are therefore insights about more complex societies—precisely the sort that emerged at the beginning of the Mesolithic—and not about the societies that preceded them.

Another problem is that there is no reason to assume that the Yanomamo are more representative of our distant past (it should be stressed that whilst others have used the Yanomamo to make more general points about war,

Chagnon himself has not) than any other primitive groups. Indeed, there is massive variation in the human experience. Bellicose societies coexisted alongside warless societies.

No matter how rare they may be, 'warless societies'—the very antithesis of the Yanomamo—have existed across human history. The Standard Cross-Cultural Sample of some 186 societies pieced together by Carol and Mervin Ember labelled more than a quarter (28 per cent) as societies where war was 'absent or rare', where absent meant not observed at all and 'rare' meant less than once a decade. Filtering out societies pacified by colonialism, the Embers' dataset identified 9 per cent of unpacified societies as ones where war was 'absent or rare'.[46] Drawing on ethnographic data from fifty societies, Keith and Charlotte Otterbein found that warfare was entirely absent in 8 per cent.[47] Quincy Wright's magisterial study of 590 societies found that war was absent from 5 per cent (no war, no weapons, no military organization). However, some 59 per cent of the total were described as 'unwarlike' or as having experienced only 'mild warfare' since 'no indication was found of fighting for definite economic or political purposes'.[48] Today, well-known and much-studied warless societies include the !Kung of the Kalahari, the Semai of Malaysia, the Inuit of Greenland, and the Yolngu (Murngin) of Australia (Arnhem Land). What this points to is the wide variation in the human experience. Some hunter-gatherer societies, such as the Yanomamo, are extremely violent; others are very peaceful. Some experienced lots of war; others no warfare at all.

The key to whether a society was warlike or more peaceful in its orientation seems to lie in its *type*. There are significant differences among hunter-gatherer types of society and these differences had an effect on how peaceful or warlike they were. The less internally coherent a group was, the less warlike it tended to be, for the simple reason that group members had little motivation to sacrifice their own interests for those of the group or its leadership. Egalitarian forager societies, what Raymond Kelly calls 'unsegmented societies', experience much less war than more sedentary, nonegalitarian, forager societies—'segmented societies', in Kelly's schema.[49] Using multiple datasets of war and peace in hunter-gatherer-type societies, Kelly found that war within and between unsegmented societies is 'typically rare to nonexistent', though it may occur in some specific circumstances such as environmental degradation or aggression by external groups.[50] Significantly, the organizational structures of most societies during the late Palaeolithic (35,000–10,000 BC) resembled those of the unsegmented societies described by Kelly.[51] One of the principal reasons why unsegmented groups were less warlike was their lack of internal cohesion.

Groups did not assume collective responsibility for the actions of individuals, meaning that individual feuds remained just that. Violent confrontations were tussles between individuals, not groups.[52] What is more, group membership was constantly in flux as members left to join or establish other groups and new members joined. This fluidity blunted competition between groups and enabled an exit option—individuals could flee or merge with other groups rather than fight.

Simple, unsegmented societies also lacked things to fight over. Nomadic as they were, they lacked territory, property, and stored resources. Violent confrontation at the group level therefore offered significant risk without much in the way of potential payoffs.[53] As societies became more complex, they developed a greater sense of group identity and shared responsibility. As they became more sedentary, they acquired more fixed assets and lootable goods. War, then, was enabled by certain types of social organization that were rare in the earliest human times. As a result, war too was uncommon.

Rare though they may be, warless societies demonstrate the possibility of peace, suggest that some of the earliest human societies may have been peaceful (a suggestion corroborated by the archaeological record), and reinforce the argument that war is social, not innate. As Marvin Harris wrote, judging from the anthropological record we have today, 'for the greater part of prehistory our kind got along quite well without so much as a paramount chief, let alone the all-powerful English leviathan King and Mortal God, whom Hobbes believed was needed for maintaining law and order among his fractious countrymen'.[54] Research also suggests that societies that fostered peaceful norms of dispute resolution at home tended to apply the same norms in their external relations—making them more peaceful in their international affairs too.[55] Some societies were more warlike than others and vice versa. Social structure was one of the most important determinants of where a particular society would sit on that spectrum. Taken as a whole, though, the ethnographic picture reflects the archaeological, with war emerging out of social change.

One thing the anthropological record conveys very strongly is the sheer variation of human society. Most obvious in this respect are the sharp differences between the warlike and warless societies described earlier. But there is also plasticity within societies themselves. Human societies have demonstrated a remarkable capacity to transform themselves from warlike to warless in relatively short periods of time (and, of course, vice versa).[56] For example, the aggressive Swedish Kingdom of the seventeenth century led by Gustavus Adolphus was transformed into a modern state—one that broadly rejected the use of force as a basic instrument of policy. More recently, in the space of a generation Japanese society shifted from one that prized aggressive militarism (a tradition that extended back to the Samurai period) to one in which pacifist beliefs were more common. Of course, societies contain elements of militarism, pacifism, and everything in between to a greater or lesser extent. They can opt to move from greater peacefulness to more prevalent belligerence just as easily. We also see immense plasticity at the level of the individual. Individual humans have capacities for aggression and violence as well as for care and empathy. They can switch back and forth between them as context dictates. Indeed, social contexts are often critical in influencing which capacity prevails, but the human brain is capable of choosing between them and of learning which to prioritize.

We should not be surprised, therefore, that warfare increased after the transition from predominantly unsegmented nomadic societies to predominantly more complex types or that warless societies are a distinct minority. On the one hand, the deepening of cooperative bonds within groups hardened the differences between them. On the other hand, as anthropological studies demonstrate well, war is contagious. Warless societies can, and often do, have war imposed upon them from outside. From the earliest times, then, societies have confronted what International Relations scholars call a 'security dilemma': the problem that by maintaining their own arms they perpetuate the possibility of war; but by disarming they risk succumbing to war's contagion.

Basic theory, archaeology, and anthropology tell us that war coevolved with society. Humans certainly have a genetic capacity for aggression and violence, but this does not equate to an innate disposition towards war any more than our genetic capacity for empathy equates to an innate disposition towards peace. Nor does the evidence support the view that war is an evolutionary adaptation or independent realm of selection as suggested by Richard Wrangham, author of the 'demonic males' thesis. Described as a 'delusion' by Lawrence Keeley, this particular theory founders on the lack of archaeological evidence of war among the earliest humans and lack of evidence of selection tendencies favouring war.[57] Indeed, the 'selfish gene' syndrome would promote cooperation, not aggression, as the best means of survival, a finding supported by game theory which shows that, over the long-term, cooperation is more beneficial than aggression.[58]

In the 1980s, a group of scientists alarmed by the march of biological determinism gathered in Seville under the auspices of UNESCO to negotiate a scientific consensus on the question of whether humans were predisposed towards war and violence. The result was a 1986 statement which held it 'scientifically incorrect' to say that we have an inherited tendency for war and are genetically programmed for violent behaviour, that evolution selects for aggressive behaviour, that humans have a violent brain, and that war is caused by instinct or any other single motivation. Biology, the statement concluded, 'does not condemn humanity to war'.[59] Largely accurate as it was, the statement did overstate the case in one respect: humans *do* have a genetic *capacity* for violence in certain circumstances, but that does not necessarily equate to a predisposition to violence, let alone the organized violence of war. After all, we have established that warfare was not a constant feature of the earliest human social life. That many of our earliest ancestors experienced peace is therefore without question. The question now is whether they also practised peace.

I have focused thus far on the coevolution of war and society, but the emergence of war occurred in tandem with the development of peaceful conflict management and resolution.[60] As groups learned to employ violence to achieve their collective goals, so they also learned ways of resolving disputes peacefully. Across history, groups have enjoyed more periods of peace than of war. They have settled their differences more often without recourse to violence than with it. It is unsurprising, therefore, to discover that the anthropological record shows that simple societies have developed dozens of ways of making and building peace between them.

We might begin with a song. In the *Descent of Man*, Darwin argued that singing would have constituted a 'musical protolanguage' that shaped early communication within and between societies. The very earliest attempts to make peace between groups may therefore have been conducted in song. Indeed, there are good reasons to think that they were. More than forty hunter-gatherer societies, including examples in every continent, utilize 'song duels' as a way of avoiding violent conflict.[61] Combined with Darwin's insights into the evolution of communication, the sheer geographic spread of the song duel, and its practice by relatively isolated yet ancient groups such as the Inuit, suggests that song may well have featured in the earliest forms of peace-making.

Beyond the song, perhaps the most obvious and prevalent form of peace-making was the negotiation of peace settlements. This involved sometimes elaborate rituals designed to signal the solemnity of the agreement and the costs of transgressing it. Drawing on anthropological studies of warring tribes in Papua New Guinea, Lawrence Keeley describes how peace overtures began with the leader of one side declaring a desire for peace, which was then reciprocated (or not) by the opposing leader. The sides would then exchange gifts or make payments to compensate for the losses of war and may agree terms to maintain peace between them. Of course, just as in modern peace negotiations, these processes sometimes failed.

Looking at tribal practices in southern Africa and amongst indigenous North Americans, Maurice Davie noted that groups sometimes exchanged gifts to facilitate peace negotiations. Among American Indians, peace treaties were usually negotiated by ambassadors from the warring tribes who brought with them pipes of peace. The pipes were solemnly smoked and passed around the ambassadors who muttered vows of commitment to the peace. Sometimes, as amongst some Hawaiian and Tahitian tribes, sacred oaths were taken, supporting the peace and pre-emptive curses placed on whoever violated the agreement first. The Angami of India swore peace with a weapon in their mouth, symbolizing that they were prepared to fall by the weapon if they did not keep their word.[62] In the Andaman Islands, peace-making involved elaborate ceremonies in which the 'forgiving party' visited the village of the group responsible for the most recent act of violence and performed a series of dances on ground prepared for the ritual with symbols linking the present to the spirits of the dead.[63] Examples of well-developed peace-making practices such as this have been found in almost every type of primitive society, including warlike pastoral-nomadic tribal societies, sedentary tribal societies including the fearsome Yanomamo, and sedentary agricultural communities.

Third-party mediation was found to play a significant role in several societies, especially 'warless' societies or those where war is rare. Within the Mbuti in the Congo, several categories of individuals are entitled to intervene to end a conflict—including elders, seniors, kin, and neighbours. Elders play a significant role in mediating quarrels within the Semai community of Malaysia.[64] Amongst the Zapotec of San Andres, the role of mediator was played by kinsmen.[65]

Sometimes, third-party intervention was more coercive. This approach takes war-fighting as an offence and looks to impose punishments on the aggressors. The Yukaghir reindeer herders of northern Siberia treated any act of violence as a wrong and accorded to the victims the right to exact revenge or compensation.[66] Members of the indigenous Mardu in Australia's Western Desert reacted similarly, instituting a variety of means—violent and non-violent—by which the victims might seek redress.[67]

Other societies attempted to regulate violence by establishing shared norms. Mervyn Meggitt's study of the Walbiri indigenous Australian desert culture found a society that 'did not emphasize militarism'. 'Communities usually respected each other's boundaries'.[68] When violent conflict did erupt, norms of conduct ensured that it was limited and directly impacted only a small portion of society. The role played by territorial norms in limiting Aboriginal war was also described by Gerald Wheeler in his 1910 study. There were, Wheeler argued, no wars of conquest precisely because of the mutually recognized attachments of peoples to their places.[69] These attachments derived from Dreamtime, the shared belief system of indigenous Australians that weds people, and their spirits, to specific places.[70] This 'territorial principle' permeated indigenous Australian society. Within it, there was simply no place for conquest.[71]

Some hunter-gatherer-type societies developed sophisticated proto-judicial means of resolving disputes without recourse to force. The Australian Mardu held 'big meetings' at which accusers and defenders would publicly present their cases. After dialogue and deliberation, the elders would arrive at a binding solution.[72] 'Big meetings' were also used as a way of managing relations between different groups. Neighbouring communities met regularly to exchange gifts, perform rituals, welcome strangers, and manage shared business.[73] Sometimes, proto-judicial proceedings included prearranged and usually harmless duels or small-group fights. The Murngin resolved conflicts by arranging ritualistic duels and fights in which contenders hurled abuse at each other or threw spears at each other from a distance unlikely to cause harm. Occasionally, though, the elders lost control of proceedings and violence escalated.[74] Torres Strait Islanders also settled quarrels with the help of ceremonial fights, which ended in peace as soon as a (usually non-lethal) blow was landed on one of the participants.[75] Similarly, Tiwi elders in northern Australia resolved disputes with spear-throwing duels that ended with the first injury.[76] An extension of this was the prearranged low-casualty battle, though these sometimes got out of hand too. One such prearranged battle among the Yokuts of central California escalated to such an extent that half of the participants were killed.[77] Sometimes, proto-judicial processes permitted violent retribution for wrongs received, as in blood feud traditions, for example.

Some societies developed elaborate systems for inhibiting war. The religious belief systems of both the Batek of Malaysia and Moriori of New Zealand, for example, forbade war: the Batek believed that war was forbidden by their ancestors and the Moriori that their hero Nunuku forbade intergroup fighting and cannibalism.[78] Arguably the most elaborate was the 'League of Iroquois' which established a loose confederation to foster peace and cooperation among the Iroquois peoples whilst boosting their collective capacity to fight off outsiders. According to political scientist Charles Kupchan, the Iroquois league achieved stable peace through institutionalized restraint, compatible social orders, and cultural commonality.[79] Other societies adopted less ambitious approaches, focused on limiting the excesses of war by inhibiting attacks on cultivators of fruit orchards (Fiji), wounded soldiers (Papua New Guinea), women (Masai), and bystanders, or by respecting the neutrality of those who did not wish to fight (Eskimos of the Bering Strait).[80] Some societies developed codes governing the treatment of prisoners. The Minuanes and Puelches of South America sometimes adopted their prisoners rather than killing them.[81]

Beyond the sheer breadth of measures adopted to promote peace and limit war, it is striking to observe their ubiquity. It appears that wherever hunter-gatherer-type societies encountered war, they developed rituals, procedures, belief systems, and even social institutions to prevent, end, or manage it. Peace, then, is not a recent invention in either thought or practice. It evolved alongside, and in reaction too, the evolution of war and is as fundamental to the human experience as its nemesis.

Are humans hard-wired for war? No. At least, no more than we are also hard-wired for peace. Humans did not evolve from their ancestors pre-formed as brutal warriors driven by a genetic disposition for war. The collective violence of war emerged only as societies developed and became more complex and cohesive. Even amidst the tumult of social change, however, some societies—albeit a minority—managed to remain warless or relatively warless, their very existence demonstrating that war is a social phenomenon, not an innate behaviour. With the coevolution of war and society came a third, often overlooked, aspect of the story of humanity: peace-making. The practice and concept of peace appeared as an immediate response to war. For no matter how bellicose, wherever societies encountered war they also developed practices of peace and exhibited a preference for it. This sentiment was captured well by the historian Thomas Arnold, who told his Oxford students at an 1842 lecture on 'war and society' that 'though I believe that theoretically the Quakers are wrong in pronouncing all wars to be unjustifiable, yet I confess that historically the exceptions to their doctrine have been comparatively few'.[82] On sober reflection, most of us would find it hard to disagree. It is precisely because we prefer peace to war that the history of world peace is as old as the history of war itself. Indeed, it is its mirror image. But the ubiquity of the art of peace should not fool us into thinking that world peace is readily achievable. Chapter 4 explains why.

CHAPTER 4

WHY WAR PERSISTS

Calm fell. From heaven distilled a clemency;
There was peace on earth, and silence in the sky;
Some could, some could not, shake off misery:
The Sinister Spirit sneered: 'It had to be!'
And again the Spirit of Pity whispered, 'Why?'

—Thomas Hardy, 'And There Was a Great Calm' (1920)

If humans are not hard-wired for war, then war—like peace—must be a social and cultural artefact. Explains British philosopher, A.C. Grayling, war is caused and sustained by 'the divisions and differences between self-identified groups with interests opposed to, or by, other groups. War is therefore a product of a sufficient degree of organization and structure to make such divisions and differences material'.[1] But divisions and differences between humans are not enough to make war a reality. Groups can, and most often have, managed their differences peacefully. Concluding his *History of Warfare*, John Keegan reasoned that war arose primarily not from human nature, economic interest, religious belief, or ideology, but from the 'institution of war itself'.[2] That war, in other words, was a kind of self-fulfilling prophecy. Yet, Keegan argued, 'it is the spirit of cooperativeness, not confrontation, that makes the world go round'.[3] So, in addition to the basic fact of human difference, a sufficient number of people within groups must also believe war to be a legitimate and effective means of protecting their values and furthering their interests for it to occur. They must believe, in other words, in the institution of war itself. These people must also be capable of marshalling sufficient resources to that end. War persists because the paths to peace forged from the embers of the Second World War have not yet sufficiently degraded this faith in war.

In this chapter, I will explain why that is. I will suggest that there are three main reasons why a sufficient number of us retain our faith in war. War persists because of the way we organize ourselves, because war has proven itself productive at times, and because war is contagious. There are many factors associated with specific patterns of war and peace, including cycles of escalation and violence caused by war itself and 'conflict traps' which make enough of us think that sometimes war is our only course of action.[4] There are also certain social and political features of our states and societies—the way we govern ourselves, our wealth, our values and ideologies—that make war more, or less, likely. Many ingredients go into making individual wars.[5] But these more proximate factors cause war only because of the way we organize ourselves, the incentive structures we build around war, and the basic problem of contagion. Unless we address them, these three underlying features of our social life will continue to bestow upon us a propensity for war. Most social institutions, including religion, can be put at the service of war *or* peace.[6] But it is these three factors that make war thinkable and sustainable. Schemes for world peace have thus far failed not only because of a political lack of will, but because they have not sufficiently addressed the underlying causes of war. We must confront them head on.

The first and most basic reason why war persists has to do with the way we have chosen to organize ourselves. Humans are divided into sub-groups that lay claim to our loyalty. Group membership is—and always has been—fundamental to human survival and flourishing. From the beginning, we were divided into familial groups. Then we developed wider kinship and, by around 10,000 BCE, political communities. Over time, the differences between groups—their values and interests—became deeply ingrained through language, culture, history, morality, religion, law, economics, and social hierarchies. Today, some groups hold radically different, and maybe directly contending, interests and values. These political communities coexist within an anarchical international setting, one without government or enforceable law akin to that which exists within communities. It is, I think, one of the great paradoxes of peace that the very social bonds that build harmony in our everyday lives within societies are so often sources of conflict between societies. It is a paradox rooted in the way we think, not in some timeless essence, yet we often like to think of the differences between groups and the potential for war this creates as immutable and unchanging facts. Writes Christopher Coker, 'we tend to believe that ... war has a nature which is eternal', whilst Azar Gat agrees that '[w]hile the forms of war may change with time, its spirit, or essence, remains unchanged'.[7]

Human society was not 'invented' out of a state of nature by self-interested and reasoning men as Thomas Hobbes imagined. It emerged out of evolutionary biology.[8] Over time, the evolution of more internally coherent human group-ings sharpened the differences between them, creating this tragic paradox: that some of the very qualities that helped promote peace *within* societies hardened the differences *between* them. As human minds grew, so learning replaced nat-ural selection as the principal driver of evolution.[9] Human groups learned to specialize and adapt to their environment in ways well beyond the capabilities of other species. They developed ways of living, cultures, moralities, and finally languages that enabled them to survive and thrive in their own particular con-texts.[10] They developed explicit teachings about the value of community and the community's values. Myths and religious beliefs helped them understand life and the world around them.[11] Social qualities such as a shared religion, something that many early political leaders tried to promote—often with themselves as the deity or in unique relation to it—helped bind early societies together.[12] The sacred and the secular emerged together, each dependent on the other. In this decidedly social context, the fittest were not necessarily the phys-ically strongest or the most cunning, but those that learned to cooperate most effectively for mutual support—something the Russian anarchist philosopher Peter Kropotkin recognized at the start of the twentieth century.[13]

With specialization came difference. We are hard-wired to recognize our closest kin and to prioritize their needs and interests above those of others. The most effective groups extended those loyalties of kinship (albeit less intensely) to the group as a whole. The group is thus held together by an internal logic that pushes its members to be more concerned about the fate of other mem-bers than they are about the fate of non-members. Underpinning all this is an evolutionary logic which holds that the stronger a group's internal coherence, the better its members can cooperate, and the greater the rewards that individ-uals reap from group membership. But internal coherence required external differentiation, sharpening rivalries and reducing the common ground between the members of different groups. 'Humanity' was no longer a salient frame of reference—it would have to be 'invented' or perhaps discovered all over again.[14] The division of humanity pitted groups internally united by bonds of belief, language, and practice against alien outsiders, who were considered to be of less importance and value than insiders. Group selection favoured those with the greatest internal coherence, since these were best placed to harness the benefits of cooperation. Indeed, in-group solidarity was enhanced by hostility to out-groups.[15] The more defined and specialized groups became, the deeper the divisions between them turned out to be. The more effectively groups provided for the wellbeing of their members and the nourishment of their shared values, the stronger became the ties that bound them. The stronger the internal ties became, the weaker became the ties between those inside the group and those outside it. Language is a case in point. Language made communication and hence deep cooperation, shared learning, and culture possible. It underpinned huge leaps in social development, technology, and human wellbeing. But it also gave forceful practical meaning to human division, for only those who comprehend a group's language could participate in the cooperation it engendered. Communication became more intense within groups and sparser between them.

Groups developed a remarkable range of different ways of living, moralities, and languages adapted by cultural evolution to the conditions in which they found themselves and shaped by their own internal and regional politics. Those groups that bonded together most tightly, held together by shared beliefs and common identities, profited more from their cooperation than those that did not, whilst the bonds that held groups together created differences between them. From our earliest civilizations, humans developed different ideas not just about what is just and unjust, but about the standard of justice itself. That is why we have no universal human account of justice and, because of that, no single vision of peace. Recall Susan Sontag's point that what we understand by peace is really just 'victory'—the triumph of our own moral vision over those of others.[16] This sceptical view of peace was ably summed up immediately after the Second World War by British political scientist, E.H. Carr, when he observed that the values that had presented themselves as 'universal' through the League of Nations system were in fact merely the preferences of the powerful masquerading as moral truth.[17] The mask of universality did not put these values beyond political or moral contestation. In this context, political leaders came to see war as a way of furthering their interests or the interests of their group. This included using violence to resist injustice and oppression. Some Marxists, for example, argued that war was both necessary and justified when it aimed to upend injustice.[18]

War endures in part therefore because groups want or believe in different things and suppose that war will help them achieve them. Groups tend to start wars to satisfy their basic needs, enrich themselves and grow, fulfil what they understand to be their rights, or correct what they understand to be grave injustices. Civil wars, meanwhile, occur when different groups—or sub-groups—compete over the boundaries, shape, and control of a political order or proffer different accounts of what values should govern that order. The underlying problem here is that justice is not an objective standard. Groups can, and do, form different accounts of what justice is and how it applies in different situations. As a result, they can always find reasons to fight.

David Hume, one of the most prominent figures in the eighteenth-century Scottish Enlightenment, helps us understand how this works. Hume argued that morality stems from sentiment rather than immutable principles.[19] How we understand morality is subjective, a product of language, culture, situation, and experience, and not objective, given from God or nature, knowable only through the application of proper method and contemplation.[20] Thus, we often disagree about how justice is to be realized in any given situation. Sometimes, justice claims are not just incompatible, they are directly opposed. Sometimes, groups might point to equally valid principles of justice to make contradictory claims. The complex, specialized, and cooperative societies which emerged in the transition from the Palaeolithic to Mesolithic came at a price: group prejudice.[21] It is not just the fact of difference that creates the seeds of war; it is the fact that groups tend to think that their interests and values should take precedence over those of others.

Group membership creates immense social pressure that pushes individuals to sacrifice their own immediate self-interests for the group. 'War would not be possible', A.C. Grayling writes, 'without arousing and directing hostility against others to the point of willingness to kill them'.[22] And, we might add, willingness to be killed by them. As groups became sufficiently strong and coherent to demand that individual members make the ultimate sacrifice, war became possible. Individual identities were subsumed into collective ones. Disputes between individuals over pride, resources, land, or women could now give rise to disputes between groups and thus to war. The struggle between Menelaus and Paris for the hand of Helen is a case in point. From an essentially private marital dispute arose the Trojan War, something that would simply not have been possible in the earliest human societies. These divisions remain with us today, now reinforced by nationalism and state power. It is this basic social fact that makes war thinkable and hence still possible. The key to overcoming it, described in more detail in Chapter 7, lies in resisting the homogenization of group identity by preserving and celebrating the multiple identities we all have.[23]

In their relations with each other, states and societies have found common ground on some shared principles to guide peaceful coexistence (international law, international organization, etc.), express shared understanding about how people ought to be treated (human rights law), and establish procedures to manage disputes. These are what political theorist Michael Walzer calls 'conventions': sets of 'articulated norms, customs, professional codes, legal precepts, religious and philosophical principles, and reciprocal arrangements' that shape judgements about morality and justice.[24] Some, especially regional groupings of like-minded states and societies, have developed into deeply rooted 'security communities', in which war between members becomes not just unlikely, but unthinkable. The European Union provides a good example of a deep and substantive security community; ASEAN in Southeast Asia is an example of a more restrictive kind. Both, however, have been associated with significant declines of war and outbreaks of peace in their regions. But there are questions about whether these communities can be extended to embrace all of humanity. As early as 1903, for example, William Sumner argued that zones of peace could never be extended to all humanity because whenever a group grows larger, animosities between insiders and outsiders grow, and war inevitably follows.[25] Indeed, some worry that rather than overcoming logics of inter-group violence, security communities simply reproduce them at the regional level. Thankfully, there is little evidence to support that view. Instead, it appears that communities of states that are able to transcend mutual fears of war bring their new norms, rules, and practices into their relationships with neighbours. In other words, security communities—and the peace they bring—might also be contagious. In both Europe and Southeast Asia, for example, the peace forged within security communities has extended to the wider neighbourhoods.[26]

Thus far, global conventions have tended to be more procedural, designed to help us manage points of difference and the disputes that inevitably arise. These conventions have contributed to the decline of war in the contemporary world but cannot by themselves resolve the problem of difference since radical disagreements over the fundamentals of justice may arise, and in those situations groups may prefer to wage war than accept the arbitration or judgements of others.

Outside security communities, war remains the *ultima ratio* of disputes between groups. As Hannah Arendt explained, 'the chief reason warfare is still with us is neither a secret death wish of the human species, nor an irrepressible instinct of aggression, nor, finally and more plausibly, the serious economic and social dangers inherent in disarmament, but the simple fact that no substitute for this final arbiter in international affairs has yet appeared on the political scene'.[27] 'For all its evil', George Orwell observed in *The Lion and the Unicorn*, war is 'an unanswerable test of strength'.[28] We have no government, no self-enforcing laws, that sit above states to regulate relations between them. As scholars of International Relations remind us, states inhabit an international anarchy—not unlike the 'state of nature' caricatured by Thomas Hobbes. Fearing for their own survival, modern states—and before them, all manner of different types of human groupings—retain for themselves the right and capacity to use force against one another. War, then, as the Prussian strategist Carl von Clausewitz wrote, is ultimately a clash of interests settled by bloodshed. It is an 'act of violence intended to compel our opponent to fulfill our will'.[29] The brutal reality is that over the course of history the capacity to wage war effectively has at times been necessary for group survival as well as an effective way of achieving the group's goals. The capacity to coerce and enforce—that is, to wage war—is essential for the exercise of law, and no such capacity exists beyond the state—much to the chagrin of the Abbe Saint-Pierre and the other schemers of world peace.

Yet war is an imperfect arbiter, for at least two, very different, reasons that were identified by two, very different, Prussians. We noted earlier that Immanuel Kant pointed out that war is an unjust and unreasoning arbiter. War turns contests over justice into contests of strength. A state's ability to wage war tells us as much about the justice of its cause as a schoolyard bully's ability to punch tells us about his. War is therefore inimical to the way that most of us would think is a fair way to settle a dispute—the application of law and reason. (Andrew Carnegie made the same argument in establishing his endowment for peace in 1911; war 'decides not in favor of the right, but always of the strong'.)[30] Carl von Clausewitz, meanwhile, observed that war is an unreliable arbiter. War is a dialectical process of attack and defence. This produces 'friction'— contingencies, uncertainties, and the unexpected, things that occur in all war—which means that once begun, war tends to be unpredictable. It generates unforeseen consequences. These qualities are the very opposite of those we normally look for in an effective arbiter of disputes.

There is another, quite different, problem that stems from the division of humanity into distinct groups, one known to political scientists and economists alike as a 'collective action problem'. Even if one could persuade states to abide by some common rules (international law) and join an international organization to arbitrate disputes and maintain the peace, there is little hope that they would expend their own resources to support the common good except in those instances where it suited their immediate interests. A collective action problem arises in situations where multiple actors (e.g. states) would all benefit from a certain good (e.g. a system of world peace) but where the cost of achieving that good makes it unlikely that any single actor would take the required steps. Thus, whilst all would benefit from a functioning system of collective security in which the whole worked together to maintain peace, in an anarchical system populated with self-interested states it is unlikely that any one state—or group of states—would be willing to pay the cost of establishing such a system.

This we have learned from painful experience. In the 1930s, the League of Nations failed to stand up to Japanese and Italian aggression, in Manchuria and Abyssinia respectively, primarily because none of the great powers at the time saw it as being in their own interest to do so. By the end of the 1930s, when the rising tide of fascism challenged the whole system, the League had been reduced to an international irrelevance incapable of offering even the mildest resistance. Its successor, the UN, has had a marginally better time, but its capacity to repel aggression, as in Korea in the 1950s and Kuwait four decades later, is dependent on the convergence of the collective interest (in maintaining non-aggression) with the individual interests of the great powers (in both cases, the US interest in protecting an ally). Where no such convergence of interests exists—as, for example, in the cases of the 2003 US invasion of Iraq, the 1980 Iraqi attack on Iran, the 1979 Soviet invasion of Afghanistan, and civil wars in Sudan (1955–72) and Nigeria (Biafra, 1967–70)—no collective action was forthcoming. In those cases, states—both individually and collectively—were not prepared to pay the price of maintaining the peace.

This is a problem that has always plagued international organizations and troubled those who developed proposals for world peace based on collective action. As Immanuel Kant recognized, international organization can guarantee perpetual peace only if its members are motivated to support it. He believed that societies governed internally by the rule of law were more likely to promote a rules-based order between them. Alfred Zimmern believed it would take more than that—a determined political commitment to peace. But they agreed that one cannot simply place diverse, insecure, and selfish states into an international organization and expect them to set aside their own interests and assume costs and risks for the collective good. This collective action problem remains a fact of international life caused by the separation of humanity into distinct and self-interested groups.

Precisely *how* we organize ourselves matters. As Kant and Zimmern recognized, some types of states and societies are more war-prone than others. Some societies are more likely to cooperate than others. Those that offer glory and renown to rulers or generals that build empires and conquer foreign lands are likely to experience more war than those that do not. Nowadays, states and societies agitated by issues of international 'esteem, just due, regard, respect or prestige' are likely to be more aggressive that those that are not.[31] The pursuit of glory and honour causes war only to the extent that societies privilege these things and see war as a means of obtaining them. Over the course of history, some societies have tended towards this view, but others have exhibited a preference to be more inward-looking and care little about matters of international status. Attitudes within societies may move back and forth over time, sometimes caring more about these concerns and other times caring less. Yet what remains constant is the fact that how we organize ourselves shapes how peaceful we are likely to be. It was this that encouraged Cicero, Augustine, Dante, and others to contend that peace must include civic order as well as the absence of war.

There is an irony of all this, as I mentioned earlier, which is that tightly knit human groups and, then, modern states proved quite successful at reducing violence within societies and at facilitating human development. There is a positive relationship between legitimate and effective states and the reduced likelihood of violent death. All manner of other social goods—health and wealth chief among them—flow from this basic relationship between internally coherent human groupings and states.[32] Yet not only does the character of those groupings shape their susceptibility to war, the very fact of them makes war possible. Most—if not all—of the twenty-first century's armed conflicts arose out of disputes over the state, about its boundaries, and about how—and by whom—it should be organized. For now, my main points are that, first, it was some of the very things essential for effective human cooperation within groups—shared language, religion, culture, etc.—and that facilitated human development and prosperity—that drove humanity as a whole apart and made war possible. Second, that some of the ways we have organized ourselves have made our societies more prone to war than they otherwise might have been. This paradox, which lies at the heart of peace, was well understood by the ancient Greeks. In the play *Lysistrata*, Aristophanes poked fun at the ascendancy of Athenian civic virtue exemplified by Thucydides' demand during a funeral oration that the citizen be a 'lover of his city'. The playwright lamented that the cult of what today we would call patriotism fashioned a war-obsessed citizenry that would ultimately destroy itself.

Before we move on to the second underlying cause of war—its potential productivity—we need to briefly consider the relationship between another type of group—the religious group—and war. I mentioned earlier that there is in fact no straightforward relationship between propensity for war and sacred belief. But that has not stopped some of war's most prominent critics from laying the blame squarely at religion's door. '[R]eligion prevents us from removing the fundamental causes of war', wrote Bertrand Russell in 1930.[33] More recently, popular science writer Richard Dawkins claimed that religion was one of the principal sources of war and violence: 'religion is the principal label, and the most dangerous one, by which a "they" as opposed to a "we" can be identified'. Were religion abolished, he claimed, there would be a 'much better chance of no more war'.[34] It is striking that a writer so outwardly committed to science would make such a strident claim when the evidence of a causal connection between religion and war is so thin. There are at least three good reasons for thinking that religious belief and identification makes little direct difference to war-proneness.

First, secular states have proven at least as aggressive as those that combine the secular with the sacred. Among the most aggressive states of the past century were two governed by entirely secular ideologies—Nazi Germany and the communist Soviet Union. Contra Dawkins, in practice the turn of European states away from the religious towards the secular did not make them more peaceful or more respectful of people.

Second, religious texts and beliefs are ambivalent on questions of war and peace. They can be made to do different things. The same religious texts and beliefs can, and have been, employed to support war, criticize war, and enjoin peace.[35] It is the uses to which religious texts and beliefs are put, not the texts and beliefs themselves, that matter. Karen Armstrong shows, for example, that Chinese legalists and strategists drew on the same sets of ideals but arrived at very different conclusions about war and peace.[36] Roland Bainton, meanwhile, has shown how a shared set of Christian beliefs has given rise to everything from the absolute pacifism of the Quakers to the holy wars of the Crusades, and everything else in between.[37] Religious belief can harden the distinctions between groups and help create the distance needed to justify violence. But it can also soften those distinctions. Religious communities tend to extend beyond national or ethnic borders. Most major religions have some concept of human equality under the heavens and traditions that value tolerance and compassion towards others. These attributes can, and do, challenge war and contribute to peace.[38] It also bears remembering that secular doctrines have proven no less malleable in this regard.

Third, given that the distinction between the sacred and the secular is a relatively recent one, it is anachronistic to isolate the religious and political causes of past wars. The Thirty Years' War, for example, certainly had a religious component, but it had equally strong political causes too.[39] Every empire of note has defined its mission—and its violence—in sacred terms, yet the *causes* of empire were altogether earthlier, having to do with the pursuit of territory, wealth, and glory. Only very rarely are conflicts primarily caused by religion. Religion played no role whatsoever in causing the Napoleonic Wars, the First or Second World Wars, or the Indochinese Wars, for example. None of the three most murderous states of modern times—Hitler's Germany, Stalin's Soviet Union, and Mao's China—killed on religious grounds. In other words, even when religion is taken out of politics, we find no shortage of reasons to continue fighting wars.

The point here is that it is the fact of human division and what we make of it—not the narrower issue of whether those divisions have theological groundings—that drives group conflict. There is little reason to think that casting out religious belief from the political world would have much, if any, effect on patterns of war and peace. Religious institutions may be important sources of group division, but they can just as easily reach out beyond divided groups and act as sources of peace.

A second reason why war persists and peace breaks down is that winning wars has proven to be quite profitable or useful. Not everyone benefits from war, of course. Overall, war tends to produce far more losers than winners, which is why so much effort has been put into the search for peace. Yet war persists because a sufficient number of people continue to believe that it is profitable and useful. They do so because war has sometimes proven itself thus (at least for some). This is part of the logic behind Carl von Clausewitz's famous dictum that war is the pursuit of policy by other means: the idea that war is a rational instrument of policy because it helps states or groups get what they want at an acceptable cost.[40] According to Donald Kagan, war is driven by the pursuit of glory, territory, and riches. It persists because in some times and places it has proven to be an effective means of achieving these goods.[41] Most obviously, war played a central role in building the ever-larger political communities necessary to establish the modern states that made the dramatic human progress of the last few centuries possible. War was central to the rise of modern states and to the formation of nations. According to John Hutchinson, wars helped create the national myths and narratives that forged separate identities, helping define the group and make it more coherent whilst distinguishing it from others. War also provided fodder for the social rituals and symbols that held nations together.[42]

For some of the winners, war has opened the door to immense wealth and privilege. Most of history's great empires, for example, were founded to some extent on war or violent conquest. European colonialism was made possible in part by advances of weapons technology, most notably the use of gunpowder, in the fifteenth century (and in part by the clever forging of alliances with local rulers).[43] For Europeans, the spoils of empire were immense. We have largely forgotten that post-Roman Europe was a global backwater riven with internal conflict, subjected to domination by the nomadic horse-people of the Steppe (Huns, Mongols, etc.), and driven out of the Middle East, the Balkans, and much of Spain by the Turks, Persians, and then the Ottomans.[44] Alongside the emergence of capitalism, the gunpowder revolution helped establish Western Europe as the first centre of truly global power, enriching its peoples and its culture. War, conquest, commerce, and empire made Europeans rich again. To the east, China is what it is today—a large, mainly peaceful, and flourishing society—thanks in part to expansionist war. The land we now call China was forged by the territorial expansion, much of it violent, of the Han. It was protected from rivals (the Japanese and Europeans among them) by force of arms. China's system of government was forged by war (a brutal civil war, which ended in 1949) and maintained by regular and massive bouts of violence (the Great Leap Forward and Cultural Revolution among them).

Success in war has helped rulers (and sometimes societies) enrich themselves. Martin Van Creveld has helpfully identified four ways how. War has inspired rapid technological advances. It has created economies of scale, thanks to the needs of war production and the possibilities of territorial aggrandizement. It has opened up new and innovative ways of making money thanks in part to the urgent need for innovation caused by war and the opening up of new markets. And war has helped stimulate ailing economies.[45]

Sometimes empire not only delivered great riches to the imperial centres and some of their peoples, but also limited violence and facilitated progress in the provinces. The example of *Pax Romana* was mentioned earlier: no matter how violent and intolerable the imposition of Roman rule on the provinces, there is no doubt that it also ushered in an unprecedented period of peace and human flourishing. According to Adrian Goldsworthy, '[M]ost of the time, over most of the empire', war and banditry 'was kept under control—a fact of life, but not a constant and serious danger to most of the population'. He continues, 'There is no doubt that the areas under Roman rule experienced considerably less war and organized violence than they did in the centuries before or since'.[46] All in all, the Roman Empire tended to be good for citizens and non-citizens alike.

But material gain is not the only way in which war has proven to be productive. War was sometimes seen as necessary to preserve peace and the common good. Waging war to protect regional or international order was often the unenviable duty of the hegemon. Indeed, sometimes order has been established and maintained only by war and violence. War is thus occasionally the pathway through which sustained peace has been achieved. Many of the arrangements and proposals for world peace—including the UN system we have today—rest ultimately on the potential for immense force to be brought to bear against any who reject or challenge the status quo. The Battle of Waterloo was necessary to restore European peace in the face of a resurgent Napoleon; the Second World War a necessary response to German and Japanese expansionism; and the war on so-called Islamic State was necessary to protect whole populations from genocide (in the case of the Yazidis). From the Holocaust to the killing fields of Cambodia, and the genocide in Rwanda, the only way to stop genocide in its tracks has been to defeat its perpetrators in battle.

Just as war enabled empire, so it has also served the cause of national liberation. Sometimes, as anti-colonial theorists such as Frantz Fanon and Jean-Paul Sartre explained, only violence can restore justice and free people from the tyrannies of material—and emotional—oppression. 'Only violence pays', wrote Fanon in the context of the Algerian war for independence from the French, whilst Sartre remarked (apparently on the strength of Fanon's work) that violence, 'like Achilles' lance, can heal the wounds it has inflicted'.[47] That is—whether or not this was true—these anti-colonial theorists maintained that only anti-colonial violence could cleanse societies of the violence of colonialism itself.[48] War, then, can be the servant of justice as much as its master. We should not assume that a world without war would necessarily be a more just one. As Nick Mansfield contended, 'we reject war because it ruins social relations, shatters bodies and savages human rights. Yet, we also look to war to preserve the social, protect threatened lives and enlarge rights. War kills and saves simultaneously'.[49]

War can give rise to other social goods, albeit indirectly. One recent history suggests that democracy itself arose out of the exigencies of war. That as rapidly improving technologies of war demanded ever-larger armies, so states were forced to concede to their people's political rights born of citizenship in return for their service and, ultimately, their sacrifice. From Athens to modernity, states able to mobilize engaged and motivated citizens to fight their wars have performed better than those that have relied on coercion or payment alone. Because of this, the rigours of war pushed some rulers to extend the rights of citizens to elect their own governments (though others, it should be said, preferred to roll them back).[50] War and mass violence may also be the best means yet discovered of eradicating inequalities of wealth within societies, albeit by impoverishing the wealthy not by enriching the poor.[51]

Indeed, economics furnishes some of the principal reasons why we fight. As long as the global economy creates losers as well as winners, there will always be those that turn to violence to satisfy their needs or their greed. The relationship between economics and war is well known, especially the argument that economic development has played a crucial role in reducing belligerency.[52] Economics has played a role in causing wars and heightening the risk of wars. Several studies have demonstrated that overall levels of wealth (measured in terms of GDP per capita) shape the likelihood of a country experiencing war, especially civil war. Simply put, the wealthier a country, the less likely it is to experience war. The reasons for this are varied and hotly disputed, but of central importance are the fact that economic wealth and opportunities direct people's energies away from military endeavours towards commercial endeavours, the greater opportunity costs imposed by war on wealthier societies, the sharper distinction between conditions in life in peace and war (the distinction being sharper among wealthier societies than among poorer), and the reduced need to acquire economic resources violently.

The likelihood of civil war is especially influenced by economics. Here, the relative economic position of groups within a country matters most. These are *horizontal* inequalities (across groups) rather than the more commonly measured *vertical* inequalities (referring to relative wealth of rich and poor measured by Gini coefficients).[53] Sometimes, conflict erupts as a result of competition between groups for scarce resources. The role that the increasing scarcity of water and grazing land, both necessary for survival in the Sudanese region of Darfur, played in sharpening the conflict there is a case in point.[54] More recently, it is perhaps no coincidence that the Syrian civil war erupted after a decade of drought and economic decline that forced upwards of 1 million people to leave their rural homes and find sustenance in overcrowded shanty towns on the edge of the country's major cities. These areas became the focal points of unrest and rebellion.

The perceived gains of war can be non-material too. It is important to understand that world peace is an ambition that coexists alongside other aspirations, including desires for justice, survival, wellbeing, love, and self-determination. These are values for which people are prepared to kill and die. During the Middle Ages, peace doctrines struggled in the face of apparently divinely sanctioned violence. Violence commanded by God cannot be easily dissuaded by mere humans. More recently, peace theorists and activists have consistently underestimated the capacity of nationalism and other collective ideologies to spur violence and self-sacrifice. In the march to the Great War, peace activists across Europe were encouraged by socialists such as Jean Jaures in France and Scottish parliamentarian Keir Hardie to call on workers to launch a general strike should war erupt. Class solidarity, Jaures and Hardie believed, would reach out across nations and prevent a calamity. They were sorely mistaken. International class solidarity was quickly swept away by a tide of patriotism. 'Unhappily for world brotherhood', historian Barbara Tuchman lamented, 'the working class went to war willingly, even eagerly, like the middle class, like the upper class, like the species'.[55] Countless numbers of people have voluntarily sacrificed their own immediate self-interest to take up arms and place themselves in harm's way in the name of social abstractions like the nation. These were people driven not by personal greed (since modern war offers few opportunities for the enrichment of ordinary soldiers) or avarice, but by a belief that their nation, its wellbeing, and that of the people within it demanded and deserved individual sacrifice: war driven not by aggression and self-regarding behaviour, but by love (of the group), cooperation (within the group), and other-regarding (sacrificial) action.

Some people actively seek out war because they find it entertaining, even exhilarating. 'I do not have it in me to write a book about peace', writes Nigel Biggar—Oxford's Regius Professor of Theology—'it is war that captures my imagination'.[56] First-hand accounts of war are suffused not just with laments of horror and suffering, but also with tales of camaraderie, heroism, excitement, and even the joy of killing. William Ehrhart, a private in the First World

War, described the first time he struck a German with a bayonet as 'gorgeously satisfying...exultant satisfaction'.[57] 'The rush of battle is a potent and often lethal addiction', wrote the war correspondent Chris Hedges, 'it can give us what we long for in life...purpose, meaning, a reason for living'.[58] We should not assume that everyone abhors war. There is plenty of evidence that many people enjoy it.

The main point in all of this is that wars happen because enough people believe it is better to fight than not, whether that is because they seek enrichment, fight for a cherished ideal, want to protect the people and things they love or help distant strangers from grave harm—or because they simply enjoy war. Whether or not a group prevails in war has tended to matter a great deal to its future prospects. Because of that, groups have tended to maintain their readiness to fight. To make war possible, a sufficient number of individuals within a group must be prepared to make the ultimate sacrifice to achieve one of these ends. If they were not, there would be less war.

There are limits to how far this line of argument can carry us, however. Just as we recognize the productiveness of some wars, we should be careful not to overstate war's appeal. War is not, for example, responsible for peace within societies. In his paean to war, Ian Morris advances a broadly Hobbesian account of life before the state and reckons that it was war that helped lift humankind out of perpetual communal conflict. In reality, as I pointed out in Chapter 3, humans never lived in conditions resembling a state of nature such as that described by Hobbes. We were always social beings. Nor was war always the engine room of state-building. Over the course of history, war has destroyed as many states as it has helped forge; its overall effect on human development is decidedly ambivalent. Some political units with long and rich heritages have disappeared entirely as a result of war.[59] Much was lost to humanity with the destruction of whole civilizations at the hands of war.

Nor must we accept the view that, on balance, empire did more good for the world than bad. In fact, the harm caused by empire remains incalculable. Thinking, for example, of the British empire, we can only wonder at what a sophisticated society such as India's may have achieved without foreign domination. What we do know is that in the eighteenth century, before empire, India's share of the global economy was equal to that of Europe's. By 1947, at the end of empire, its share had decreased six-fold.[60] We cannot begin to understand the travails of the contemporary Middle East or sub-Saharan Africa without understanding their painful and bloody colonial past. A different past would have made their present very different too.

Nor are soldiers always willing volunteers, prepared to sacrifice themselves for a noble cause. Recall that in Chapter 3, we noted that most societies exhibit a strong preference for peace. Many—if not most—soldiers across human history were forced to fight. Conscription, often forcible, remains a common practice. States conscripted soldiers to fight in the First and Second World Wars, and in Vietnam, precisely because they could not find sufficient volunteers. The regular Iraqi Army that was so devastatingly crushed by an international coalition in 1991 was composed almost entirely of conscripts. Serbia's 'nationalist wars' of the 1990s were not well supported by Serbs. Men had to be forcibly drafted into the military; more than two-thirds of Belgrade's military-aged men dodged the draft.

The value ascribed to war is at least partly manufactured. Why does war appear so honourable and exciting? Part of the answer lies in the fact that almost everywhere in the world, war is presented that way in collective narratives backed by the full power—and resources—of the state. Chris Hedges and historian George Mosse refer to this as the 'myth of war'. 'The old lie: Dulce et decorum est pro patria mori', wrote Wilfred Owen from the trenches of the First World War: 'it is sweet and right to die for your country'. War is institutionalized. We are taught in schools to valorize our nation's military successes, to honour its heroes. Honouring war is a national ritual. War is romanticized.[61] Monuments and statues are erected to honour those who served and died in war, never to those whose efforts helped societies avoid or limit war. War is the subject of popular films, books, and serials. It appears honourable and exciting precisely because that is how it is presented to us. It is normalized. The tenaciousness of the mythology excoriated by Owen stems not from its raw persuasiveness, but from the efforts and resources put into sustaining it.

The way we see war is framed by institutionalized narratives, images, and modes of thinking. All of this creates powerful social psychological incentives for individuals to comply when asked to fight for their country or their group. Ironically, these incentives stem from our very sociability—our in-built need for inclusion within our social group—not from our aggressiveness. Through a series of famous experiments in the 1960s and 1970s, social psychologists like Stanley Milgram and Philip Zimbardo demonstrated that the urge to 'fit in' created a strong disposition to comply with the requests and demands of authority figures. They showed how certain social contexts and cues (for example, narratives about the justice and necessity of the cause and how individual acts could serve it, narratives about reverence to particular types of authority, narratives about the immorality of the enemy, etc.) can push individuals into taking actions, such as inflicting pain on others or accepting a higher risk to themselves, that ordinarily they would not.[62] The institutionalization and romanticization of war help establish the social contexts and cues that normalize and encourage participation in it. It explains why ordinary people sometimes do extraordinarily inhumane things in times of war.[63]

The reality of war, though, is quite different from the popular imagery. It is a reality often kept out of view. After the First World War, the authorities in Britain and France tried to keep from sight the tens of thousands of men who suffered horrific facial injuries, the sides of their faces obliterated, their noses smashed, their eyes missing. Very few photos were circulated of those whose injuries were considered too gruesome for public consumption. Still today, the mainstream media censors out raw images of war's destructiveness, judging that their audiences—often in places untouched by war—may be distressed by such sights.[64] For all the talk of the 'media-ization' of modern war, war's basic realities, the nature of the deaths and injuries it inflicts, the fear it engenders, remain largely hidden from view. Because of that, only those with first-hand experience of war have any sense of its brutal reality. So, if war seems to be a legitimate tool for satisfying interests or pursuing values that is at least in part because it has been made to look that way by narratives and institutionalized practices that hide its full reality. These are themes I will return to in Chapter 7.

None of this, however, displaces the basic point that groups engage in war because a sufficient number of people within them believe it to be a reasonable and effective means of achieving their goals. War persists because enough of us still believe that it is useful, enriching, and necessary—even if that support is manufactured by states and societies. True, soldiers are often coerced into action—sometimes under pain of death—but some of the most successful armies have tended to include large numbers of true believers. However, the evident limits to this way of thinking do suggest that this ordering of values is not impervious to change.

The third inescapable reality is that war is contagious. Peaceful societies can, and often do, have war imposed upon them from outside. The Phoenicians, for example, survived as independent political entities for close to 1,000 years, despite having no army of their own. But they could not survive invasion by Alexander the Great. Whether theirs was a wholly peaceful society or not, the Minoans of Crete suffered a similar fate. Weakened by a series of natural disasters, the Minoans were colonized by the more aggressive Achaeans from mainland Greece. Even extreme remoteness is an imperfect barrier. We once thought that the Rapa Nui civilization on Easter Island caused its own demise by destroying the island's ecology. And that then, unable to grow or catch enough food to sustain themselves, the Easter Islanders descended into internecine conflict and cannibalism as different tribes fought to stave off starvation.[65] We now know better. The Rapa Nui deforested their island, but they adapted. There is no archaeological evidence of famine or the war and cannibalism it was said to have produced. What devastated the Rapa Nui was violent contact with outsiders. In the 1860s and 1870s, nearly half the population was carried into slavery by Peruvian slave traders; others were killed outright by Peruvian and European sailors. When the Peruvians were forced to return surviving slaves to the Islands, they brought smallpox with them, devastating what was left of the population.[66] War and conquest, it seems, can reach even the remotest outposts of peace. Any system of peace has to barricade itself against the contagion of war.

War coevolved with society in different ways, at different times, in different parts of the world. It was spread from one group to another, irrespective of whether it was welcome or not. When one group raids its neighbours, those neighbours have a limited range of options with which to respond. They can choose to fight, turn to flight, or submit to their attackers. In prehistory, when people were less tied to land and space was plentiful, flight was a common response, its availability going some way towards explaining how the earliest humans avoided war. With demographic growth, the rise of agriculture, and the establishment of organized societies, flight became less of an option. Societies with fixed assets could either resist aggressors or submit themselves and/or their assets to them. As the differences between groups grew, so submission became less attractive. Wars spread. To protect themselves from raiders and aggressors, groups developed their own military capabilities. This, in turn, made their neighbours feel insecure, prompting them to develop their own military capacities. From the earliest times, then, societies have confronted what I described earlier as a 'security dilemma': the problem that by maintaining their own arms they perpetuate the possibility of war; by disarming they risk succumbing to war's contagion. In this context, wars may be caused by misperceptions: the persistent fear that another's preparations for defence might in reality be the portents of attack and misplaced belief that the use of war pre-emptively might remove such crippling uncertainty.[67] This radical uncertainty about the intentions of others also helps explain John Keegan's view that war springs not from human nature, divisiveness, or poverty, but from 'the institution of war itself'.

As I mentioned in the introduction, war is its own self-fulfilling prophecy. It recurs because we believe it will, and in the categories and definitions it creates.[68] Thus, it sows the seeds of its own future. Jane Addams (1860–1935), one of the first modern peace intellectuals—responsible for coining the terms 'positive' and 'negative' peace—recognized the point well. War, she argued, 'reverses the process of cooperating good will', 'arouses the more primitive antagonisms', and undermines friendship and mutual understanding.[69] It destroys the very things that make peace possible. War begets war. It leaves in its wake the bitter sentiments needed for its own recurrence, obscures all thought of alternatives, and stymies hope of social progress. War enables nationalism and jingoism, and vice versa. War justifies 'radical assaults on basic civil liberties; abuse of immigrants; and legally sanctioned vigilantism' against minorities, pacifists, and others.[70] It is, in other words, a self-sustaining evil that can be mitigated only by sustained social action best led, Addams believed and not without good reason, by women.[71]

War has an escalatory logic. There is a tension between the imperative to win and the imperative to fight well. When the two come into stark relief, the former tends to triumph over the latter. There are moral principles such as the 'just war tradition' and laws of war designed to moderate war and prevent its worst excesses. But war's nature is towards escalation, especially when the stakes are high. After all, those waging war do so to win and sometimes the costs of failing may be huge and irreversible.[72] As each side seeks a knockout blow against the other, they increase and widen the scope of violence they are prepared to use to achieve it. Mutual animosities grow with every act of violence. As they do, moral restraints fall away. Soldiers seek vengeance for the loss of their comrades; civilians cheer them on, keenly aware of their own losses but emotionally removed from the losses their own side is inflicting. The accidental killing of our civilians pushes us to take revenge on their civilians, which pushes them in turn to exact a greater toll on ours. 'Every war', writes George Orwell, 'suffers a kind of progressive degradation with every month that it continues'.[73] Inflicting unspeakable suffering on the enemy seems justified by the suffering of our own. In war, we tend to blame our own atrocities on the provocations of the enemy. This logic of escalation is underwritten by an uncomfortable but inescapable strategic reality that—all other things being equal—the group prepared to use any means whatsoever to succeed has an advantage over the group whose actions are inhibited by moral or legal constraints.[74] In an international system composed of self-interested states free to act more or less as they please—or as they can physically get away with—there is little material incentive to limit how we wage war.

Nor is there much incentive to limit our capacity to fight. In fact, as Hedley Bull observed in the late 1950s, states would be acting irrationally if they limited themselves thus.[75] 'You may not be interested in war, but war is interested in you', Leon Trotsky is reputed to have said. For that reason, states have a duty to remain prepared for it, and to be prepared to do whatever it takes to win. In a lecture given immediately after the First World War, German sociologist Max Weber showed how the necessities of leadership can push even those that abhor violence towards acceptance of war. Writing about political leadership as a vocation, Weber argued that when an individual assumes a role as head of state they are compelled to set aside any personal commitment they have to pacifism and to accept the necessity of war when needed. Personal morality is one thing, Weber maintained; political responsibility is another thing entirely. Where any single state retains the capacity to use force against another, meeting that challenge becomes the responsibility of all. The alternative is to meekly accept injustice imposed by others.[76]

The contagion of war remains with us today. Datasets show that, all other things being equal, a country whose neighbours experience war is far more likely to succumb to war itself than a country whose neighbours are at peace. The potential spread of civil war, one recent study found, threatened neighbouring states like nothing else.[77] There are a number of reasons why this might be. There is some evidence that violence itself is contagious—that violence begets violence, pushing societies and their neighbours into cycles of viciousness from which it is difficult to escape. Civil wars reach across borders as supply chains for arms, ammunition and soldiers, and political, kinship, and ideological affinities stretch across national boundaries. The civil war in Syria provides a good example of this. Not only did it give rise to renewed violence in Iraq, and potential violence in Lebanon, it also drew in Turkey, Qatar, the United Arab Emirates, and Saudi Arabia on one side, and Iran, Iraqi shi'ites, Hezbollah, and Russia on the other. Another example is the impact the civil war in Liberia in the 1990s had on that country's neighbours, two of which—Sierra Leone and Côte d'Ivoire—were dragged into their own civil wars.

One of the reasons for war's contagiousness may well be the proliferation and technical advancement of armaments, but the picture is far from straightforward. Recognizing that the flow of arms contributes to war, calls for general disarmament or at least the control of arms have figured prominently in the demands of peace activists since the nineteenth century. In *World Without War*, first published in 1958, J.D. Bernal—a renowned British scientist whose work on X-rays is overshadowed today by his Soviet sympathies and acceptance of the 'Stalin Peace Prize'—argued that world peace could be achieved by abolishing military research and development and by funnelling the funds into civilian science instead.[78] Hard-nosed diplomats too have sometimes conceded that the path of war is paved with arms. Reflecting years later on his time as Britain's foreign secretary at the start of the First World War, Sir Edward Grey remarked that the race to acquire arms and the militarism that accompanied it had made war 'inevitable'. 'Armaments were intended to provide a sense of security in each nation...What they really did was to produce fear in everybody'.[79]

But whilst controlling the supply of weapons can contribute to world peace by making it more difficult to fight (see Chapter 8), it is probably not determinative. At the root of the problem is the fact that there is no established empirical relationship between arms control and greater peacefulness. What is more, the causal relationship between peace and arms control runs in the wrong direction: not from arms control to peace, but from peace to arms control. Except when imposed by external actors, arms control, typically, is what happens when parties either trust each other sufficiently or share sufficient common interest in limiting their destructive capacity. Neither of these conditions is likely to be satisfied in wartime. Peace is a prerequisite. What is more, the increasing destructiveness of modern weaponry, especially nuclear, helped increase the costs of war and thus make it much less useful and efficient. As Hannah Arendt observed, with the advent of nuclear weapons, '[t]he technical development of the implements of violence has now reached the point where no political goal could conceivably correspond to their destructive potential or justify their actual use in armed conflict. Hence warfare...has lost much of its effectiveness and nearly all its glamor'.[80] It is better to see arms control and disarmament not as standalone limitations on the contagion of war, but as elements of a broader campaign to make war more difficult to wage.[81]

Proposals for world peace have tended to include provisions for an international organization to tackle the problem of war's contagiousness. Within these schemas, any state looking to spread war would find itself confronted by the community of states as a whole. But whilst international organization has a role to play in the management of contagion, bitter experience teaches that their capacity to effect change is inhibited by the collective action problem mentioned earlier and their inability to prevent defections. For some, the problem lies in the imperfection of global governance. From this arise all manner of proposals for reforming the institutions we already have (for instance, by furnishing the UN with its own military capabilities) and suggestions for new institutions altogether (such as world parliaments or federations, or judicial institutions with the authority to compel states to act in certain ways). But this way of thinking gets things the wrong way around.

The problem is not the nature of international organization but the units (self-interested states) that have to be managed and the (anarchical) environment in which they operate. International organizations perform quite well when the values and interests of their most powerful members are aligned. They do much less well when those with the most power fail to agree, as the fate of the League of Nations and the impasse over the Syrian civil war show. The problem is that international organizations are what might be called 'secondary' institutions in world politics, since they are composed of states (the 'primary' institutions). For as long as humans divide themselves into separate and sovereign political entities that jealously guard their own prerogatives, prioritize their own ways of seeing and doing things even at the expense of others, and see war as a sometimes-useful instrument of national policy, international organizations will succeed only in preventing some wars and coordinating somewhat more effective responses to them. As the UN's second (and still one of its most revered) Secretary-General, Dag Hammarskjold, commented: the UN was meant to save humanity from hell, not take it to heaven. International organizations are a necessary part of the world peace equation, but their role is a secondary one. Fulfilment of their potential relies on developments beyond their control, especially developments in the way that states and societies organize themselves. This was a point well understood by Immanuel Kant, who recognized that relations between states could not be governed by law until relations *within* states were.[82]

War's contagiousness also explains why the path to world peace cannot lie exclusively in pacifism—though the right of individuals and groups to choose pacifism must be privileged and protected, for reasons I will explain in Chapter 8. If war spreads from one society to another, and if only some and not all adopt pacifism, then those that do leave themselves defenceless against predatory attacks. Indeed, the adoption of pacifism by some but not all societies would have the perverse effect of increasing the likelihood of aggression by significantly lowering the costs associated with it. Pacifists have never satisfactorily resolved the question of how the renunciation of violence brings peace in a world that produces characters like Hitler and Stalin who are only too willing to use extreme violence to get their own way. This point was understood by one of John Dewey's colleagues in the American pragmatist school of philosophy, Sidney Hook. Hook explained the problem eloquently in a book published at the height of the Second World War in 1943. 'The pacifist argument that it pays everyone not to have wars', he pointed out, 'runs up against the fact that it would pay some people in a world where others are pacifist, to make war on the pacifists'.[83]

Although each individual war has a specific set of ingredients, war itself persists because humanity is divided into different and distinct groups that privilege the interests and values of insiders over those of outsiders, because enough of us still think that war can help them (or their group) achieve what they want, and because war is contagious. Using this as our starting point, we can begin to think about the steps that could be taken to move us towards world peace in three clusters. They shape the remainder of this book.

The first are questions about how we organize ourselves into groups. This involves thinking about how states and societies establish peace within themselves and how they organize their relationships with one another to limit contagion.

The second relates to the hard rationalities of war; its costs and payoffs. It involves thinking about the goods reaped from war and the costs imposed by it. It challenges us to think about the steps that might be taken to make war more expensive and peace more rewarding.

The third relates to how we relate to one another: the social bonds, cues, and practices that push us closer together or drive us further apart. We need to think more about the factors that push individuals towards or away from war, about which social attachments we privilege and which we discard—and why.

These, I think, are the building blocks upon which world peace can be based. Chapters 5–7 consider each in turn.

CHAPTER 5

THE STATE

Warmaker and Peacemaker

For by this authority, given to him by every particular man in the commonwealth, he hath the use of so much power and strength conferred on him, that
by terror thereof, he is enabled to form the wills of them all, to peace at home,
and mutual aid against their enemies abroad. And in him consisteth the essence
of the commonwealth which is, to define it, one person, of whose acts a great
multitude, by mutual covenant one with another, have made themselves every
one the author, to the end he may use the strength and means of them all as he
shall think expedient, for their peace and common defence.

—Thomas Hobbes, *Leviathan*

The state is a paradox. It is simultaneously the most awesome warmaker and
the most effective peacemaker ever devised. It helps resolve the problems
of day-to-day anarchy that so animated Thomas Hobbes, but it also exacerbates the problem of human difference and gives rise to an international system
that makes war contagious and sometimes rewards predatory behaviour. The
state as warmaker story is relatively well known to us; recall that Immanuel
Kant doubted whether peace would ever be possible without fundamental
changes to the state. The state as peacemaker, however, is a more contested
proposition, but one for which there is just as much evidence. This chapter
examines both sides of the paradox, focusing mainly on the state's role in
building peace *within* societies. I will suggest that in helping establish and maintain legitimate social orders, the state—for all its faults and all its violence—is
indispensable to the cause of world peace. States establish monopolies of force
and underpin rule-governed societies that have tended to be less violent than
the alternatives. Certain types of state, of course, do this better than others. We
will unpick those differences. All states, though, instantiate the problem of war
between them. I will focus on that in Chapters 6 and 7.

War, I explained earlier, emerged as hunter-gatherers began to establish
sedentary, hierarchical, and political communities. Modern states too were

often forged in fire, prompting sociologist Charles Tilly to remark famously that 'war made the state, and the state made war'.[1] Referring specifically to the formation of modern European states from the Middle Ages onwards, Tilly argued that the imperatives of war forced rulers to establish ever-more capable and coercive powers over ever-larger territories. The more powerful lords imposed their will on 'fractious rivals', sometimes through co-option but often through 'pacification' and 'elimination'.[2] From this sprung the ultimate war-fighter—the modern state. Bureaucracies were established to collect taxes, the majority of which was expended on preparations for war. Thus, the modern state, Tilly argued, was effectively a by-product of efforts to perfect the machinery of war. It is unsurprising, then, that war became one of its primary instruments.[3] Yet by concentrating the use of force in the hands of a single sovereign, the state also brought 'peace to a people'. The formation of larger, national, states in places such as France, Britain, Russia, and Germany, and then of their global empires, owed much to wars of conquest spanning centuries. International Relations theorists connected to the so-called 'English School' argued that this model of the modern, bureaucratic, state was carried beyond Europe by colonialism until it was adopted, or imposed, almost everywhere.[4]

As they developed, modern states fashioned, facilitated, or were accompanied by the rise of national identities that bound peoples together as communities of fate and legitimized demands for ever-greater sacrifice on the field of battle.[5] England and France led the way, the others forced to follow suit or perish. Some apologists for nationalism such as the political philosopher G.W.F. Hegel believed that war played a crucial and positive role in binding people together and forging productive and wholesome communities. War tied individuals firmly into national communities and destroyed degenerative forces born of property ownership, private wealth, and individualism. Wrote Hegel in 1802, thanks to war, 'the ethical health of peoples is preserved ... as the movement of the winds preserves the seas from the corruption into which they would be brought by settled calm, and the peoples by a lasting, not to say, perpetual peace'. Governments, Hegel wrote five years later, should plunge their societies into excoriating war from time to time to weed out pernicious forces and renew the national spirit.[6] Even if nations managed to join together in political unions or alliances, he argued in 1821, they would still clash in opposition and enmity.[7] Later in life, Hegel claimed that these exhortations to violence were mere philosophical reflections, not practical guides.[8] Yet, 'the origins of Europe', Michael Howard reminds us, 'were hammered out on the anvil of war'.[9]

Ultimately, nationalist ideals undermined the legitimacy of multinational empires, first the Austrian and Ottoman, then the British, French, and Italian, and finally the Russian/Soviet. As a result, today we live in a world of sovereign states, most of which are at least nominally tied to nations that squabble almost as much about the symbols of nationhood as they do about material concerns.[10] Most states expend significant portions of their national wealth maintaining a capacity to wage war. With the rise of the state, humans militarized group difference and made war itself an international institution.

There is much, therefore, to commend the first part of Tilly's aphorism—that war made the modern state. But we also have reason to doubt it. Or, rather, to doubt whether *all* states share a violent heritage. Many quite successful states were *not* forged in war. The Phoenician city-states, for example, were built primarily on trade, not war. Sometimes war prevented states from emerging or caused the collapse of proto-states.[11] As for 'English School' talk of the global 'expansion' of the European states system, this view of history largely ignored the fact that the non-Western world had its own political formations stretching back well beyond colonization and that some of them, including imperial China and Mughal India, were advanced and state-like in form.[12] Europe's prowess at trade and the co-option of local rulers were at least as important to its imperial rise as its superiority in war.[13] Some communities adopted the modern bureaucratic state model not because of its military proficiency or because it was imposed on them, but simply because this was the most fashionable and legitimate form of government at the time.

The second part of Tilly's famous aphorism—'the state made war'—portrays the modern state as a mega-sized protection racket. This notion was a mainstay of anarchist philosophy in the nineteenth century. One of anarchism's first protagonists, Jean-Pierre Proudhon (who later described himself as a 'federalist'), wrote that states and private property were the principal obstacles to peace.[14] In *La Guerre et la Paix* (*War and Peace*) he argued that more, and more capable, states meant only more and deadlier war. The sort of industrial-scale warfare envisaged by Proudhon reached its apogee in the mass slaughter of the trenches during the First World War. And it was not only war that modern states perfected. According to Mark Levene, genocide too developed directly out of the European state-building and colonization projects.[15] Even the Holocaust, sociologist Zygmunt Bauman famously claimed, was the logical corollary of the modern state: the perfection and bureaucratization of mass extermination, not its antithesis.[16] Hannah Arendt's arresting portrayal of Adolf Eichmann, an *SS-Obersturmbannführer* who played a major role in the killing of Jews during the

Holocaust, as a bland technocrat blindly fulfilling his role within an anonymous bureaucracy of mass extermination made the point most vividly.[17] The modern state has unparalleled destructive capabilities, yet makes evil appear 'banal' by disguising agency and distorting morality. The modern state itself, by this account, is a war-making, genocide-executing, machine. 'Statism'—the idea that states should be sovereign and command the loyalty of their populations— writes Ken Booth, one of the pioneers of 'critical' approaches to 'security studies', allowed states to 'behave badly at home and compete for power abroad (using war if they must) within a global system of mistrust and competition that they themselves created'.[18]

But as we know, the emergence of more and more capable states did not produce ever-more and deadlier war. As Ian Morris points out, war may have made the modern state, but the modern state—by and large—made peace. It did so at home first and then internationally.[19] Drawing on different sets of data and examples, a raft of recent books—including John Mueller's *Retreat from Doomsday*, Robert Muchembled's *History of Violence*, Azar Gat's *War in Human Civilization*, Joshua Goldstein's *Winning the War on War*, and most famously Steven Pinker's *Better Angels of Our Nature*—have shown that the likelihood of our dying violent deaths declined with the rise of modern states. That is not to say that there are no examples of non-state societies maintaining and sustaining peace—there are, as the Rapa Nui of Easter Island attest—but only the state has achieved the scale necessary to sustain peace within large societies. With the emergence of the state came a reduction of our overall chances of dying in war, even if the process of state formation sharply increased the chances of some people dying violent deaths in the immediate term.

Beyond the claim that war between states is in decline, something I discussed in Chapter 1, the argument here is that lives are more peaceful within modern states than they are, or have been, outside them. If this claim were true, it would lend credence to our view of the modern state as central to the goal of world peace. Indeed there is significant evidence to support it. Whether or not we accept Pinker's overall thesis, it does seem clear that our chances of dying a violent death have declined with the rise of the modern state.[20] A significant part of the reduction is accounted for by the decline of violent crime. In 1981, Ted Gurr published a landmark essay charting the decline of homicide in London. In the thirteenth century, the city's homicide rate stood at forty-five per 100,000 (and an alarming 110 per 100,000 in Oxford), falling to about ten per 100,000 by the sixteenth century, and around one per 100,000 by the twentieth century.[21] Whilst critics have picked at Gurr's numbers, his overall thesis has withstood the test of time, supported by research drawing on the experiences of other countries that show more or less the same trajectory: that the establishment of modern states and rule by law reduced the incidence of homicide dramatically.[22]

But there is another, I think more compelling, piece of evidence pointing to the contribution of the modern state to human welfare. Life has grown longer. At 71.5, global life expectancy is today more than thirty years longer than the life expectancy of individuals in any society, anywhere, before the twentieth century. It is not just that modern states reduced violence, it is also that they created the peaceful space needed for scientific discovery, prosperity, and public health well beyond anything achieved by any other form of political organization.

A final argument is that modern states have proven particularly effective in helping societies achieve the conditions necessary for peace. The systems of laws and judicial decision-making enacted by states are in effect processes for the non-violent resolution of conflicts. They also played a crucial role in facilitating the economic exchanges and innovations that contributed to economic growth. Similarly, as Thomas Nagel has argued, the very idea of human rights is possible only if there are institutions with the power and authority to enforce them.[23] None of this is to say that there are no possible alternatives. There are, and many have been pursued in different times and places. It is just to say that none yet has proven so effective on such a grand scale as the modern state.

What, though, of the argument that it was the modern state that perfected the arts of genocide and mass killing? That it is primarily an architect of death, not a sustainer of life? Genocide's long pre-modern history suggests that humans were perfectly capable of exterminating each other without the help of modern states. When the ancient Athenians seized the island of Melos, they killed all the men and sent the women and children into slavery. When Rome finally defeated Carthage, the city was razed and every last inhabitant killed. Whatever drives the impulse to massacre and exterminate, it is not necessarily the modern state and its bureaucratic banalities. Genocide predated both.[24] With the wisdom of hindsight, we now know that Hannah Arendt, who coined the term 'banality of evil' to express how the Holocaust arose was organized by modern bureaucracies, was taken in by Adolf Eichmann's own pleas of mitigation. 'I was not a responsible leader and as such do not feel myself guilty', Eichmann wrote in his pardon plea. '[P]eople like me [were] forced to serve as mere instruments in the hands of the leaders'. But Eichmann was not forced to serve. He volunteered. Papers show that as early as the early 1930s, Eichmann believed that Germany needed to destroy the Jews. He joined the Nazi party before 1933 and volunteered for service in the SS in 1935. He assumed responsibility for Jewish affairs in 1939 and oversaw the deportations and mass killing of Poles and Jews. Far from merely following orders as he claimed, so intense was Eichmann's commitment to the extermination of the Jews that in November 1944 he circumvented a direct order from Himmler to cease deportations from Hungary and ensured that they continued until the Germans were forced to retreat from the advancing Red Army. Eichmann often expressed pride at his role in the Holocaust before his arrest by Israeli agents in 1960.[25] Adolf Eichmann was thus no bureaucratic cog in the machine of modernity as so often claimed. He organized the extermination of Jews because he was an ideological fanatic in the service of anti-Semitism. Eichmann was not an 'ordinary man' twisted by circumstance and social pressure to conform in the service of the state; he was one of those responsible for twisting the state to the service of genocide.

The modern state is a tool, a human artifice. It can be used in the service of great evil, but that does not mean that the modern state itself is an evil. States can be, and have been, used to drive or facilitate giant leaps in human prosperity, welfare, and freedom. What matters most is the nature of the state and the ends to which it is put. Establishing sound institutions can make the difference between peace and prosperity, and violence and poverty.[26] This requires that states be guided by ideas and ideologies that sustain these things.

How, then, can the modern state be made to better serve the cause of peace? As I pointed out in Chapter 2, many of the earliest thinkers believed that peace began at home—that peace entailed civil order. It was in taming the daily violence of pre-state life and creating conditions that allowed human cooperation that states made their most significant contribution to peace. The ancient Egyptians, for example, saw peace as a primarily domestic issue—what mattered most to them was the absence of internal strife, even if that came at the cost of perpetual war overseas.[27] Likewise, *Pax Romana* connoted a condition of peace within the provinces, but it was a peace enjoyed inside the empire whilst the legions fought incessant wars at its boundaries.

In *Leviathan*, Thomas Hobbes argued that individuals created states in order to escape the 'state of nature' and its perpetual 'warre' of all upon all. It was not God, nature, or biology that brought society into being, but human self-interest. Humans were not bellicose by nature but were driven to aggression by the freedoms and fears caused by the state of nature. Yet humans were also endowed with rationality enough to understand that perpetual 'warre' was disastrous for all. Safety could be found only in political association through the establishment of a 'common power'—the state—or, as Hobbes called it, the *leviathan*. The leviathan derived its authority, and the brute power that underwrote it, from a social contract between the people who set it above themselves. By agreement with one another, individuals conferred upon the state unlimited sovereignty over them. In return, the sovereign—be it an absolutist monarch (as Hobbes preferred), oligarchy, or democratic republic—conferred its protection upon the people. Once constituted, the state enjoyed unlimited rights over individuals within its domain and had but one responsibility: ensuring their safety. The state's untrammelled rights, Hobbes thought, were necessary for its proper functioning. The people were not entitled to claim that their state treated them unjustly and nor were they permitted to rise in rebellion against it. Overthrowing the sovereign would undermine the very reason for which the state had been established in the first place. Because every individual was an author of the sovereign, any complaint of injury against the sovereign was effectively a complaint against its author. The state's ability to establish order out of 'warre' depended upon the sovereign's authority and its power to compel obedience.

But there was a hole in the armour of absolute sovereignty, arising out of the purpose for which the state was contracted: the safety of the people. According to Hobbes, the sovereign was established by the people and granted power and authority over the people for 'the procuration of the safety of the people', to which end he is 'obliged by the law of nature' and 'to render an account thereof to God, the author of that law, and to none but him'.[28] The sovereign may enjoy absolute power on earth, but is obliged to guarantee the safety of the people and remains subject to the judgement of God. Sovereignty, in other words, came with responsibilities for public safety as well as rights.[29] And there was an earthly sting in the tail for the sovereign. For should the sovereign power imperil its own subjects, their natural right to individual self-preservation—the right for which they had formed the state in the first place—permitted them to resist. For Hobbes, though, this was only ever an *individual's* right to resist, not a collective right. Beyond that, there was relatively little that a people could do to protect itself from a tyrannical state.

The problem, one of the great liberal theorists of the Enlightenment, John Locke, argued, lay in Hobbes' overly reductive account of natural law in the state of nature. Hobbes insisted that in the state of nature every human battled every other in a condition of perpetual 'warre'. Their *right* to wage perpetual 'warre' on one another arose out of their natural right to self-preservation. But for rights to have practical meaning, Locke pointed out, they must entail corresponding duties. It makes no sense for an individual to be said to enjoy a right to life if there is no corresponding duty on others to not kill, or positive duty to prevent killing by others. In the state of nature as described by Hobbes there was no hierarchy or authority. No one could dictate how others lived. In such conditions, either nobody had a right to self-preservation, because rights themselves could not exist, or everybody did. And if Hobbes was right in claiming that self-preservation was a natural right enjoyed by all, then, Locke reasoned, everyone must also have a corresponding duty towards the preservation of all others. This duty entailed not just an obligation to refrain from killing but also a duty to protect others from harm, including by punishing those who kill. Locke believed that natural rights extended beyond the mere preservation of life to entail the preservation of liberty and property as well, for in the state of nature no one could rightly impose their will on others or claim rights over property inhabited by any other. Individuals therefore had natural rights which preceded the state and which imposed duties on others; rights that individuals were entitled to vindicate on their own account.

As Locke explained, in his *Second Treatise of Civil Government* (1690):

> that all men may be restrained from invading others right, and from doing hurt to one another, and the law of nature be observed, which willeth the peace and preservation of all mankind, the execution of the law of nature is, in that state, out into every man's hands, whereby everyone has a right to punish the transgressors of that law to such a degree as may hinder its violation.

Locke recognized that it would be difficult in practice to realize these rights in a state of nature. It would be equally difficult, though, for individuals to relinquish their natural rights to a Hobbesian leviathan, since this would create a powerful tyranny no more conducive to self-preservation than the state of nature. Locke's elegant solution was the idea of a state established to preserve the natural rights of people, rights which individuals retained even when they entered into a contract establishing a sovereign over them. Government was thus granted authority to legislate for the 'public good of society' and the preservation of natural rights.[30] Should the government break that trust by acting against the public good or by trespassing on the natural rights of its people, the people had not just a right but a duty to overthrow it and install one better able to satisfy their rights.

This had implications for relations between states as well. For if the state of nature was riven with the mutual hostility described by Hobbes, then neither was the space in which different groupings interacted. The division of humanity into different territorial entities was not forged in war, Locke maintained, but through positive agreements and reciprocal recognition of each other's existence, rights, and territories.[31]

Sovereignty, then, entails responsibilities both to citizens and to the wider community of sovereigns. Recall that Montesquieu described the 'first law of nature' as peace. The first principle of government, therefore, is the security and liberty of the people. This view rests on the idea that individuals have *inalienable* natural rights—human rights in today's language—that may never be rescinded. These rights are universal, not culture specific. They are also prior to politics. As such, an individual's basic rights are never secondary to the rights of national or any other kind of groups. According to Lynn Hunt, these rights have three innate qualities: they are *natural* (inherent in human beings), *equal* (the same for everyone), and *universal*.[32] This is often touted as a new or radical conception of sovereignty. But it is neither new nor all that radical. The doctrine of sovereignty as responsibility was written down by Thomas Jefferson and proclaimed in America's Declaration of Independence on 4 July 1776. Thus:

> We hold these truths to be self-evident, that all men are created equal, that they are endowed by their Creator with certain inalienable Rights, that among these are Life, Liberty and Happiness.
>
> …to secure these rights, Governments are instituted among Men, deriving their just powers from the consent of the governed,—That whenever any Form of Government becomes destructive of these ends, it is the Right of the People to alter or abolish it, and to institute new Government…
>
> …when a long train of abuses and usurpations, pursuing invariably the same Object evinces a design to reduce them under absolute Despotism, it is their right, it is their duty, to throw off such Government, and to provide new Guards for their future security.[33]

Governments that fail to protect the fundamental rights of their citizens or subjects or that wantonly abuse those rights fail in their sovereign responsibilities. This gives the people, as individual sovereigns, the right and duty to overthrow the government and replace it with one more conducive to the satisfaction of their rights. These ideals were repeated thirteen years later by the French National Assembly which, in 1789, proclaimed the 'Rights of Man and the Citizen', insisting that 'the principle of all sovereignty rests essentially in the nation. No body and no individual may exercise authority which does not emanate expressly from the nation'.[34]

These ideas were not widely supported in their own time—in a world of absolute monarchs, these notions struck at the heart of aristocratic privilege. And of course, America's founding fathers believed that only white males were deserving of these rights, but ideas about human equality were carried forward in the US and elsewhere. Nor did they give rise to peace. American independence was won by force of arms, not the power of persuasion. The French Revolution gave way to the 'Terror', Napoleonic despotism, and imperial expansion. Paradoxically, the Napoleonic wars discredited popular sovereignty whilst simultaneously spreading its ideals across Europe, inspiring later Italian, Hungarian, Croatian, and German nationalists. Although its meaning and fortunes ebbed and flowed, sovereignty as responsibility survived into the twentieth century. Among its champions were three members of the Roosevelt dynasty.

In May 1918, former US president Theodore Roosevelt insisted that the massacre of Armenians by the Turks invalidated Turkey's claim to rule over Armenia (ironically, he did not think that the extermination of indigenous Americans, which he occasionally championed, invalidated Washington's claim to rule over their lands). In the Armenian case, Roosevelt argued that 'the perpetuation of Turkish rule is the perpetuation of infamy', continuing, '[w]e are guilty of a peculiarly odious form of hypocrisy when we profess friendship for Armenia and the downtrodden races of Turkey, but don't go to war with Turkey. To allow the Turks to massacre the [Armenians] and then solicit permission to help the survivors...is both foolish and odious'. He ended by referring to America's reasons for joining the First World War: 'when we now refuse to war with Turkey we show that our announcement that we meant "to make the world safe for democracy" was insincere claptrap'.[35] After the war, Woodrow Wilson defended the idea that sovereignty be based on the principle of self-determination, the idea that government be based on the consent of the governed. But this did not extend to self-determination for Armenians because Congress rejected a proposed American trusteeship, or to colonized peoples. That would come later.

In the 1941 Atlantic Charter, Franklin Roosevelt persuaded the great imperialist Winston Churchill to accept, albeit grudgingly, the principles of self-determination and individual human rights. The Charter proclaimed 'the right of all peoples to choose the form of government under which they will live' and that the Allied powers would establish a peace in which 'all the men in all the lands may live out their lives in freedom from fear and want'.[36]

After the Second World War, a third Roosevelt, Eleanor, played a key role in cajoling world leaders into adopting a *Universal* Declaration of Human Rights, by chairing the UN Human Rights Commission and shepherding the draft declaration through eighty-three commission meetings and some 170 amendments.[37] The Declaration proclaimed that 'recognition of the inherent dignity and of the equal and inalienable rights of all members of the human family is the foundation of freedom, justice and peace in the world'—principles central to decolonization. Article 1 declared that 'All human beings are born free and equal in dignity' whilst Article 3 insisted that 'Everyone has the right to life, liberty and security of person'. Missing was the second component of sovereignty as responsibility: the idea that a government's failure to satisfy these rights granted others a responsibility to ensure their realization. That idea has proven much more difficult to institutionalize.

For all its faults, the modern state has done a relatively good job at protecting the right to life of its inhabitants and at reducing war. Homicide, civil war, and domestic strife, and with it the chances of dying violent deaths, declined. Alternatives do exist, but we have yet to find one that can perform better on a sufficiently large scale. Precisely *how* states achieved these feats remains the subject of conjecture, but there are at least four principal explanations.

First, by replacing the anarchy of the 'state of nature' with a law-based order, states decisively altered the balance of consequences between conflict and cooperation in favour of the latter. Prohibiting and punishing homicide made killing a much less attractive route to riches than it once was, whilst a system of laws helped establish the trust needed to allow cooperation to flourish.

Second, by concentrating coercive power in the hands of a few, the rise of states dramatically reduced the number of actors capable of employing organized violence. Whilst the Hobbesian state of nature may never have actually existed, it is certainly the case that for much of history, in many parts of the world, every minor lord or landowner worth his salt could raise an army and wage war—and often did so in pursuit of glory, land, and riches. By imposing a monopoly of legitimate force, states centralized violence, limited the number of actors that could legitimately employ it, and thereby reduced its incidence.

Third, with the concentration of power and authority in their hands, modern states became far more capable, and destructive, as war-fighters than anything that had gone before. Wars became more expensive and therefore less appealing as an instrument of policy.

Fourth, the commercial, industrial, and scientific advances made possible by modern states—in short, the process of 'modernization' itself—made peace more profitable than war. Modernization dramatically increased the rewards of peace, at first influencing judgements about costs and benefits and then pushing whole societies further away from belligerency.[38]

States are not universally good at fostering peace. Some are better than others.[39] Tyrannies such as the fascist and communist dictatorships of the twentieth century produced much more violence than peace, whilst liberal democracies have tended in the opposite direction. Immanuel Kant, recall, argued that it was not states per se, but a particular kind of state—those with republican constitutions—that would give rise to perpetual peace. He reasoned that republican states waged war only with the consent of the people. '[N]othing is more natural', he thought, 'than that they should weigh the matter well before undertaking such a bad business. For in decreeing war, they would of necessity be resolving to bring down the miseries of war' upon themselves. A tyranny, by contrast, would think nothing of waging war since all the costs would be borne by others.[40] Napoleon's republican aggression shattered this particular Kantian theory, for it transpired that when injected with enough nationalist fervour, citizens could be easily persuaded willingly to endure the costs of destructive war. Yet I think his broader point, that the nature of states matters, remains true. In fact, there is considerable evidence to support it.

The 1997 report of the Carnegie Commission on the Prevention of Deadly Conflict, a report that continues to shape the way that the UN and others approach conflict prevention, held the same view. Peace, it argued, rests on the establishment of 'capable states with representative governance based on the rule of law, with widely available economic opportunity, social safety nets, protections of fundamental human rights, and robust civil societies'.[41] More recently, the relationship between governance and peace was recognized by the UN General Assembly in its 'Sustainable Development Goals', agreed in 2015. Goal 16 calls upon states to 'Promote *peaceful* and inclusive societies for sustainable development, provide access to justice for all and build effective, accountable, and inclusive institutions at all levels' (emphasis mine). Five characteristics of a state are particularly important for fostering peace: a monopoly of legitimate violence, the accountability of government, the protection of fundamental human rights, the maintenance of a basic floor of economic justice, and gender equality. States that exhibit or promote these five attributes are more likely to sustain peace than those that do not.[42] Such states can become the bedrock of world peace. Let us look at each of these attributes in turn.

Monopoly of legitimate violence. It is a defining feature of states, German sociologist Max Weber taught, that they hold a monopoly of legitimate violence. It is through the centralization of violence in the hands of the state that daily anarchy is escaped. By monopolizing violence, the state is able to bring immense force to bear against any who would violate its laws. As a result, most of us choose not to violate the law. At the same time, by organizing coercion in ways regarded as legitimate by societies, states laid the foundations for the cooperation and innovation necessary for economic development.[43] Legitimacy also explains why most states, most of the time, do not succumb to civil war. It is not just that the state is capable of using force; it is that most of us believe that the state has a right to do so. That it is justified.

Accountability. If Hobbes and Locke were right, then the domestic peace established by states rests on a contract between government and governed. For many if not most states, this is more than a matter of pure political theory. It is a relationship embedded in constitutional law. Take, for example, India's constitution. The preamble signals that the state is constituted by 'the people of India' for the purpose of securing justice, liberty, equality, and fraternity for all its citizens. Turning to the specific purpose of the state, Article 38 declares it as being 'to promote the welfare of the people by securing and protecting as effectively as it may a social order in which justice, social, economic and political, shall inform all the institutions of the national life'. The Brazilian state too was formed by the representatives of the people for the purpose of 'ensuring the exercise of social and individual rights, liberty, security, well-being, development, equality and justice' (preamble). Article 3 identifies the first objective of the state as being 'to build a free, just and solidary society'. Russia's constitution expresses the point in decidedly Lockean terms: its first substantive article (Article 1 covers the state's official name), Article 2, declares that: 'Man, his rights and freedoms are the supreme value. The recognition, observance and protection of the rights and freedoms of man and citizen shall be the obligation of the State'. The social contract is no Western liberal fiction. It is evident in the constitutions of most states, including leading non-Western powers like India and Brazil; even the Russian constitution declares that the rights of individuals precede the state and that the state is *obligated* to protect the rights and freedoms of man.

If the state is constituted by the people (however defined) to protect their fundamental rights and achieve their common goals, it stands to reason that one of the most fundamental principles of state is accountability; its foremost institution, the rule of law. Whilst the former ensures that government is answerable to the governed for the fulfilment of its fundamental purposes, the latter ensures that this relationship is not arbitrary. Political stability, human rights, and economic prosperity are all premised on the rule of law. When there is no rule of law, or its rule is weak, civilian populations become subject to the arbitrary exercise of power by government. Governments that are unaccountable or that are not subject to the rule of law have fewer inhibitions (and bureaucratic obstacles) about using violence to achieve their goals or maintain themselves in power. Sometimes, governments have argued that ideology should trump the rule of law and accountability. In the past few decades, governments captured by fascist, Marxist-Leninist, extreme anti-communist, Islamist, racist, and extreme nationalist ideologies haven proven themselves to be especially violent, to their own populations as well as to their neighbours. Many non-state armed groups operate in similar ways, combining unaccountable decision-making with violent extremist ideologies. Accountability deficits also breed arbitrariness. It is often the case that in autocratic governments and non-state armed groups, the executive leadership exercises arbitrary power, with no institutional checks and balances. When there is limited accountability, those with the capacity to use violence will be repeatedly tempted to do so, especially when it offers a seemingly efficient way of resolving problems. What is more, weakness in the rule of law reinforces cultures of impunity that are especially important for persuading agitators to launch acts of violence. Where there is limited accountability, and impunity is permitted, state violence can be normalized and its power put into the service of violence. The legitimate state, Christopher Coker reminds us, is one that can reconcile differences through the fairness and accountability of its decision-making, not one that abolishes such differences.[44]

Adherence to the rule of law provides accountability even in the face of discriminatory policies by governments, ensuring a safety net for targeted individuals and groups. An accountable system of government contains institutional and ideational deterrents that impede political elites from attacking their own populations. Even semi-democracies are less likely to experience civil war or to launch wars of aggression than autocratic regimes, but they at least have some checks on the exercise of arbitrary power.

We should not, though, succumb to the belief that accountability and the rule of law necessarily entail Western-style democracy. Democratic governments are often said to be more legitimate, effective, stable, and—hence—peaceful than their non-democratic counterparts. It is certainly true that, as proponents of the 'democratic peace theory' claim, democracies tend not to wage war on each other (though even this is hotly disputed, with much hinging on what we mean by 'democracy'). It is also true that democracies are much less likely to succumb to civil war than non-democratic states. All told, a world composed of thriving and established democracies would likely be a more peaceful one. Their peacefulness tends to grow with their level of democracy. The more democratic, the more peaceful. Yet, democratic states have exhibited few inhibitions about attacking those they judge to be non-democratic and democracies have sometimes collapsed into violence. What is more, the road to democracy is a bumpy and sometimes violent two-way street. Societies making the transition to democracy are amongst the most vulnerable and the most violent.[45] Those that have recently made the transition often face a great risk of violent reversion. And democracy has a 'dark side'. Democratic reform can unleash nationalist and xenophobic passions as the 'people' look to carve out their own national living space. All too often, democratization has gone hand in hand with violent ethnic cleansing.[46]

But the principal reasons why I think democracy—however much I value it in its own right—is not necessarily essential for world peace are that democratic forms of government are not the only ones capable of holding governments accountable, and that sustained peace has sometimes been achieved in the absence of democracy. Democracy is a good thing in itself, and when established makes peace easier to sustain, but it is not a prerequisite for peace. The road to a less violent world is not necessarily, therefore, paved with Western values and styles but it is paved with relations of accountability between a state and the society within it.[47]

Human rights. The third attribute of a peace-supporting state relates to how it treats its own people. States contribute to peace when they protect a basic floor of human rights for their peoples. Basic rights are important because without them other rights cannot be met. The satisfaction of basic rights is also the minimum standard of 'public safety' that states should achieve to fulfil their part of the great sovereignty bargain with their people. Two rights stand out as being particularly important: the right to freedom from arbitrary violence (rights to life and liberty) and the right to equal treatment (principle of non-discrimination in all its forms, including racial and gendered). At a minimum, governments should refrain from killing, abusing, and torturing their populations, should ensure a basic level of public safety, and should treat their peoples equally.

Where governments actively discriminate between specific groups, be they ethnic, political, socioeconomic, or religious, the promise of safety that gives the state its reason for existing in the first place is left unfulfilled. In such situations, the individuals and groups discriminated against sometimes see little reason to obey the state and may instead rebel against it. These problems are aggravated where the state itself is active in discrimination and/or not bound to the rule of law. States that do not protect a basic floor of rights are more likely to be genocidal, to succumb to civil war, and to lead foreign aggressions than those that do. I mention genocide deliberately, as this crime always begins with hate speech and targeted discrimination.[48]

Discrimination takes many different forms, including the denial of basic political rights (such as the right to a fair trial, the right to vote, freedom of speech, freedom of association) on grounds of race, religion, gender, and nationality, amongst others; the denial of citizenship, freedom of religion, and self-identification, and limitations on basic social or civil rights (such as freedom from discrimination on grounds of race, ethnicity, religion, etc.); economic discrimination such as unequal access to economic opportunities, land and other resources, employment, food, shelter, or healthcare; gender discrimination, which includes the denial or inadequate protection of basic rights relating to physical security and the status of women, compulsory birth control, and unequal access to services and property; and racial discrimination. Persistent discrimination establishes entrenched social divisions that serve both as a material cause of and a perceived justification for group violence.

Basic economic justice. Governments have an important role to play in ensuring that their populations enjoy a basically decent standard of living.[49] Among other things, this involves the fair distribution of public goods (including healthcare and education), provision of secure livelihoods, and mitigation of gross inequalities. Overall levels of wealth (measured in terms of gross domestic product [GDP] per capita) matter inasmuch as a society's susceptibility to civil war declines markedly as its wealth increases, but the relative economic position of groups within a country also matters. These are horizontal inequalities (across groups) instead of the more commonly measured vertical inequalities (referring to the relative wealth of rich and poor measured by Gini coefficients). These economic inequalities increase risk indirectly by raising the stakes of intergroup competition. Moreover, disaffected groups may have a lower commitment to peace. Sometimes, however, the causal path can be unusually direct; for instance, when violence is used in a competition between groups for scarce resources. The mismanagement of income secured from natural resources, for example, can also become a key point of dispute between groups. The role the increasing scarcity of water and grazing land, both necessary for survival, played in sharpening the conflict in Darfur that erupted in 2003 is a case in point. States that can satisfy their population's right to subsistence, promote economic growth and wellbeing, and mitigate divisions do more for world peace than those that do not.

Gender equality. Gender-equal societies are far more peaceful than patriarchal societies. Patriarchy is a system of social and political organization that places power and authority in the hands of men and that privileges values and attributes commonly associated with masculinity above those commonly associated with femininity. Across human history, the great majority of states and societies have been patriarchal ones. They still are. The problem for us is that patriarchy makes societies more militaristic and war-prone. In other words, war persists in part because it is enabled and facilitated by how we manage relations between genders.

Gender equality is strongly associated with peace. Over more than two decades of research, using different datasets, and focusing on both civil and interstate wars, studies have repeatedly demonstrated a strong connection between gender equality and peace. Mary Caprioli showed that more gender-equal societies were much less likely to lead wars of aggression on others than less equal societies.[50] Others found that states with higher levels of violence against women tended to have poorer relations with their neighbours.[51] Another study found that women were significantly more likely than men to believe that international organizations were an effective means of resolving interstate disputes.[52] Another showed that the more common violence is against women within a society, the less likely that society was to comply with international norms. Erik Melander found that gender equality had a strong pacifying effect on society. Melander used three measures for gender equality— the number of women in senior leadership, female representation in parliament, and male–female education ratios—and found that whilst female leadership made little difference, there was a strong correlation between the other two measures and greater peacefulness. More equal societies tend to be less vulnerable to civil war than unequal ones.[53] In their landmark book *Sex and World Peace*, Valerie Hudson and her collaborators demonstrated that the level of violence against women in a society was a better predictor of state peacefulness, internally and internationally, than other variables such as democracy, wealth, and ideology.[54] Gender equality is also positively linked to effective peace-making and non-violent resistance.[55] Peace processes that include women as equal partners tend to produce more sustainable peace than those that do not.[56]

There is also much to be said for the argument that militarism and war rest on foundations of patriarchy and what might be called 'hyper-masculinity'. Whilst there are plenty of examples of women who were just as enthused by and involved in war as men, one of the most consistent features of opinion polling about war is that men tend to support it to a far greater extent than do women.[57] The relationship works in the other direction too—war is supportive of patriarchy. War has, historically, been associated with the violent male domination of females. Indeed, rape and the kidnapping of women were among the principal goals of early warfare, as the fable of the Rape of the Sabine Women attests. Until quite recently, looting and rape were considered ordinary accompaniments of war. But the relationship between patriarchy—the privileging of men and masculine identities—and war goes deeper than this. First, war has, historically, tended to rely on the same rigid delineations of male and female roles in society as patriarchy which gave rise to deeply entrenched ideas about masculine and feminine stereotypes: the former privileging aggression, strength, resilience, and other virtues necessary for war and the latter privileging beauty, humility, and compassion; and the former taking precedence over the latter. Societies that reinforce these stereotypes are, thus, more likely to be 'warlike', or at least more likely to view war as a noble and necessary endeavour, than those that do not.[58] Second, both patriarchy and war depend upon violence. They are both manifestations of a common problem: social violence. There is no a priori reason why human societies should privilege males over females, yet over the course of history the great majority of societies have done precisely that. These systems owed their endurance to the powerful social norms that underwrote them but also to the violence they often sanctioned. That is why many feminists continue to argue that war should be understood not as a distinct social practice but as part of a continuum of violence 'running from bedroom, to boardroom, factory, stadium, classroom, and battlefield, traversing our bodies and our sense of self'.[59]

There is a strong connection between patriarchy and war; and conversely between gender equality and greater peacefulness. There is clear evidence, for example, that the world's more gender-equal societies are also the world's more peaceful—a logical corollary of patriarchy's association with violence. None of this is to suggest that women are not just as capable as men of supporting war, waging war, and committing horrific atrocities. We know that they are.[60] What is more, anthropological evidence suggests that matriarchal societies—those where females dominate males—are just as war-prone as patriarchal societies. The point is that the way in which most societies organize themselves (patriarchies) sustains, and is sustained by, war.[61] When that relationship is ruptured by social relations based on gender equality, societies become less war-prone.

Simply put, the more gender equal a society is, the more peaceful it tends to be, and vice versa. Precisely *why* this relationship holds is more difficult to ascertain. It is not that women are naturally more peaceful than men; women can be just as violent, aggressive, and jingoistic as their male counterparts. Nor is there something necessarily warlike about patriarchal societies; some of the most famous peaceful societies of the past were patriarchal—as, of course, were some of the most violent. The key seems to lie in the influence that equality has on cultural practices and attitudes and, through that, on state behaviour. That is not to say that patriarchal societies cannot be peaceful. We know they can. But it is to say that gender-equal societies are *more likely* to be peaceful. Two principal reasons stand out. First, because the cultural norms nourished by more equal societies favour human rights, equality (including gender, racial, religious, etc.), inclusiveness, rule by law, accountability, and non-violent conflict resolution (and these norms are *required* for a society to become more gender equal in the first place) and challenge entrenched hierarchies, patterns of violence and abuse, and economic and social discrimination. These norms, in turn, impact on the way governments think and act. Research on genocide and mass atrocities shows that mass violence is more likely when a country's decision-making elite is centralized, non-democratic, and drawn from a small sector of the community.[62] Gender equality necessarily involves more diffused and inclusive forms of decision-making, in which a wider range of perspectives are brought to the table. States that encourage greater gender equality help reinforce domestic peace and inhibit tendencies to see war as a viable and efficient instrument of policy, reducing the pernicious effects of group difference and war's contagiousness.

In sum, states that hold a monopoly of legitimate violence, are accountable to their people, protect their basic rights, facilitate a basic degree of economic justice, and foster gender equality provide a more solid foundation for world peace than those that do not. Precisely how states and societies understand and pursue these goals rightly differs across time and space, since there is no monopoly of wisdom and legitimate states are attuned to the cultural preferences of their peoples. Every revolution or state ideology has tended to assume that it has found the answer, only to discover that dogmatism tends to lead to new rounds of violence. We should think of these five characteristics not as absolute values but rather as anchorages identifying broad ambitions and guiding judgements about whether states are moving closer towards or further away from promoting peace.

The state is nothing if not a paradox when it comes to war and peace, and although the consolidated and legitimated state is a bedrock of peace, the process by which states were built was often incredibly violent. War features large in the annals of state-building. In *Against the Grain* (2017), James C. Scott argued that violence and subjugation were at the heart of the earliest state-building projects in Mesopotamia. New states, he alleged, were driven by the need for manual labour to irrigate and farm land for grains and generate a surplus for the new aristocracies. They achieved this through systems of forced labour. Armed groups were formed to capture new slaves, writing a propensity for war into the state from the very outset. Other technologies of control, such as writing, soon emerged, all designed to strengthen the rulers' capacity to control 'their' peoples.[63] From these inauspicious beginnings, war, conquest, and empire played pivotal roles in establishing ever-larger political groupings—the great empires of Rome, Mughal India, and Han China, and the states that later emerged from their ruin. But, in turn, these political orders gave rise to huge leaps in human development by fostering internal cohesion and cooperation.[64] The Roman Empire is a classic example of the paradox of peace at work. Within the empire, levels of everyday violence were much lower than they were outside it or before it, because Rome enacted and enforced laws. Commerce, trade, and wellbeing thrived. However, the process of making and sustaining the empire was incredibly violent; warfare was deeply embedded in the structure of civilization itself.[65] Yet through war, a political system reduced daily violence, improved wellbeing, and extended lives. Subsequently, wars were waged—and genocides sometimes committed—to form 'national' states and to align national identities with state boundaries. Yet through this bloody process, humans were organized into political entities that tended to make them safer and richer than they had been before.[66]

State-building remains an incomplete global project and therefore one of the greatest tasks for those committed to world peace. In many parts of the world, it is an endeavour still less than a century old. Most of today's wars are conflicts over state formation and consolidation—wars about what the boundaries of the state should be, what ideological and constitutional form it should take, who should control it, and on what basis. These contests are sometimes fuelled by the very same principle—self-determination—that gave rise to statehood independent of colonial authority in the first place. Having used self-determination to assert their independence from European powers, new national elites found others trying to apply the same principle to win independence from them.[67] As a result, many post-colonial states were plunged almost immediately into civil wars. Many have barely—if ever—exercised legitimate control over the whole of their territory. In places like Afghanistan, Sudan, South Sudan, Somalia, the Democratic Republic of Congo, the Central African Republic, Mali, and Myanmar there have been many more years of war than of peace since independence. In these countries, atrocity crimes have been widespread and systematic in part because of their practical utility and in part because the association of peoples and territories lay at the core of their disputes. Convulsions in the Middle East, meanwhile, are driven by the one thing that governments there share: their illegitimacy. Across that region, governments are controlled by unaccountable authoritarians who pay lip-service to the rule of law, maintaining order (such as it is) only through systems of repressive rules, intrusive surveillance, and massive doses of violence, including torture. These wars on unfinished and contested state-building are the 'remnants of war' mentioned earlier.[68]

After the end of the Cold War, the international community got into the business of helping rebuild states broken by war, or sometimes to build them from scratch. In a few cases, such as in Kosovo and East Timor, this assistance took the form of temporary trusteeships through which international bodies assumed sovereign authority whilst the situation was stabilized and basic *institutions* constructed, before transferring that authority back to local actors. More often, however, international agencies have worked in support of, and with the consent of, existing national authorities. That these efforts have had decidedly mixed results—ranging from relative success in places such as Cambodia, Namibia, Guatemala, Liberia, and Sierra Leone to ongoing failure in places like South Sudan, Afghanistan, and the Democratic Republic of Congo, and much that sits somewhere between the two poles—should not surprise us.

State-building is a risky and long-term project. It was always unlikely that societies afflicted by decades of civil war would transform themselves into havens of stable peace in a generation. What matters is that they begin the journey and stay on the road even when crises and setbacks emerge. International assistance can help, but if we expect miracles, we are bound to be disappointed.

Civil conflicts drive unvirtuous circles of despair. Often themselves responses to incomplete state-building, civil war and violent rebellion tend to further weaken states, damage livelihoods, and fuel the passions of future conflict. Civil wars are often especially barbarous precisely because the combatants know each other so well. 'The personal motives that infuse civil strife make the conflict palpable and the stakes obvious', writes Russell Jacoby.[69] What is more, because civil war is a violent contest over who should govern and on what terms, it entails a collapse of social order itself. For that reason, thinkers have long ascribed it as an especial evil because it involves not just the violence of war but also a reversion to a pre-civilized state. Thus, the Greek philosopher Plato argued that there was no greater evil than civil wars, the Roman poet Lucan that civil wars brought no triumphs, and the Christian theologian Augustine that these were wars of a 'worse kind'.[70] Rome, of course, was ultimately undone by civil wars. They were, David Armitage reminds us, Rome's curse, one which writers from Caesar to Augustine tried in vain to understand.[71]

The perils of civil war, and their attendant horrors, were well described by Thucydides. The renowned historian of the Peloponnesian War recounts how Corcyra's privileged elite rose against the city's democratic government in an attempt to sever its alliance with Athens and establish a new union with Sparta. After a series of violent clashes, the Athenian fleet intervened on the side of the democrats, tilting the balance decisively in their favour. With the state and its rules of law overthrown, there followed a bloody massacre. 'Death raged in every shape; and, as usually happens at such times, there was no length to which violence did not go; some were killed by their fathers, and suppliants dragged from the altar or slain upon it; while some were even walled up in the temple of Dionysus, and died there'.[72] The cause of this bloodletting, Thucydides tells us, was human nature itself, set free when 'the ordinary conventions of civilized life [were] thrown into confusion'. Human nature, 'always ready to offend even where laws exist, showed itself proudly in its true colours, as something incapable of controlling passion, insubordinate to the idea of justice, the enemy to anything superior to itself'. The 'cause of all these evils', he writes, 'was the lust for power arising from greed and ambition'. Such suffering would be repeated 'so long as human nature remained the same' and unbound by the civilizing power of the legitimate state.[73] What mattered for Thucydides was that the breakdown of the state—the *polis*—caused a collapse of social order and with it the very possibility of justice or morality.

Thomas Hobbes also regarded civil war—the breakdown of the state—as a source of great calamity. Hobbes argued that the very purpose of political philosophy was to prevent 'confusion and civil war', a task for which civil government 'was ordained'. From civil war, Hobbes wrote in *De Copore* (1655), stemmed 'all such calamities as may be avoided by human industry', including 'slaughter, solitude, and the want of all things'. Its prevention, therefore, was among the first jobs of government.[74] For Hobbes, as for Augustine more than a thousand years earlier, the sovereign's primary responsibility was to deliver people from the tyrannies of 'warre' and civil war.

Recent experience shows that state-building and modernization can provoke opposition. Pankaj Mishra recently argued that the contemporary rise of violent extremism is merely the latest phase of a backlash against modernization and globalization that goes back centuries and included the anarchists who terrorized Europe in the nineteenth and early twentieth centuries.[75] Mishra maintains that Western-style modernization uprooted traditional cultures and societies but failed to replace them with new locally grounded and legitimated ideas about how to live. That was not much of a problem for those who benefitted materially from the global transformation, but it created a reservoir of resentment amongst those who did not, those on the receiving end of the ever-widening inequalities between rich and poor. Extremist ideologues—entrepreneurs of disenchantment—exploited this resentment to their own advantage. Romantics responded to modernity with nationalism and mythology; anarchists, communists, and fascists with wildly utopian visions of a world reordered; Islamists with dreams of the caliphate and the restoration of their own—extremist—accounts of Sha'ria. In Mishra's vision, today's jihadists and white extremists are simply contemporary manifestations of the same forces that brought anarchist terrorism, socialism, and fascism to the streets of Europe in the nineteenth and early twentieth centuries.

This account is illuminating inasmuch as it points to the inevitability of violent resistance to transformational change and shows that, far from being unique and novel, the extremism of today draws from the same reservoirs of human resentment that drove extremism a century ago. It also helps explain why political extremists and especially their leaderships tend to come not from the very bottom of society but from the educated middle classes, those often acculturated by the modern but who, for one reason or another, chose to rebel against it in the name of the genuinely disenfranchised. But it is a one-sided accounting of the contemporary world that pays insufficient attention to the goods wrought by modernization, not least among them sharp declines in poverty, increases both in the quality and length of life, and greater peacefulness.

Mishra's thesis is also too general in its explanation and has difficulty accommodating different experiences. Why, we might wonder, has this violence emerged only in some places and not in others that underwent similar transformations? The answer may lie in the role of ideologues—and the ideologies they peddle—which may play a more significant role than Mishra suggests.[76] So too, in all likelihood, do local conditions. The rise of Boko Haram in Nigeria, for example, had next to nothing to do with industrialization and modernization and everything to do with local politics and the authorities' mistreatment of opposition activists. Likewise, it was not 'modernization' that sparked the Sunni rebellion in Iraq that eventually gave rise to Islamic State. After all, many of Iraq's Sunnis profited under Saddam's modernization schemas. Rather, it was the collapse of Saddam's regime, their loss of privilege, wealth, and security, and the sometimes brutal discrimination against them by the Shi'ite-controlled government in Baghdad that drove their resentment: all of this a product of the US decision to invade in 2003. However, Mishra's account exposes how radical social and economic transformations can give rise to violent backlashes. It reminds us that state-building, consolidation, and modernization can be violent processes, that can give rise to opposition—itself often violent.

Once states are established, legitimized, and consolidated, civil wars within them become much less likely. Legitimate and capable states that hold a monopoly of violence, are accountable, protect the fundamental human rights of their people, maintain a basic floor of economic justice, and promote gender equality rarely fall into collapse or civil war—though history is rarely unidirectional and these conditions, and with them the chances of war, can worsen as well as improve. Peace, therefore, begins with the state but so too does war. Much of the war we experience today stems from problems associated with states. States and societies can help one another by supporting the capacities that make states legitimate and capable. They can help states and societies recover from civil war and create the sorts of institutions, rules, and practices needed to avoid a recurrence—the stuff of peace-building. They can also create international environments conducive to state consolidation by recognizing each other's right to territorial integrity and non-interference (principle of independence). International institutions can also step in to prevent conflicts from escalating. All this can help states fulfil the role for which they were established—the provision of public safety and maintenance of the peace.

Yet the state is not only a peacemaker; it is also a supremely effective warmaker. It is a paradox of peace that the more internally coherent a state and its people are, the sharper the differences are likely to be between them and their neighbours. The ties that bind people together within states are usually stronger than the ties that bind them to those outside, and this very fact—the fact that humans are organized into different and discrete polities and prioritize the welfare of their own over that of others—is what makes war between states possible. As such, how a state comports itself on the world stage matters. States that abide by international law on the use of force and fulfil their legal obligations to the UN's collective security system, states that support free and fair trade and avoid mercantilism, states that adopt an internationalist outlook by helping other states develop the capacities they need to become effective and legitimate do more to support world peace than those that do not. Precisely how states and societies relate to one another, and what this means for world peace, is the question to which we now turn.

CHAPTER 6

THE COSTS OF WAR

For I dipt into the future, far as human eye could see,
Saw the Vision of the world, and all the wonders that would be;
Saw the heavens fill with commerce, argosies of magic sails,
Pilots of the purple twilight dropping down with costly bales;
Heard the heavens fill with shouting, and there rain'd a ghastly dew
From the nations' airy navies grappling in the central blue;
Far along the world-wide whisper of the south-wind rushing warm,
With the standards of the peoples plunging thro' the thunder-storm;
Till the war-drum throbb'd no longer, and the battle-flags were furl'd;
In the Parliament of man, the Federation of the world.
There the common sense of most shall hold a fretful realm in awe,
And the kindly earth shall slumber, lapt in universal law.

—Alfred, Lord Tennyson, 'Locksley Hall' (1835)

In Lord Tennyson's evocative poem 'Locksley Hall', the protagonist envisions a world ripped apart by war and rebuilt once more. Tennyson wrote the poem shortly after Rosa Brookes had refused his proposal of marriage in favour of a wealthier man. At its heart, 'Locksley Hall' is a critique of societies that value wealth above love. Like Tennyson himself, the protagonist is rejected by his beloved Amy in favour of a rich but boorish man. Arriving at Locksley Hall, where he had spent many a happy time during his childhood, the protagonist reflects on the greed and self-destructiveness of materialist society, seeing that greed unchecked would lead nations into a great and devastating war. Violence would know no bounds, even taking to the air—'airy navies' battling in the 'central blue' (interestingly, Sir John Slessor, Marshal of the Royal Air Force during the Second World War, used 'central blue' as the title of his autobiography).[1] Offering a forewarning of the destructiveness of twentieth-century innovations such as indiscriminate bombing and nuclear weapons, Tennyson described 'heavens filled with shouting' raining down a 'ghastly dew'. At the last, however, hope emerges from the devastation. When 'the war-drum throbb'd no longer', common sense drives people to recognize war's folly and establish a 'Parliament of man' that would govern through 'universal law'. The 'kindly earth' falls into a presumably peaceful slumber.

The idea that the immense costs of war could eventually persuade societies and their political leaders to embrace peace is a long-standing article of faith for peace activists. It is also the logical corollary of the idea that war persists because it helps some individuals and groups get what they want at a reasonable cost. If war were no longer productive, if it delivered only 'ghastly dew', it would be less attractive and therefore less common. 'To abolish war', writes Martin Van Creveld, we need only make sure 'it can no longer serve the objectives of policy/politics'.[2] In this, at least, there is evidence of significant progress. The spiralling costs of war and increasing rewards of peace, combined with the increasing difficulty of translating battlefield success into favourable political outcomes, mean that war is becoming less profitable financially and less rewarding politically. Peace, meanwhile, has helped deliver staggering progress in human wealth and wellbeing in many (though not all) parts of the world. If war does have a future, it will likely not be as a rational instrument of policy.

In Chapter 3, I argued that war persists in part because a sufficient number of us continue to see it as productive—an efficient means of securing or advancing interests. In a classic statement of this view, Donald Kagan argued that war was caused by the pursuit of glory, territory, and riches.[3] Kagan—whose analysis looked backwards into history rather than forwards into the future— was right to point out that warfare arose as a way of achieving short-term benefits. First taking the form of predatory raiding, war then evolved into tussles over territory, which became more pronounced because in so many parts of the world land held the key to economic wealth. As Ian Morris contends, war built states and empires which, as we saw in Chapter 5, drove social development and brought with it greater peacefulness. War also sometimes helped to reverse great wrongs, and offered groups a way of resolving their differences through tests of strength. War permeates human history because it has occasionally proven itself to be useful, enriching, and efficient.

But what if social and economic changes reduced war's capacity to deliver these goods? What if, by increasing the payoffs of peace and the costliness of war, modernization—as Azar Gat calls it—has fundamentally altered the ledger? What if war no longer paid? What if the costs outweighed anything that could be gained? When war no longer pays, it loses one of its principal rationales and ceases to recommend itself as an option. This is not idle speculation. There are clear signs that this is already happening—that war is becoming a costly and inefficient way of resolving disputes or furthering interests; that war is becoming too expensive to be useful. These are trends we can reinforce if we so choose. In this chapter, I will show how war can be made still more expensive and thus less attractive as a political instrument.

The idea that the path to peace lay in the increasing costs of war is not new. One of the first to think systematically about this was Jan Gotlib Bloch (1836–1902). (Another, incidentally, was Karl Marx's collaborator, Friedreich Engels, who, unlike most military commentators at the time, understood what the US civil war portended for Europe: the superiority of defence and the war of attrition.) Jewish by birth, Bloch lived in Poland and in adulthood converted to Calvinism, though he never forgot his roots and was a staunch campaigner against anti-Semitism in Russia as well as an advocate of Zionism. Bloch studied at the University of Berlin before returning to Warsaw where he worked as a banker. He then moved to St Petersburg, where he supported the financing and planning of Russia's railways. He was fascinated by modern technologies such as railways and armaments and by new developments in warfare, and he became increasingly concerned about the devastation that could be wrought by industrial-scale warfare. He was one of the few who saw fleeting hints of what was to come during the Franco-Prussian War of 1870–1. Having made a small fortune, Bloch left the banking world and dedicated himself to the study of war and advocacy of peace.

In 1898, Bloch published an encyclopaedic book on the changing economics of war. *Is War Now Impossible?* anticipated both the nature and consequences of the First World War with astounding accuracy. Bloch argued that new weapons such as smokeless gunpowder, heavy artillery, better rifles, and machine guns would make traditional wars of manoeuvre obsolete. These technological innovations vastly increased the range at which armies could engage one another, greatly extending the area on which battles could be fought. The capacity of industrial economies to churn out vast quantities of arms and ammunition meant that wars would no longer be settled by a single decisive battle or operational manoeuvre. Of all these developments, Bloch believed that the most horrifying was coming in the field of artillery. A single shrapnel shell fired at great range, he found, inflicted as much damage on the enemy as 1,000 bullets fired at close range. Bloch quoted Prince Hohenlohe, a Prussian artillery commander in the Franco-Prussian war, as declaring that 'a battery placed against a road fifteen paces in width might annihilate a whole mass of infantry on this road for a distance of 7700 yards, so that no one would even think of standing there'.[4] With such immense firepower, capable of firing at such great distances, future industrial wars would inevitably become entrenched and attritional. They would cause casualties on an unprecedented scale.[5] 'The destruction produced in the ranks of armies will be immense', reasoned Bloch.

Bloch anticipated that militaries would respond to these technological developments by improving their defensive capabilities. In other words, they would perfect the art of digging in. He foresaw that:

> In the future war every body of men appointed for defence and even for attack—if it is not to attack at once—must immediately entrench itself. It must dig, so to speak, in the earth its line of battle, and, if time permit, must raise a whole series of defensive points, taking advantage of natural obstacles and perfecting them with defensive works. Sheltered behind such works and in a position to devote all their energy to fire against the enemy, the defenders will sustain losses comparatively slight, only their heads and hands…being exposed, while the attacking bodies will be exposed to the uninterrupted fire of the defenders, and deprived almost of all possibility of returning the fire.[6]

These ideas ran contrary to the prevailing military thought of the time, which emphasized the power of the offensive and kept faith with the idea that a decisive early blow would be sufficient to knock an enemy out of a war. Yet Bloch rightly saw that artillery and machine gun technologies favoured the defence. Defenders could sit in protected bases and pour down shrapnel and bullets on their enemies. New munitions were much more likely to hit oncoming targets than those of the past thanks to improved range and accuracy, the possibility of rapid fire, and the sheer volume of metal that industrial power could bring to bear.

To make offensive war possible in these conditions, industrial nations would have to massively increase the size of their armies. Already, he observed that armies had grown significantly. By the end of the nineteenth century, most European armies called on the services of millions of men. Larger armies with greater firepower would make it more difficult to achieve a decisive victory in battle, resulting in longer and more attritional wars. Wars would become extended duels of industrial power that imposed vast costs. Their outcomes would be determined not by prowess on the battlefield, feats of courage and honour, or superior tactics, but by bloody attrition: the capacity of one side to grind down and destroy the other's ability to fight. These wars would demand ever-greater sacrifices: soldiers sacrificed to attrition; resources exhausted to sustain mass armies; national finances bankrupted by the cost. Bloch wrote, 'Difficulties in the satisfaction of the vital needs of populations, interruption or stagnation in the employment of the productive forces of the population—these are the factors which will influence statesmen against undertaking war, or if war be undertaken, these are the factors which will at one moment or another decidedly veto its continuation'.[7]

The extraordinary demands placed on national populations by major war would cause massive social dislocation, including famine and disease. Eventually, societies would be able to bear no more. Social order would collapse as societies lurched towards rebellion, revolution, and disaster. 'For certain states yet another danger appears', wrote Bloch, 'the danger of revolutionary moments, not only political but also socialistic'. Pushed to the brink by the sacrifices of war, populations would rise up against their governments and establish new regimes whose first acts would be to take themselves out of the war business. So, Bloch argued, when its consequences were thought through to their logical conclusion, it was clear that major war ran contrary to the interests of the Great Powers. Such war would be long, bloody, politically indecisive, exhausting, and prohibitively expensive; the sacrifices demanded of ordinary people would provoke them to revolt. Since no government wished revolution upon itself, all would be forced by self-interest to renounce war as an instrument of policy and to settle their differences peacefully.

Read today, Bloch's work stands among the most prescient and far-sighted of all accounts of future war.[8] His views reportedly influenced Tsar Nicholas II's decision to summon the first Hague Peace Conference in 1899 but they gained little traction beyond that. They were unable to stop several of Europe's Great Powers succumbing to the very traps he had identified.

A decade later, another book was published, this time in Britain, that made a similar argument. It was written by the British academic and politician, Norman Angell, and it was called the *Great Illusion*. The 'illusion' that Angell identified was the idea that nations could still benefit materially from war, militarism, and conquest, when in reality wars between industrial powers had become exercises in futility. Angell argued that growing trade and economic interdependence made war costly and imprudent because conquering powers could no longer simply steal resources from occupied land and exploit local productive power. 'What is the real guarantee of the good behavior of one state to another?', Angell asked. 'It is the elaborate interdependence which, not only in the economic sense, but in every sense, makes an unwarrantable aggression of one state upon another react upon the interests of the aggressor'.[9] Major war,

Angell argued, had become economically irrational since the financial burdens it imposed were enormous and the potential payoffs slight: war indemnities were not easily collected, trade could not be forced through war, and colonies were unprofitable. War had put itself out of business. 'The day for progress by force has passed', he argued. From now on, 'it will be progress by ideas or not at all'.[10] The solution, he argued, lay in international law and the promise of a world court.

Warmly received in Britain, where Angell's case was taken in some quarters to be a defence of Britain's global hegemony (more recently, Niall Ferguson called it a 'liberal imperialist tract') and where universities established study groups to propagate its ideas, the book was less well received in Germany.[11] Angell travelled to Germany in 1913 for a speaking tour at universities, armed with 2,000 copies translated into German. Turnout was low; the reception frosty. At the University of Gottingen, twenty-five students walked out in protest as Angell was about to speak. Things were worse in Berlin. The meeting there ended in a fracas, with Angell complaining that professors had encouraged their students to heckle him. Students then complained to the police that Angell had organized a political meeting in a foreign language.[12] Many Germans, it transpired, were reading another book, one that offered a very different perspective on the value of war: General von Bernhardi's *Germany and the New War*. As popular in Germany as Angell's book was in Britain, Bernhardi's was the antithesis to Angell's. It insisted that war was 'a biological necessity', a national right, and a duty.[13]

It must be said that Bloch's ideas were better received than Angell's, but he too struggled to arouse the interest of Europe's publics. After his death in 1901, a Museum of War and Peace was established in Lucerne, Switzerland to promote his ideas. It was closed in 1919 because of a lack of visitors.

What we think of Bloch's and Angell's theses today is obviously affected by the fact that in 1914 the European powers found major war anything but impossible.[14] Not only did they choose war; they found ample support amongst their populations. But neither Bloch nor Angell had argued that war was physically impossible, only that it would be futile or suicidal. A sense of futility was an emotion often expressed by those on the frontline, especially, but not only, during the First World War. 'Often I used to gaze around the wintry landscape and marvel at the futility of it all', wrote George Orwell of his time on the frontline in the Spanish civil war in early 1937.[15] But just because something is futile, it does not mean that governments, militaries, and publics will avoid doing it. Bloch, in particular, recognized the human capacity for supreme irrationality.

'I do not…deny', he observed in his preface, 'that it is possible for nations to plunge themselves and their neighbours into a frightful series of catastrophes which would probably result in the overturn of all civilized and ordered government'.[16] But major war could not be decisive. Nor could it be waged in a way that would not prove disastrous even for the victorious power. War, then, 'has become impossible, except at the price of suicide'. Shortly before his death, Bloch warned that nationalist politics were encouraging war and that the entrenched mindsets of Europe's elites would not be easily swayed from their irrational course.

Bloch's and Angell's views were ultimately borne out by events. None of the powers that went to war in 1914 emerged from it stronger in 1918. Three empires were destroyed: Russia collapsed into communist revolution; Austria-Hungary collapsed and was dismembered; the Ottoman Empire collapsed and was also dismembered. Germany lost its Kaiser, its empire, and some of its own home territory, and had a punishing peace imposed on it. The victorious allies, Britain and France, hung on to their empires a little longer but were crippled financially and materially. Both began to lose their grip on their global empires. Indeed, so weak had they become that they were unable to enforce the peace terms agreed in 1919, unable to prevent German remilitarization, unable to prevent the rise of Nazism, and unable to hold back the tide of German aggression in 1939.

Not all the leaders sleepwalked into war in 1914. There were some who recognized the dangers at the time. One of those who did was Britain's Foreign Secretary, Sir Edward Grey. Grey expressed his fear that:

> The possible consequences of the present situation were terrible. If as many as four Great Powers of Europe…were engaged in war, it seemed to me that it must involve the expenditure of so vast a sum of money and such an interference with trade, that a war would be accompanied or followed by a complete collapse of European credit and industry…this would mean a state of things worse than that of 1848, and, irrespective of who were victors in the war, many things would be completely swept away.[17]

Afterwards, the devastation wrought was all too obvious. Winston Churchill himself spelled out the terrible wages of the First World War. In his 1931 account of the eastern front, *The Unknown War*, Churchill remarked that 'both sides, victors and vanquished, were ruined. All the Emperors or their successors were slain or deposed…All were defeated; all were stricken; everything they had given was in vain. *Nothing was gained by any*'.[18] Others recognized the point too.

Reflecting on the bloody first day of the Somme in 1916, poet Edmund Blunden observed that neither side 'had won, nor could win the War. The War had won'.[19] Of the major powers, only the United States—which joined late and avoided a home front—emerged stronger from the war, yet for it too the costs were sufficiently high to prompt a retreat from global affairs almost as rapid as its entry in 1917.

It was Europe's rulers, not Bloch and Angell, who had gotten things badly wrong. The verdict of history has been damning. 'They knew the risks in 1914, but didn't really understand or *feel* them', wrote Christopher Clark in his aptly titled study of the march to war: *Sleepwalkers*.[20] Great power war had changed fundamentally. Armies were massive, their firepower unparalleled in history. But the way in which rulers and generals thought about war—their assessments of cost and benefit, their strategies, their tactics—had not. They lacked the imagination to comprehend just how catastrophic the war would be, writes Margaret MacMillan.[21] Europe's rulers were not so glib in 1939 and the balance sheet continued to shift in favour of peace after 1945, as the rest of this chapter will demonstrate.

When we think today about the costs of war, we think principally of three things: the direct costs in terms of people and finances, the opportunity costs in terms of lost trade, and the political and reputational costs. In each of these three domains, the modern balance sheet has shifted against war. Let us examine each in turn.

First, and most obviously, we are drawn to ask questions about the direct cost of fighting wars—the proportion of national wealth directed to armaments, the material devastation wrought, and the chances that war can turn a profit. According to the Institute for Economics and Peace, which produces the annual 'Global Peace Index', the direct economic costs of war, and maintenance of readiness for war, are staggering. It calculates that in 2016, violence cost the world $14.3 trillion, or around 12.6 per cent of world GDP. The majority of that, close to $10 trillion, was accounted for by global spending on the military and security forces, with a little over $1 trillion accounted for by the losses of armed conflict and more than $2 trillion by violent crime.[22] Whilst some defence spending is clearly necessary for a state to maintain its monopoly of legitimate violence, the sheer scale of spending is colossal. It represents a more than $5 a day per person loss as a result of violence, more than half of which is accounted for directly by war and preparation for war. In terms of the opportunity costs arising from that, just a 10 per cent reduction of global violence would be sufficient to double global foreign direct investment or triple global spending on slowing and mitigating climate change. War, then, imposes an immense financial cost. Of course, these figures are global averages. In practice, the most war-prone societies bear a greatly increased share of the global burden. For example, in 2016, more than half of the national economies of Iraq, Afghanistan, and Syria were consumed by war.

Beyond these raw figures, the idea that modern warfare has become excessively expensive is most obviously exemplified by nuclear weapons. The world has enough nuclear firepower to destroy all human life, and to make all life on earth impossible for hundreds of thousands, if not millions, of years. What cause could ever justify even a fraction of that terrible cost? Nuclear weapons did inhibit superpower conflict during the Cold War, encouraging the US and Soviet Union to step back from the brink when they might otherwise not have done so. Nuclear weapons may also have helped to keep some uneasy regional settlements—though the evidence here is less compelling. Relations between India and Pakistan, North and South Korea, and Israel and its hostile neighbours have been held in check somewhat by local, nuclear-armed, deterrence. That is not to say, though, that we should join Kenneth Waltz in 'thanking our nuclear blessings'.[23] For one thing, recent history might have unfolded just as it did without nuclear deterrence, the likely costs of conventional war between the Great Powers doing the job of deterrence by itself. For another, nuclear deterrence did nothing to stop the superpowers fighting proxy wars. And what is more, the proliferation of nuclear weapons could itself become a cause of future war—over Iran or North Korea, for example—or could one day help extremist non-state armed groups hold the world to ransom or worse.

But perhaps the most important reason for thinking that nuclear weapons are more a menace than a peacemaker is the knowledge of just how close to Armageddon they brought us. The Cuban missile crisis in October 1962 stands out in our memory as a moment when the world stood on the precipice. The dangers were real and intense. But it was not the closest we came to nuclear war. That came on 26 September 1983. On that day, Stanislav Petrov, an officer in the Soviet Air Defence force, might have saved the world from nuclear disaster. At a moment of heightened tensions, Soviet systems detected the launch of what it thought were five American nuclear missiles. Soviet doctrine demanded an immediate massive nuclear retaliation, which may in all likelihood have triggered all-out nuclear war. But Petrov, who was on duty that day, hesitated. His civilian training taught him to distrust his instruments. He also knew that retaliation would bring devastation. What is more, he thought a genuine American nuclear attack would involve more than five missiles. So Petrov did not report the apparent launches to military commanders who may well have ordered a retaliation. He waited and then reported, rightly, that they were false alarms.

No matter how beautiful nuclear deterrence might look in Waltz's theory, the reality is that it relies on human systems, perceptions, and actions—all of which can be flawed and compromised. For all the sophisticated theorizing of nuclear experts, a different person at the desk on that fateful day in 1983 could have produced a very different response. A faulty radar reading could have triggered nuclear catastrophe. That is no way to organize world peace.

Thankfully, we can sustain an argument about the prohibitive costs of modern war without the need for nuclear weapons. Carl Kaysen argued that whilst for much of human history war could be profitable for the victors, industrialization has fundamentally changed that fateful calculus.[24] This argument recalls Bloch's point that industrial-age warfare places whole societies under enormous strain in ways that most pre-modern wars did not. Forced to ask more of their citizens, states had to grant them more rights and freedoms but also had to fight for nobler reasons such as national self-preservation, fundamental rights, or peace itself.[25] All this made war more difficult to sustain except in the rarest of circumstances.

The second way in which costs have dampened our appetite for war are through the opportunity costs to trade and economic growth it imposes. As the economic payoffs of war have declined, so the payoffs of peace have improved thanks in large part to industrialization and commerce—activities that thrive in peace. There are at least four ways in which commerce encourages states and societies to prefer peace to war: by making peace more financially lucrative than war, by offering a less expensive way of acquiring resources than war, by increasing the interconnectedness of people in different groups, and by allowing groups more ways of competing and trying to influence one another. In the modern world, war makes states and societies miss out on all sorts of possible goods.

Whatever the economic advantages of war in the past, evidence suggests that modern war—especially civil war—is best characterized as 'development in reverse'.[26] Modern wars ruin economies, rich or poor, setting back human welfare and development. They do so by forcing societies to redirect their resources and energies away from productive enterprise and towards destructive actions that yield few material rewards. Today, it is widely understood that, all other things being equal, war reverses economic development and economic success inhibits war.[27] The 2017 *Global Peace Index* includes case studies on the economic impacts of war in Liberia, Rwanda, Sierra Leone, and Syria, showing that in each case the outbreak of war plunged the national economy into a nosedive. Despite nearly a decade of sustained peace-building, only in 2007 did the Liberian economy return to the level it had been on the eve of civil war, twenty-two years earlier. It remains well behind where it would have been had the economic trend of the mid-1980s (hardly impressive in itself) not been interrupted by war. The pattern is very similar in Sierra Leone. The economic consequences of the 1994 genocide in Rwanda were somewhat different because economic trends were already poor and the violence was extremely sharp, but quite short-lived. Nevertheless, more than two decades on, the Rwandan economy is not close to being where economists project it would have been without war. As for Syria, its economic nosedive after the outbreak of civil war was more severe than that of any of the other cases and the *2017 Index* reported no signs of recovery.[28]

The problem is compounded by the fact that war, especially civil war, has a multiplier effect—an observable aspect of war's contagiousness. It was once commonly thought that economic development made violent conflict more likely because rising powers tended to adopt expansionist foreign policies in order to acquire the territory, access to markets, and resources needed to sustain their growth.[29] In the past few years, however, there has been an outpouring of research showing that the effect of economic development on violent conflict runs in the opposite direction: that poverty, economic inequality, and sharp declines in wealth make war more likely, whilst growing wealth breeds greater peacefulness.[30] Countries with strong and growing economies, and stable governance, that have enjoyed peace for more than five years are extremely unlikely to experience war, be it international or civil war. By contrast, countries with stagnating or shrinking economies, factionalized governments, and recent histories of violence are as much as thirty times more likely than the average to experience war.

The causal link between economic weakness, inequality, and war is well established. So too, as the *Global Peace Index* case studies demonstrate, is the causal chain running in the opposite direction: from war to deprivation. In what Paul Collier describes as the 'conflict trap', contemporary civil wars tend to significantly reduce a society's economic prosperity. They also destroy social infrastructure such as housing, health, and education, meaning that subsequent generations tend to suffer its costs as well. This in turn makes civil war more likely, because wars occur more often when economies are weak, fragmented, and unequal. War therefore creates an economic trap: it destroys national income and capital stock and thereby increases the chances of future war. So war today (whatever its result) increases the risk of future war. This puts societies into a dangerous downwards spiral from which it is very hard (but not impossible) to escape.[31]

The conflict trap is something that affects the poorest communities afflicted by civil wars more than the wealthiest, whose wars tend to be international in nature, but contemporary war can impact negatively even the wealthiest of states. The US-led war against Iraq, for example, pitted a major power against a weak one. Yet the war cost the US in excess of $3 trillion, plunging the American government into a deeper debt crisis that has contributed to falling investment in public infrastructure, education, and much more, with long-term negative effects. The US economy may have been able to sustain this cost, but whether it could sustain the costs of fighting multiple weak states simultaneously, let alone a well-armed state like China, is another question entirely.

The European Union stands out as the global exemplar of how trade and cooperation can give rise to peace. So successful was the EU that all too many take its goods for granted and forget the reasons behind its creation. Indeed, it was to remind us of the EU's remarkable contribution to peace that the Nobel Committee awarded it the peace prize in 2012. Arising out of the ashes of a second cataclysmic war in less than three decades, European integration was a product of its times and the environment it confronted, one made hostile not just by the Soviet threat but also Western Europe's own history. As one of its progenitors, Jean Monnet, put it as the Second World War raged: 'There will be no peace in Europe if states reconstitute themselves on a basis of national sovereignty...European countries are too confined to ensure prosperity and essential social developments for their people'.[32] Or, as political scientist Ole Wæver observed, 'the European idea was to a large extent shaped as a revolt against Europe's own past'.[33]

For Monnet, European integration and the construction of a common European identity was not about balancing or trading sovereignty and national identity, but creating a new type of political community. As Monnet himself put it, 'don't speak in terms of giving up sovereignty...the truth is we are creating a common sovereignty'.[34] This common sovereignty would be manifested in political and economic institutions. In keeping with the 'functionalist' ideas of David Mitrany, discussed in Chapter 2, European economic cooperation and the building of institutions to make that more effective would create mechanisms for resolving disputes peacefully—in the first instance. Over time, these habits of cooperation would lead to the harmonizing of interests and forging of common identities and values. From this, a European community would emerge. War between its members would become inconceivable. Cooperation would breed peacefulness and greater wellbeing. Monnet was right. In the space of a few short decades, trade, economic cooperation, and political integration propelled Europe from being the world's most bellicose continent into its most peaceful.

It is also instructive to compare the experience of different regions on this point. Etel Solingen did just that in a landmark study that compared postcolonial East Asia with the Middle East. Both had emerged from colonization around the same time, both were plagued by territorial disputes and ideological fissures, and in the 1950s they had similar types of highly centralized authoritarian states. They both had societies dominated by conservative feudal lords and military elites. In some respects, the Middle East's starting position was better than East Asia's since it enjoyed a higher degree of cultural similarity and fewer sharp ideological divides. From that point on, however, the two regions took very different paths. Most East Asian states consciously prioritized economic development through industrialization and trade. National resources and government energies were directed towards supporting industrialization. Intra-regional trade grew strongly, creating its own demands for regional stability and establishing national elites with international interests. The region developed strong anti-war norms of non-interference which helped stabilize relations between states. Middle Eastern governments, on the other hand, preferred self-sufficiency over trade, state-led rather than state-supported entrepreneurship, and privileged the military, the military-industrial complex, and militarized conceptions of security over the civilian economy.[35] In the Middle East, war remained a persistent feature of political life. In East Asia, it declined dramatically. The incidence of armed conflict in the Middle East was some five times greater than in East Asia. The principal cause of this marked difference, Solingen found, was the prioritization of economics by East Asian governments and the outward-looking and trade-focused path to development they embraced. The prioritization of 'economic development' in East Asia, Rosemary Foot writes, 'reflects a widely held belief among many of the elites in these states that there is a reciprocal relationship between economic growth and the promotion of regime and state security'.[36]

This brings us to a second way of counting the costs of war: the opportunity costs. East Asia's economic growth depended on manufacturing goods and trading them. This focus on trade gave states a stake in stability, its natural pre-requisite. For example, it encouraged governments to restrain defence spending, with the effect that East Asian states committed much less of their wealth to armaments than did-states in the Middle East. This created a virtuous cycle, since spending less of their national wealth on arms allowed East Asian states to invest more heavily in civilian infrastructure and the national economy. With increasing interaction between countries, domestic business coalitions took on transnational characteristics, strengthening their capacity to influence and their restraining effects.

The best-known critiques of what might be called the 'commercial peace' hold that trade poses no barrier to war and that unequal or hegemonic trade practices might actually cause war. For evidence, we need look no further than Europe on the eve of the First World War. In 1913, European trade had reached unparalleled levels; undocumented travel across borders was the norm. Still this proved insufficient to hold back the tide of war. This is a powerful reminder of why we cannot rely on a single mechanism, such as commerce, to carry the burden of world peace. But there is also reason to think that contemporary trade is qualita-tively different, and more peace-inducing, than earlier twentieth-century forms.

Whereas, in the past, economic interdependence simply involved the trading of goods between countries, its modern globalized form comprises global production chains where individual components, rather than finished prod-ucts, are manufactured in different countries. One effect of this is that the real-ization of a product's value, and hence the value of each of the components, is dependent upon each part of the chain.[37] Thus, as East Asian specialist and political economist John Ravenhill points out, countries depend upon the inputs of others to realize the value of their own production. This effect is com-pounded by the additional value of global brands and marketing which impact significantly on the value of a component or product. As a result, the potential costs associated with the disruption of trade flows within the global economy have never been greater.[38]

The final point here is also perhaps the most obvious one. In the modern era, national wealth and wellbeing are achieved primarily through the production and trade of goods, services, and ideas. It is also through these means that states can best achieve their own goals. In what Arendt described as a 'complete reversal' in the relationship between power and violence, 'the amount of violence at the disposal of any given country may soon not be a reliable indication of the country's strength'.[39] Again, East Asia is a case in point. Increased trade and peacefulness helped lift 1 billion people there out of poverty and has improved living standards significantly. To give but one example, at the time of independence, South Koreans were, on average, only half as well off as the average Nigerian. Not until 1962 did South Korea catch up with Nigeria. In the years that followed, peace (of sorts), industrialization, and trade propelled the average South Korean's income to thirteen times that of the average Nigerian. This transformation began in the absence of democracy; but it would not have been possible without peace.

The third type of costs relate to legitimacy and how what we think about war influences our capacity to translate battlefield successes into sustainable political successes. John Mueller famously argued that the frequency of war had declined primarily because our attitudes towards it have shifted. That is, because where we once believed that war was a legitimate and useful means by which to advance the national interest, we now see it as an increasingly illegitimate aberration.[40] But Mueller's approach surely exaggerates the extent to which war is abhorred: some wars remain very popular in some parts of the world. Even the unlawful and morally dubious US-led invasion of Iraq in 2003 carried the support of more than half of all surveyed Americans, at least for a time. Surveys revealed strong support at home for Russian military interventions in Ukraine (2014) and Syria (from 2015). Mueller also underestimates the role played by material forces in driving attitudes to war. It is perhaps not surprising that war would lose its appeal as it became costlier and less decisive. As Azar Gat argues, rather than ideas changing practice, might it not be that social and material changes have impacted upon our ideas?[41]

One way this may have happened is in the changing relationship between states and their citizens. One of the innovations of the modern nation-state, Michael Howard writes, was the granting of citizenship to individuals in return for their military service. This bargain between state and society was perfected by Napoleon, allowing him to field mass armies of committed soldier-citizens. But in the twentieth century, this model was gradually undermined by technological advances and military professionalization, which gave rise to the professional volunteer army as a realm distinct from civilian society. As a result, societies became less militarized and more peaceful, putting downwards pressure on the incidence of war. Writes Howard:

> The intense popular commitment that had made possible the wars of nations and the building of those nations themselves was predicated on an individual commitment, however notional, to dying for one's country, or at least identifying oneself with, and supporting, those called upon to do so. War was the great audit of national efficiency and morale...But by the end of the twentieth century death was no longer seen as being part of the social contract...War was now fought by highly trained specialists.[42]

The changing material nature of war caused social changes which, in turn, tilted the balance of ideas away from war and towards greater peacefulness.

We need not follow Mueller the whole way in order to recognize how changing ideas about appropriate behaviour have contributed to increasing the costs of (at least some types of) war and diminishing the payoffs. We can, instead, recognize that ideas sometimes change as a result of material transformation and still see political and reputational costs as one important part of the calculus tilting the balance sheet of war towards peace.

To understand how ideas shape costs, we need to look more deeply at how societies think about the legitimacy of war. Legitimacy is a much-debated concept, but I take it to mean a shared understanding within a group about the appropriateness of a particular state of affairs or action. The important elements of legitimacy to bear in mind are group consensus and the notion of appropriateness. To say something is legitimate or illegitimate is to comment not on one's own opinion but the prevailing views of a particular group. Because of this, things are rarely wholly legitimate or illegitimate because there is often disagreement within the relevant group. We think, then, in terms of degrees of legitimacy, yet legitimacy is no less powerful because of that, for what the group thinks affects how individuals within it behave. Legitimacy judgements are expressly normative—judgements about what is right and what is wrong. These judgements are informed by law but are not reducible to the simple applications of rules, because whether we think something is right or wrong is not determined by whether it is lawful or not. The Jewish uprising in the Warsaw ghetto in 1945 was, strictly speaking, unlawful, yet I would defy anyone to argue that it was illegitimate. Likewise, a child stealing a loaf of bread from a well-fed person to feed her starving family would in most societies be judged unlawful, but legitimate. This is because judgements about whether something is legitimate are a composite of three types of normative reasoning: legal, moral, and prudential. To ascertain whether something is legitimate, we ask whether it is legal. But the law may be unjust or its application in a particular scenario may produce outcomes we think are unjust, so we also ask whether it is moral, drawing upon whatever codes of ethics are relevant to the situation. But this too does not exhaust the calculation since some things that are lawful and moral may also be terribly counterproductive, politically destabilizing, or technically impossible. So, legitimacy refers to whether a group thinks some action or state of affairs is justified or not, taking into consideration its legal, moral, and prudential qualities.

Legitimacy matters because these judgements influence how we respond to external events. When we believe a decision to be legitimate, we are more likely to voluntarily comply with it, even if it impacts negatively upon us. More legitimate actions tend to receive more voluntary compliance and support; less legitimate actions tend to generate opposition. It is not difficult to see how this relates to the costs of war. If war itself becomes less legitimate, then it becomes more difficult for actors to legitimize specific wars. The less legitimacy a war enjoys, the harder it will be to prosecute since it will enjoy less support and engender more opposition within the population.

In each of the three domains of legitimacy—law, morality, and prudence—we can see a progressive tightening of what can be achieved by war and of how war may be waged. The law provides the most obvious constraints. From the earliest civilizations until 1945, states enjoyed a legal right to wage war whenever and wherever they saw fit. Though international lawyers argued about the conditions under which war might be 'justified', they accepted that states had an ultimate right to fight and that only God could sit in judgement on the decisions of sovereigns. Immanuel Kant famously derided the international lawyers (specifically Hugo Grotius, Samuel von Pufendorf, and Emmerich de Vattel) as 'sorry comforters', arguing that the legal arguments of such wise men had no practical bearing on state practice and that regarding any war as potentially 'just' resulted simply in 'confusion and harm', since it opened the door for every war to be so considered.[43] The League of Nations Covenant, agreed in Paris in 1919, tried to limit the exercise of this right to wage war—by requiring that states submit to a period of compulsory arbitration before resorting to war—but the right itself remained intact. In practice, states seldom—if ever—submitted themselves to the League's cumbersome procedures, often preferring to ignore them or simply leave the League. Had they followed the rules, they would surely have used the arbitration period merely as an opportunity to prepare their forces for battle. As it was, by the time general war returned in 1939, neither the US, nor the USSR, nor Germany, nor Italy, nor Japan were members of the League.

1945 changed all of this. The Charter of the new United Nations imposed a legal prohibition on the use—or threat—of war by states (Article 2(4)). It allowed just two exceptions. States retained their inherent right to self-defence in the event of an armed attack (Article 51) and the UN's Security Council was entitled to authorize war for the purpose of maintaining or restoring international peace and security (Article 39)—a system known as collective security. From 1945 onwards, any war waged not in self-defence or in pursuance of a mandate issued by the Security Council would be deemed illegal and treated accordingly. This prompted Christopher Greenwood to write, nearly two decades before he was appointed as a judge to the International Court of Justice, that it was now doubtful 'whether it is still meaningful to talk of war as a legal concept or institution at all'. From a legal perspective, 'the state of war has become an empty shell', he argued.[44] In some cases, as North Korea and Iraq found to their cost when they invaded South Korea and Kuwait respectively at either end of the Cold War, the international community would unite around the victims of aggression, bringing forth coalitions of force to repel the invaders. That such extreme measures were the exception, not the rule, does not diminish the fact that states considering armed aggression after 1945 had to at least contemplate the possibility of a grand coalition rallying against them.

But it was not just in the outlawing of war that the new UN system attacked its legitimacy. New laws made it much more difficult for the victors of war to legitimize their spoils—and especially their territorial gains. The outlawing of territorial conquest, prohibition of armed secession, the rule that boundaries cannot be changed by force (uti posseditis), and the principle of self-determination all made it much more difficult to translate successful war into legitimate political outcomes.[45] Let us consider each in turn.

Territorial conquest and colonization—once a right of states—was rendered illegal.[46] No longer could territories be added to a national homeland by force. Colonies could not be seized and bent to the will of the colonial centre. By 1945, almost the whole of the inhabited planet was divided into recognizable political entities, be they states, trusteeships, or colonies. For one to take over another was now forbidden. What this meant in practice was that attempts to conquer another territory would likely draw international censure, if not outright military opposition, and even if successful could not be translated into a new political fact. Russia's recent occupation of Crimea demonstrates the point nicely. Though dominant on the battlefield, prevailing without loss of life, and supported by a large majority of the population of Crimea, Russia has failed to translate its victory into a recognized legal fact. Crimea remains 'occupied territory', with Russia subjected to economic sanctions and Crimea's citizens unable to travel freely around the world. Turkey faced a similar problem following its invasion of northern Cyprus in 1974. Despite Ankara's best efforts to establish a state there, the UN Security Council has stuck by its decision to never recognize it. As a result, the territory lives in a legal limbo, dependent on its ties with Turkey for its economic wellbeing. Over time, its economy has fallen further and further behind that of the internationally recognized Cyprus situated in the mainly Greek south.

Armed secession was also judged to be unlawful. Most of the new costs of war described in this chapter relate to interstate rather than civil wars, where the dynamics are quite different. This may explain why the former but not the latter has declined so much. But one of the new rules that did impact on civil war was the prohibition of armed secession. During the nineteenth and early twentieth centuries, secession by force was one of the principal ways in which new states were born. Greece, Serbia, and Romania, for example, all owed their independence to wars waged against the Ottoman Empire (the latter by aligning with Russia in the Russo-Turkish war of 1877–8). Before that, the US won its independence from Britain thanks to a secessionist war. All of these states were recognized as sovereign shortly after their military successes. There is nothing to suggest, for example, that the international community would not have recognized the Confederacy had it emerged intact from the US civil war. In the early twentieth century, this right began to disappear as states recognized its potential to create great disorder. After 1945, the right disappeared entirely. Recognition and mutual agreement, not armed force, would be the engine of secession. Only if all the relevant parties agreed to secession would it be permitted. In practice, parties rarely do agree—the partition of Czechoslovakia into the Czech Republic and Slovakia remains a rare exception. According to one study, the success rate of armed secessionist movements—never good— declined from 12 per cent before 1945 to 2 per cent afterwards, the great majority of the 2 per cent tangled up in the process of decolonization.[47] This 2 per cent also includes the collapsed state of Yugoslavia, although international judges found that this state—a federal union of constituent republics—had 'dissolved'. A European arbitration panel set up to untangle the legal mess found that Slovenia, Croatia, Bosnia, Macedonia, and then Montenegro were successor states, not secessionist states.

If we look at some recent cases, we can see just how difficult it has become to translate secessionist war into actual secession. The world's newest state, South Sudan, waged a decades-long war for independence from Khartoum. For most of that time, South Sudanese not government forces controlled most of what is now South Sudan—at least the territory outside the major towns and cities. Yet secession only happened once the Sudanese government agreed to it, in a comprehensive peace agreement. The same was true for Eritrea. It took thirty years of war (1961–91) to persuade Ethiopia to accept Eritrean secession, and only then was Eritrea granted international recognition of its sovereignty. Meanwhile, there are many examples of secessionist movements that did not succeed because their opponents chose not to relent. Most obviously, in the Middle East, the Kurds of Iraq, Syria, Iran, and Turkey are no closer to achieving statehood despite decades of armed conflict and, in some parts of the region, significant periods of autonomous rule. The Igbo of Nigeria, Matebele of Zimbabwe, Chechens of Russia, Karen and Shan of Myanmar, Ossetians of Georgia, and Serbs of Bosnia are among the dozens of other groups that have launched unsuccessful armed insurrections to secede from their state.

The principle of the inviolability of borders, known by its Latin name *uti posseditis*, was also underscored after 1945. This principle holds that new international boundaries must follow the lines of existing administrative borders. It arose out of a prudential calculation stemming from decolonization, as the major powers recognized that allowing borders to be redrawn would be a recipe for war and chaos. As such, they decided that whilst the status attached to borders might change (i.e. internal boundaries becoming national ones), the position of the border itself could not—unless the affected parties all agreed. Thus, it was agreed that either whole colonies—such as Libya—should be granted statehood or colonies should be divided along pre-existing boundaries—as with India and Pakistan. For our purposes, what matters is that new and arbitrary boundaries, perhaps based on ethnic distribution, were prohibited. New boundaries imposed by force would not be recognized by the international community. This created a powerful disincentive for war. States or other armed actors could not, therefore, simply translate success on the battlefield into new political facts as they once had. Nor could they (in principle at least) use genocide or mass ethnic cleansing to change the ethnic or religious makeup of a population and then draw new boundaries around them (though this did sometimes happen in practice). The norm promoted peace by providing a simple way of delimiting border disputes in a manner consistent with the law against conquest, by reducing uncertainty about where boundaries might be drawn, and—in cases where borders were changed by consent—giving negotiations a shared reference point at the beginning.[48] *Uti posseditis* also had profound effects on the way peace was negotiated after war. Most obviously, where peace treaties had once often involved the exchange of land and populations, after 1945 they did so only very rarely.

The principle of self-determination is concerned with the relationship between the state and the people it governs. Article 1 of the UN Charter identifies respect for the 'equal rights and self-determination of peoples' as one of the purposes and principles of the organization. Simply put, self-determination relates to the right of a people to determine its own government. It is, in this respect, the logical corollary of the idea, espoused by Thomas Hobbes and John Locke, that the state arose out of the voluntary agreement of individuals. If the state was brought into being by the people to serve the people, it stands to reason that its form and character be determined by the people. Much hinges, though, on how we ascertain 'the people' that enjoy a right to self-determine. As conceived by nineteenth-century nationalists in Europe and US President Woodrow Wilson after the First World War, self-determination referred to the rights of nations to govern themselves free of imperial oversight. But as Wilson discovered when he arrived in Europe intending to build a world peace based upon self-determination, the principle was not only impractical, it was dangerous. European populations were so intermixed as to make delineation on national grounds impossible without heavy doses of ethnic cleansing. 'Why should I be a minority in your country, when you can be a minority in mine?', Europe's peoples asked one another. The problem was no less pressing in the non-European world where decolonization frequently gave rise to violence between groups vying for control of the state. In response, self-determination gradually evolved to become less about the rights of nations to their own states and more about the rights of individuals and groups to find cultural recognition and respect within their existing state. We may not always agree on precisely what self-determination looks like, but we do agree on what it does *not* look like. It does not look like conquest, or armed aggression, or colonialism. Self-determination means that a state can govern a territory only with the consent of a large part of its population— though we still disagree about how that consent should be ascertained.

Taken together, these new rules inhibited war by making it more difficult to justify and more difficult to translate military victories into legitimate and sustainable political victories. Naturally, there are many examples of states breaking the rules and seeking to create new facts on the ground. There are even examples of them succeeding. In 1961, Indian forces rolled into the Portuguese enclave of Goa and integrated the area into the Indian state. Indonesia had less luck with East Timor. It too sought to correct an imperial anomaly by annexing a former Portuguese colony but unlike the Goans, who largely welcomed Indian rule, the East Timorese were bitterly opposed to rule by Jakarta. Only a handful of states recognized the annexation and a bitter war of insurgency and counter-insurgency erupted which cost, by some accounts, the lives of a quarter of the territory's population and imposed heavy financial and political costs on Jakarta. Eventually, Indonesia was forced to succumb and East Timor achieved its independence in 2002.

East Timor's dogged resistance to Indonesian occupation points to another way in which the costs of war have increased and the payoffs declined in war, a cost associated with the rise of nationalism and self-determination. Victory on the battlefield translates into political victory only if the defeated side accepts the results of battle. If national groups refuse to accept defeat, as they have been increasingly reluctant to do in the age of nationalism, then the defeat of an army may result not in peace but in the emergence of insurgency, irregular armed opposition. Whatever the legitimacy of their cause, foreign invaders break the link between territory, people, and government and create a powerful incentive for 'the people' to take up arms against them.[49] Napoleon found this to his cost in Spain—that nationalism breeds a deep sense of shared identity that pushes communities to resist invaders with all their might. During the peninsular war, the Spanish devised the perfect means of resisting a more powerful enemy—the *guerrilla*—literally 'little war'. Guerrilla war involved the use of hit and run tactics, the avoidance of battle, and the use of civilian populations as cover. Though incapable of defeating the enemy outright, guerrilla tactics significantly increase the costs of occupation and reduce the payoffs, often wearing the more powerful side down. Because guerrillas avoid battle, the stronger side is unable to deal their enemy a decisive blow. Unable to distinguish the guerrillas from the civilian population, they sometimes turn to retribution against civilians. This, of course, is almost always counterproductive since these patently unjust tactics only increase local support for the guerrillas. Meanwhile, Western governments confronted by insurgencies in Afghanistan and Iraq failed to note one of Clausewitz's principal lessons: that as aims become more ambitious, so war becomes more intense.[50]

Guerrilla tactics were used by French civilians (*francs-tireurs*) after the defeat of the French army in the Franco-Prussian war and employed, with differing degrees of success, by partisans across occupied Europe during the Second World War. Insurgency tactics were then employed to good effect in numerous anti-colonial struggles and notably by the Viet Cong against the US and by the Afghan *mujahedeen* against the Soviet Union. In these cases, insurgents effectively defeated the ambitions of each of the world's superpowers. More recently, the Taliban's insurgency in Afghanistan prevented the US from translating its military success there in 2002 into a political success.[51] The post-2003 insurgencies in Iraq helped produce an outcome antithetical to the dreams of the American neo-conservatives who launched that war. In these and other cases, communities doggedly resisted foreign occupation and imposed significant costs on major powers. Armed with the tactics of guerrilla warfare, the conquered can make occupation and conquest prohibitively expensive. This is a lesson that almost every great power has had to learn at some point over the past two centuries.

Between them, these four rules—non-aggression, no armed secession, *uti posseditis*, and self-determination—imposed new restrictions on the circumstances in which force could be legitimately employed. When states or non-state armed groups violate them, their actions are likely to be judged illegitimate. Armed aggression might be reversed by a grand coalition of armies or made prohibitively expensive by economic sanctions; armed secessionists may struggle for international support and recognition; and those looking to change borders or colonize populated areas will find it almost impossible to translate battlefield victories into new and sustainable, lawful, and legitimate political facts. Each of these rules makes war more difficult to wage by either increasing its costs or decreasing its political utility.

International rules have also made it more difficult to wage war legitimately. Beginning in the nineteenth century but accelerating after the Second World War, new humanitarian laws—backed by the possibility of international criminal prosecution—were introduced to regulate the conduct of war and protect civilians and other non-combatants from its ravages. The repeated violation of these rules has, in recent times, prompted a surge of support for the view that unless war can be fought precisely, lawfully, and justly, it should not be fought at all. This 'contingent pacifism', Larry May tells us, concedes the possibility of justified war, 'but not at the current time or into the foreseeable future due to the contemporary nature of armed conflict and geopolitics'.[52]

The political leaders responsible for crafting the world order which emerged from the ashes of the Second World War were cognizant of what, 150 years earlier, Immanuel Kant had described as the problem of the 'sorry comforters': that international law would be 'law' in the proper sense of the word only if provisions was made to enforce it. It was for that reason that the Great Powers created the UN Security Council, a body granted sweeping and unprecedented global authority to maintain international peace and security.

Article 24 of the UN Charter confers upon the Security Council 'primary responsibility to international peace and security'. It awards the Council almost unlimited discretion to define its own business and repertoire of measures. Indeed, the Council is not obligated even to follow international law in the pursuit of its mandate. Instead, the Council determines the legality of its own actions. Article 24(2) requires only that the Council discharge its duties in accordance with the purposes and principles of the UN, identified in Article 1 of the Charter, and that it utilize the powers set out in Chapters VI (peace measures), VII (enforcement measures), VIII (regional arrangements), and XII (trusteeships) of the Charter. As David Bosco argues, 'the Council's terms of reference were designed to provide all the authority it would need to preserve peace around the world'.[53] It is, former UN Assistant Secretary-General Edward Luck agrees, 'a Council for all contingencies'.[54]

This freedom of action has given rise to an inevitably selective and uneven approach to the world's security problems, but it has also ensured the continuing cooperation of the Great Powers (US, Russia, and China). When the Council is at its best, it is this latitude that explains its capacity for innovation. But it can also contribute to gross inaction in the face of emergencies and inconsistency when the Great Powers are unable to find common ground.

World peace is the Security Council's business. Article 39 states that the Council 'shall determine the existence of any threat to the peace, breach of the peace, or act of aggression' and shall decide what 'recommendations to make' or measures to adopt to maintain or restore international peace and security. There are three important points worth stressing here. First, it is for the Council itself to determine when a threat or breach of the peace exists. This is a political, not a legal, decision and is not subject to judicial review. Second, Article 39 awards the Council an explicitly preventive function by referring to *threats* to international peace and security and requiring action to *maintain* the peace: the Council need not wait for threats to materialize (i.e. for the peace to be broken) before it acts. Third, Article 39 awards the Council a discretionary *right* to adopt measures to maintain international peace and insecurity but does not impose any *obligation* upon it to do so.

Although the Security Council enjoys far-reaching authority to maintain world peace, it also confronts significant practical and political limitations. Most importantly, the work of the Council and the effectiveness of its resolutions depend to a great extent on its capacity to persuade states to implement its resolutions. Since it cannot compel, much less expect, obedience from states, the Security Council must persuade them to implement its decisions. The Council has few material resources at its direct disposal and therefore relies almost entirely on the goodwill of member states to provide the (sometimes extensive) resources required to implement its decisions. It must therefore rely on its ability to persuade states to commit the resources, capabilities, and political capital necessary to implement its decisions. For this reason, the implementation of Council decisions has been patchy at best.

It is also important to underscore that the Council is a *political* (not judicial) body composed of sovereignty-wielding states whose ideologies, interests, allegiances, and preferences influence the positions they adopt on particular issues and which change over time. When the Great Powers are united, the Security Council can be an immense force for world peace, as it was in response to Iraq's invasion of Kuwait, for example. But when they are not, the Council is no more able than anyone else to make or impose peace. Its recent experience in Syria is a chilling case in point. The broader point here, though, is that the world today is relatively well endowed with the laws and institutions needed to make aggressive war a prohibitively costly business for those that undertake it.

One of the reasons war persists is the widely held assumption that it can produce decisive political outcomes at a reasonable cost. The utility of force, General Rupert Smith reminds us, is measured by its ability to achieve political goals.[55] The idea of the 'decisive battle' is deeply ingrained in the way we think about war's purpose and the way in which strategists and generals think about fighting them.[56] Yet the central ideal of war, the decisive battle, was always something of a myth. Hannibal defeated Roman army after Roman army, yet still could not land a decisive blow until, at the end, he succumbed. Napoleon, the great general who scored so many decisive victories and from whom strategists and historians have learnt so much, was ultimately a political disaster for his country, which he left broken and thoroughly defeated. If that was true of the past, the increasing costs associated with war mean that nowadays, wars rarely deliver decisive political victories, even for the powerful. The US failed to translate its military might into lasting political gains in Indochina, Afghanistan, or Iraq; the Soviet Union similarly failed in Afghanistan; China failed to impose its will on Vietnam by war; Saudi Arabia struggled to defeat Houthi rebels in Yemen. War, it would seem, is becoming less decisive.

War is also becoming more expensive as the direct costs, opportunity costs, and political/reputational costs soar. Few emerge from war—be it international or civil—in a stronger position than they were in beforehand. As Pierre Hassner—a Holocaust survivor, refugee, and one of France's leading experts on war and politics—observed after the end of the Cold War, war 'has already lost its justification' and 'its meaning'.[57] If these trends continue, war is likely to appeal less and less as an efficient and effective means of acquiring riches or resolving disputes. Piling on additional costs in the future will help make war 'less central to political life' and tip the ledger still further in the direction of peace.

CHAPTER 7

LEASHING THE PASSIONS
OF WAR

Farewell all, farewell!
When we fall for you and for our future,
Let these words re-echo as our last salute:
Farewell all, farewell!

—Heinrich Lersch (1914)

When we brothers
went to war,
from our eyelids
hung bitter tears

—Ber Horowitz (1914)

If Clausewitz had been right about war being the (rational) 'continuation of policy by other means', it would have been eliminated by now.[1] But on this point at least, Clausewitz was wrong. War, as John Keegan reminds us, is shaped by culture and emotion. It is driven by human passions, not cold calculation alone. War is a collective enterprise and as such requires a good deal of consent. That is, it requires that a sufficient number of people believe it to be legitimate. After all, war demands that large numbers of people put themselves in harm's way—something few of us would do without good reason. Sometimes, of course, soldiers are compelled to fight. But war has always found willing volunteers, too. In the eighteen months after August 1914, nearly two and a half million British men volunteered to fight in Kitchener's new army—the largest volunteer force ever amassed. Beliefs about the virtue and necessity of war are shaped more by human emotions than cold rationality. Human emotions enable the individual aggressive impulses and sense of group cohesion that give rise to violence. But they can also inhibit these impulses. In fact, emotions play an obvious and omnipresent role in political and social life, including in decision-making about whether, and how, to wage war and in the individual choices made by soldiers. World peace cannot, therefore, be built on institutional arrangements or economics alone. It must also live within the hearts and minds of people, in the values of our communities, and in the ways we manage relations with one another. Leashing the passions of war is a task far more difficult than that of leashing the institutions and economics of war. It is at once larger and more complex, a task for which we are yet to find good answers.

When Argentina invaded the Falkland Islands on 2 April 1982, British Prime Minister Margaret Thatcher's advisers and her Defence Minister, John Nott, told her that the situation was hopeless and that the best Britain could hope to do was negotiate an honourable transfer of authority. Britain, they reasoned, was no longer a great power capable of projecting force across the globe. It no longer had interests in the South Atlantic. Losing ownership of the Falklands would make no material difference to national security or wealth. It would actually make a modest positive contribution to the government's budget-cutting agenda. Any attempt to retake the islands by force would be difficult, risky, and expensive. There was no rational reason why Britain should not just give up the islands. Indeed, that was precisely why Britain had withdrawn HMS *Endurance* from the Falklands in 1981 and opened negotiations with Argentina on the transfer of sovereignty, talks derailed by the vehement opposition of Falkland Islanders themselves.

Whitehall's torpor was shattered by Sir Henry Leach, the First Sea Lord and Commander of the Royal Navy. Alarmed, Leach burst into the Prime Minister's residence at 10 Downing Street. 'The Navy could do it', he exclaimed to Thatcher. It would be a high-stakes venture but liberating the Falklands was possible. The Royal Navy could quickly assemble a powerful task force, deploy to the South Atlantic, and retake the Falklands. There was a moral imperative to act, Leach argued. National honour was at stake. 'Because if we do not, if we muck around, if we pussyfoot, if we don't move very fast and are not entirely successful, in a very few months' time we shall be living in a very different country whose word will count for little'.[2] This was exactly what Thatcher wanted to hear. The task force was dispatched and the Falklands retaken at the cost of 255 British and 649 Argentine lives. British honour apparently restored, and national pride reinvigorated, Mrs Thatcher—who before the crisis had been languishing behind the opposition in the opinion polls—went on to a crushing victory in the 1983 general election.

It is not only the big decisions made by political leaders about whether to fight that are shaped by emotions. Social psychology tells us that emotions drive all human behaviour; that emotional impulses can push people to place their own material interests in jeopardy. I have already mentioned Kitchener's army. When war was declared in 1914, Britain was woefully underprepared, its army of 250,000 dwarfed by Germany's 4 million troops. Lord Kitchener, the newly appointed Secretary for War, moved quickly to build a new mass army of volunteers. The call went out: 'your country needs you'. Two and a half million answered the call. Some were undoubtedly deluded about what volunteering actually meant, about the very real risks involved. Few at this stage understood the gravity of the situation or the true nature of industrial war. Yet when news reached home of the fall of Mons in August 1914 and of the terrible toll of death and injury inflicted on the British army there, the number of volunteers surged.

My home city of Sheffield quickly raised a battalion of university and professional men; the industrial heart of Britain's war machine, Sheffield's workers were needed in its factories. In short order, 1,100 professionals and students volunteered for service in August 1914. The fall of Antwerp in October 1914 propelled a new surge of volunteers. On some days, as many as 10,000 people around the country volunteered for service. By Christmas 1914, 1 million soldiers lay dead on the battlefield—the war of manoeuvre inflicting a toll just as terrible as the war of the trenches—yet still people volunteered to fight. They volunteered because they believed the war to be just, because they believed it was their duty to fight, because their friends signed up, and because society expected them to. 'It will be hell to be in it, and hell to be out of it', wrote the poet Robert Brooke. Few of them signed up because they thought it would help their social or professional advancement, for monetary compensation, or for any other rational expectation of reward. The soldiers of the Sheffield City Battalion were volunteers doing what they thought was the right thing to do. They went over the top on the first day of the Somme, 1 July 1916. Nearly half of them were lost that day.[3]

The average British soldier serving on the Western Front in the First World War had a more than one in two chance of becoming a casualty of war, whether killed or injured. The odds were even worse for the French. Yet they kept volunteering and, with the notable exception of the French mutiny of 1917, scarcely objected to the travails imposed upon them.[4] To understand why, we need to understand how emotions can push people into war—and how emotions can be created, shaped, and manipulated to achieve that effect. I will also show how some of these forces are more fragile than we might think and how emotions might be harnessed to reject war and build peace.

For leaders, soldiers, and civilians alike, decisions about war and peace are driven as much, if not more, by passions as by cold rationality. Yet the place of emotions in sustaining peace or waging war has been overlooked until relatively recently. Sentiments bind us together, but also drive us apart. They can foster transnational solidarity, support for universal human rights, activism for international peace, and dedication to humanitarian action. But they can also give rise to fear, hatred, aggression, and vengeance. To make matters more complex still, emotions are double-edged swords. They can impact upon us differently in different situations. None are necessarily 'good' or 'peaceful'; none wholly 'negative' or 'belligerent'.

Take the feeling of love, for example. Love is typically juxtaposed to hate, the former associated with peace and harmony, the latter with war and violence. Yet love is an extremely powerful sentimental attachment to particular others that overrides self-interest. We are often prepared to sacrifice our own interests to protect those we love. In practice, love can be associated with positive emotions such as joy and pride when times are good, and negative emotions like fear and anger when loved ones are imperilled. Love, then, can just as easily give rise to belligerence as to joyfulness. Sometimes, love even *demands* aggression. Love inspires parents to react aggressively to protect their children. Humans are not wholly self-regarding precisely because love sometimes impels us to act contrary to our own immediate interests. It can also impel us towards violence and aggression, because love is necessarily selective. We love some more than others. 'Identification can make sacrifice for loved ones a rational choice and likewise can make the killing of those who in some way threaten the well-being of our group equally rational'.[5] In this sense, 'our hatreds are the reflection of our loves'.[6]

People that volunteer for military service are driven mainly not by the joy of killing or dreams of loot but by a sense of moral purpose and responsibility. Writes Roland Stromberg of those that volunteered to fight in the trenches of the First World War: 'Doubtless they found hell, but they did not go seeking it; rather than an itch to kill, hurt, or torture their fellow men, as Freud claimed, they felt something much more akin to love'.[7]

Empathy, another staple of the international peace movement, is equally Janus-faced. It refers to our capacity to understand what another person is feeling, to feel what it is like to walk in their shoes. Empathy is considered so important to peace that there is a 'Centre for Empathy in International Affairs', led by a former UN negotiator, that works with the US Institute of Peace. In some quarters, empathy is judged fundamental to the success of peace processes and even 'as the key to world peace'. Yet, like love, empathy can sometimes be selective. We tend to feel it most strongly for those who are most like us. Feeling the pain of those who are most like us breeds feelings of enmity towards those we hold responsible for that pain. As such, empathy can just as easily give rise to racism, xenophobia, and hatred as it can to solidarity, since it fosters a politics that pays more heed to the near stranger than to the distant stranger. That is why Paul Bloom recently argued that we need less empathy in public life and more rationality and compassion.[8]

The ties that bind us to communities are also ties that keep communities apart from one another. These ties are partly institutional, as I showed in Chapter 5, but they are also emotional, underpinned by feelings such as love and empathy. These ties can be thought of as concentric circles of commitment, with those closest to us on the inside, moving out to wider family, local communities, regions, nations, and beyond. Whether consciously or not, humans tend to value the lives and interests of those in the inner circles more highly than those in the outer. Part of this is to do with our hard-wiring. We are genetically programmed to recognize difference and privilege sameness. Recognizing kin, after all, was crucial to the development of early groups, the possibility of cooperation, and through those things, human survival and flourishing. But as societies grew and evolved, the power of that genetic programming declined, only to be replaced by some far more powerful social engineering—engineering that allowed us to see sameness and difference across vast communities. We personally know only a tiny fraction of our fellow citizens, yet we identify with them nonetheless. People typically feel more pain, fear, and anger when their co-nationals are killed by terrorists than they do when even a far greater number of foreigners are killed in the same way. As François Poulain de la Barre, a Cartesian and early feminist philosopher, explained in the seventeenth century, '[e]veryone believes that his country is the best because he is used to it; and that the religion in which he is reared is the true one that must be followed, even though he has perhaps never paused to examine it or to compare it with others. One always feels more amity for one's countrymen than for strangers'.[9]

These predispositions are reinforced—sometimes consciously so—by the way we organize ourselves (into states) and the (national) stories we tell. Points of difference are constructed and reinforced by social practice, language, education, and other aspects of national life that create powerful connections between individuals and groups within societies but also equally powerful distinctions between insiders and outsiders. As nineteenth-century German philosopher J.G. Fichte—one of the earliest theorizers of nationalism—explained, through the nation 'each single person becomes part of an organized whole and melts into one with it'.[10] Nations help individuals find their place in the cosmos and associate their individual actions with the meanings and purposes of the nation as a whole. This is such powerful stuff because the urge to social conformity and acceptance is one of our principal sources of motivation. Nations establish a 'common life' that binds them together in the daily lives of their members but that also marks them out from one another. Volunteers in national armies experience this common life to the full, bound together by shared commitment and common destiny. At once, these commonalities create the bonds of love and trust that encourage political leaders to value such intangibles as 'national honour' and encourage their followers to sacrifice their own self-interest for those of an essentially abstract community—the nation.

War reinforces, and is reinforced by, these collective identities and commitments. By these forces, 'whole societies', Barbara Ehrenreich reminds us, 'may be swept up into a kind of "altered state" marked by emotional intensity and a fixation on totems representative of the collectivity'. War sometimes inspires 'a veritable frenzy of enthusiasm among noncombatants and potential recruits alike, and it was not enthusiasm for killing or loot or "imperialist expansion" but for something more uplifting and worthy'—the protection of the nation, its people and values.[11]

In the modern world, nationalism (and patriotism), national identity, and other powerful collective ideologies help distinguish us from them, friend from foe. These ideas help differentiate and vilify the enemy. They valorize killing and dying in war. They help create and justify the social pressure that pushes ordinary people to commit brutal acts of violence against an enemy army or people or to cheer on others that do so. George Orwell opens *The Lion and the Unicorn* with a powerful reflection on how national loyalty and patriotism construct deadly enmity between individuals with no personal axe to grind:

As I write, highly civilized human beings are flying overhead, trying to kill me. They do not feel any enmity against me as an individual, nor I against them. They are 'only doing their duty', as the saying goes. Most of them, I have no doubt, are kind-hearted law-abiding men who would never dream of committing murder in private life. On the other hand, if one of them succeeds in blowing me to pieces with a well-placed bomb, he will never sleep any the worse for it. He is serving his country, which has the power to absolve him from evil.[12]

It is not just that we have different identities—or markers of difference—it is that one *particular* marker rises to prominence over all others. We all belong to different groups and therefore have multiple identities. The pilot trying to bomb George Orwell may have been a writer before the war, or a civil servant; he may have been a member of the working class conscripted into a war he had played no part in starting; he may have shared Orwell's appreciation for fine cigars. But in that moment, the only identity that mattered was the identity of Orwell and the pilot as opposing soldiers at war with one another. Patriotism, Orwell points out, is adept at narrowing the diversity of identity.

Nationalism is similarly potent. Fascism and communism did the same on racial and class grounds respectively. This, remember, is the essence of war: violent conflict between *groups*. Only coherent, organized groups that can exert social or coercive power sufficient to persuade enough people to sacrifice their own immediate interest in survival for the supposed collective good of the group are capable of waging war. The conflation of our multiple identities gives rise to bellicosity by eroding the ties that unite us and amplifying one particular thing that divides us. Of course, identities are not wholly malleable. They are in large part ascribed to us by others. But there is an element of choice. We can choose, for example, to amplify the significance of our belonging to different groups.[13]

Time and again, peace activists and theorists have underestimated the capacity of nationalism to reorder people's priorities. Norman Angell, whose *Great Illusion* won him the Nobel Peace Prize in 1933, argued that the principal divisions in humanity lay between democracy and autocracy, individualism and socialism, the oppressors and the oppressed, and not between nations. The lines of division ran within nations, not between them, Angell believed. Yet liberalism, working-class solidarity, civil service rationality, and the peace movement itself proved far too weak to withstand, or provide a plausible alternative to, the surge of nationalism in 1914.[14] To those on all sides who volunteered for war in 1914, nationalism instilled a culture of voluntary self-sacrifice that would be rationally inexplicable without it; and amongst the wider population it encouraged the setting aside of normal politics for the sake of national unity.

The threat of war can turn nationalism into hyper-nationalism, ideological sympathizers into zealots, and the peace-loving into trigger-happy soldiers. War ties individuals to communities and gives them a sense of higher purpose. This idea of war as a communal experience, writes George Mosse, is perhaps the most seductive part of what he describes as the 'myth of war' for it allows the common person to transcend ordinariness and fulfil a higher purpose. The soldier transcends death itself in the loyal service of a timeless nation.[15] It creates a sense of meaning and purpose not experienced in peacetime. As one Italian writer noted when his country entered the war, 'confused by so many books, I have found again the freshness of a new humanity, courageous, pure souls'.[16]

When the First World War erupted, some British feminists, including Emmeline and Christabel Pankhurst, set aside their long campaign for women's suffrage, embraced nationalism, and committed themselves to supporting the war effort. 'If you go to this war and give your life', Christabel Pankhurst told a crowd in Plymouth, 'you could not end your life in a better way—for to give one's life for one's country, for a great cause, is a splendid thing'.[17] 'Pacifists [are] a disease' born of 'over-prosperity' and 'false security', she wrote in the periodical Britannia two years later.[18] Across Europe, even some committed pacifists like the Viennese novelist, Stefan Zweig, were overcome by the collective emotions of war. He described the temptation to join that 'awakening of the masses' which seemed to him to be 'grandiose' and 'ravishing'. 'All differences of class, rank and language were swamped', he argued, 'by the rushing feeling of fraternity'. The individual, he wrote, experienced the 'exaltation' of being no longer isolated but part of a bigger whole. He felt as if his life had taken on new meaning. 'In spite of all my hatred and aversion to war, I should not like to have missed the memory of those first days', wrote Zweig.[19] Austrian writer, Robert Musil, also observed how 'beautiful and fraternal' the war had turned out to be. Meanwhile, figures as unlikely as Gandhi and Sigmund Freud rallied behind the war efforts of their respective countries.[20]

Modern war helped forge the national identities that then drove war forward. 'Could a nation...be born without a war?' asked historian Michael Howard.[21] No, answers German philosopher and nationalist G.W.F. Hegel. Nations, Hegel insisted, are living organisms held together by the emotional attachments of their members. Nothing made a nation bind together more strongly than the sacrifice of its citizens in war. Nothing weakened it more than peace. 'In time of peace', wrote Hegel, 'civil life expands more and more, all the different spheres settle down, and in the long run men sink into corruption, their particularities become more and more fixed and ossified. But health depends upon the unity of the body and if the parts harden, death occurs'.[22]

National identities bind communities together but they also mark them out from one another. Communities have different ways of life, moral values, and interests. They have things to fight over. The differences between them are only sharpened when fights erupt. In war, political struggles within societies tend to pale into insignificance when set against the differences between enemies.[23] But here again, emotions defy easy categorizations. Identities, even national identities, are fluid—both their meaning and content being subject to change. Ultimately, all nations will be forgotten; all cultural practices changed.[24] What is more, individuals can, and often do, have multiple overlapping identities and may be forced to choose between them.[25] Thankfully, the human mind is quite pliable. Identities can be learned and re-learned. Once established, identities need not be unchanging. With political will, differences can be managed or even overcome. This creates the hope of peace. But differences can be exacerbated and exploited. And this creates an enduring fear of war.

It is not the simple fact of the similarities or differences that drive war or peace, though, but the meanings assigned to them. As I mentioned in Chapter 5, one powerful strain of thought suggests that civil wars are so brutal precisely *because* the combatants are so familiar with one another. In *Civilization, Society and Religion*, Sigmund Freud argued that communities with adjoining territory, similar characteristics, and close relationships engage in constant feuding with one another because of their hypersensitivity to minor points of difference. This need to exaggerate differences might stem from the need to preserve a sense of self-identity and separateness. Proximity can also breed envy and fear as much as harmony. The 'narcissism of minor difference' helps establish points of differentiation where there may be very few. It explains why seemingly minor differences can give rise to war. It also points to why some civil wars are so much more savage than international war. The US civil war, for example, killed more Americans than the First World War, Second World War, Korean War, and Vietnam War combined. More Russians died in the Russian civil war than in the First World War that helped cause it. At least 4 million Chinese were killed in that country's civil war, which ended in 1949. A similar number died in the Democratic Republic of Congo's civil war which began in 1998.

Civil wars also tend to be more consequential for the daily lives of ordinary citizens. Not only are our neighbours more likely to kill our loved ones than distant strangers are, but they are also more likely to impose their ways of life upon us. It might be easier to fear distant strangers, but we are more likely to be threatened by those closer to home. That fact can be exploited by making small differences and disputes appear anything but, thanks to the narcissism of minor difference. The emotions that pull neighbours apart are especially difficult for peace activists to address.

These points notwithstanding, the argument that proximity breeds contempt (and war) has been exaggerated. It overlooks evidence suggesting that greater difference between combatants inhibits constraints in war. If we factor in the violent depredations and genocides committed against distant 'others' in the name of imperialism and colonialism over the past 200 years, we find a toll of death and destruction much greater than that resulting from civil war. We see the distinction even when we compare US bombing strategies in the European and Asian theatres during the Second World War. In the European theatre, the US exhibited a keen interest in limiting civilian casualties and was opposed in principle (if not always in practice) to targeting cities. It exhibited no such inhibitions when it came to Japan.

Emotional attachments do not just exist in nature. They are actively fostered. War is valorized and normalized in a way that peace is not. 'Battles give crowns and take them away…[they] render the conqueror immortal', wrote the Habsburg General Montecuccoli in 1703.[26] It is not a coincidence that across the world, more than fifty countries have erected shrines to the 'Unknown Soldier' that command extraordinary reverence. That soldier is a timeless and nameless—and very democratic—symbol of the individual's sacrifice to the nation.[27] These attachments are further sustained by a permanent readiness for war. Writing in 1910, William James observed that 'battles are only a public verification of the mastery gained during the peace interval…[The] preparation for war by nations is the real war, permanent, unceasing'.[28]

A sense of social responsibility and longing to contribute to a higher purpose may be what drives many to volunteer for war service but other, less noble, passions are sometimes also displayed. The American strategic thinker, Martin Van Creveld, thinks that war has often been considered 'a highly attractive activity for which no other can provide an adequate substitute' since it provides unparalleled opportunities for men to test 'his ultimate worth' against mighty opponents. 'However unpalatable the fact', argues Van Creveld, 'the real reason why we have wars is that men like fighting them'.[29] War diaries tell not only of the horrors of war, but also of its delights. Arguably the most famous German diarist of the First World War, Ernst Junger, recalled that having '[g]rown up in an age of security we shared a yearning for danger, for the experience of the extraordinary. We were enraptured by war'. Junger found battle to be like an 'opiate whose immediate effect is to stimulate the nerves though the subsequent is to deaden them'. He went on to describe fleeing British troops whom he and his comrades gunned down in March 1918 as 'hunted game'. For his comrades, too, 'it is quite jolly. Many of us take quite a sporting interest in the job'.[30] Soldiers on all sides expressed similar views. F.R. Darrow found bayoneting Prussians to be 'beautiful work'. A New Zealander described his 'sickening yet exhilarating work' as 'joy unspeakable'. Henry de Man describes the time he scored a direct hit on the enemy's trench as among 'the happiest moments of my life'.[31] Evidently, for some of those that experienced it, killing was not just fun, it reinforced their sense of masculinity. After volunteering to join the German army, Otto Braun wrote in his diary that 'I believe that this war is a challenge for our time and for each individual, a test by fire, that we may ripen into manhood, become men able to cope with the coming stupendous years and events'.[32]

These views need not make us despair. These hyper-masculinized superhero-style accounts of war are usually precisely that—attempts by soldiers, usually written after the events themselves, to find meaning in their sacrifices and justification for their actions. They are often not accurate accounts of what actually happened or representations of how the main characters were feeling at the time. Often, these individual accounts are inconsistent with what we know from history about particular battles. As a picture of the overall attitudes of combatants, these tales of heroism and derring-do are also inconsistent with the basic fact that most soldiers in the First and Second World Wars (and the US civil war and Vietnam wars too) never fired their weapons in anger.[33] Artillery, machine guns, and, by the Second World War, aerial bombing—death and destruction dealt from a distance, often a great distance—were the principal causes of death in their wars, not the type of close-quarter rifle and bayoneting duels often described.

It may be that the joy of killing speaks to an individual's psychological state (psychopaths, for instance, might be expected to enjoy war), but these sentiments also tell us something more broadly about how war intoxicates. 'The chance to exist for an intense and overpowering moment, even if it meant certain oblivion, seemed worth it in the midst of war', writes Chris Hedges, a war correspondent for the *New York Times* who has covered conflicts in Sudan, Libya, Central America, and the Balkans. Yet that sentiment, so powerful in the midst of war, felt 'very stupid' once the war ended. Taking a step back from the daily horrors and excitements of war, Hedges found that whilst war exposed the latent potential for evil and aggression that lies in each of us, exposure was not a wholly natural or biological phenomenon. Wars, he argued, and the sentiments they stir up, are 'manufactured', socially produced. They are 'born out of the collapse of civil societies, perpetuated by fear, greed and paranoia, and they are run by gangsters, who rise up from the bottom of their own societies and terrorize all, including those they are purporting to protect'. Nationalism is among its driving forces. It can push people to the absurd. In Argentina, for example, nationalist rhetoric and war for the Falklands galvanized public support for a military dictatorship responsible for the deaths of thousands, if not tens of thousands of Argentines. British rule of the Falklands, by contrast, had resulted in the deaths of no Argentines. War's logic today, argues Hedges, is the same as that identified by Scottish Enlightenment thinker, David Hume, in 1740. War makes saints of us and demons of our enemies; our violence is just and necessary, theirs evil and barbarous.[34] We will return to Hume later.

Valorization involves a confidence trick: the sanitization and trivialization of war. Those of us who have never experienced war first-hand have no comprehension of what it is like or of what its effects look, feel, and smell like. War comes easily to people precisely because they have little sense of its horrors.[35] 'War is sweet to those who have no experience of it', the Greek poet Pindar pointed out around the fifth century BCE. Indeed, states and societies *make* war appear sweeter. Yet its reality is 'messy, confusing, sullied by brutality, and an elephantine fear'.[36] Far from smelling sweet, war, recalled George Orwell of his time in the anarchist militia during the Spanish civil war, has a 'characteristic smell' of 'excrement and rotting food'.[37] What we who have never served are presented with, George Mosse writes, is a trivialized vision of war.[38] An image of war controlled by commemoration and official narratives, supported by often carefully staged pictures and photos, an industry of toys and games that create the thrill of war without any of its horrors, and military histories and battlefield tourism full of the derring-do exploits of soldiers minus the stuff that induced the psychoses of shell-shock and post-traumatic stress.

As Chris Hedges points out, we do not 'smell rotting flesh, hear the cries of agony, or see before us blood and entrails seeping out of bodies'.[39] Not for nothing is the suicide rate of US army veterans more than double that of the US population as a whole. It is greater still amongst veterans that experienced direct combat. Among New Zealanders who returned from the First World War, the suicide rate was at least double and maybe as much as four times greater than the rate amongst the same-aged male population generally. Another study showed precisely the same pattern in Queensland, Australia.[40]

The pure horror and terrible fear evinced by war is a part of its character that is kept firmly out of view. If we could all see, hear, smell, and feel war, we would be more fearful of it.

War often plays a significant role in the collective memories that define societies and nations. But collective memories are always selective memories, sometimes even carefully curated by official commemoration. Modern national identities were sometimes shaped by official narratives and rituals drawn from selective interpretations of war. Historian Jay Winter reminds us that national remembrance, in many countries an official annual event whose meanings are taught to children from the earliest age, helps those who were not there construct their own—rather safer—image of war.[41] Acts of collective remembrance are therefore also acts of collective forgetting. What we choose to remember is shaped (though not determined) by whatever memories political and social elites choose to promote. Sometimes, narratives are designed self-consciously to support national goals and promote military service. Other times, these effects are achieved unconsciously. The key point is that what societies remember in their official commemorations of war is not war itself but a selective interpretation of it, one that reflects more the concerns and fashions of the times than the actual realities of war.

Soldiers are not born. They are made. Often quite literally through the training they receive. Basic military training teaches soldiers to suppress compassion, humility, independent thought, and fear, and to elevate hyper-masculinity, aggression, commitment to the unit and the cause, and bravery. Few have expressed this point more eloquently than the military historian Richard Holmes, whose histories were among the first to convey the realities of the battlefield to those that have never experienced it:

> A soldier who constantly reflected upon the knee-smashing, widow-making characteristics of his weapon, or who always thought of the enemy as a man exactly as himself, doing much the same task and subjected to exactly the same stresses and strains, would find it difficult to operate in battle...Without the creation of abstract images of the enemy, and without the depersonalization of the enemy during training, battle would become impossible to sustain...if...men reflect too deeply upon the enemy's common humanity, then they risk being unable to proceed with the task whose aims may be eminently just and legitimate. This conundrum lies, like a Gordian knot linking the diverse strands of hostility and affection, at the heart of the soldier's relationship with the enemy.[42]

Perhaps with his mind on the Christmas truce of 1914 (more on which below), Graham Greene observed, 'noone said that we couldn't like them, they just said we had to kill them. All a bit stupid isn't it?'. An enemy 'had to remain a caricature if he is to remain at a safe distance: an enemy should never come alive'.[43]

The Russian writer, Tolstoy, also understood that soldiers did not just exist, but had to be made. In *The Kingdom of God Is Within You* (1894), Tolstoy vividly portrayed how war, and its myths of patriotism, put whole societies to work in its service, creating social conditions that made it all but impossible for men to refuse to kill—and die—for their country. Religious institutions ('The bells will peal and long-haired men will dress themselves in gold-embroidered sacks and begin to pray on behalf of murder'), newspapers (whose editors will 'set to work to arouse hatred and murder under the guise of patriotism'), manufacturers, officials, military commanders, and even idle men and women (who will 'fuss about, entering their names in advance for the Red Cross and getting ready to bandage those whom their husbands and brothers are setting out to kill') all contribute to this terrible end, the result being that:

> hundreds of thousands of simple kindly folk, torn from peaceful toil and from their wives, mothers, and children, and with murderous weapons in their hands, will trudge wherever they may be driven, stifling their despair in their souls by songs, debauchery, and vodka. They will march, freeze, suffer from hunger and fall ill. Some will die of disease, and some will at last come to the place where men will kill them by the thousand. And they too, without themselves knowing why, will murder thousands of others whom they had never before seen, and who had either done nor could do them any wrong.[44]

All society thus reinforce the myths of patriotism that tear kindly folks from their hearth and put them to work as purveyors of death and death's potential victims. It is as if war and patriotism hypnotize whole armies, pushing individual soldiers to do things that they would never ordinarily choose. They are hypnotized, W.B. Gallie tells us, first by their government and then by each other.[45]

We need, then, to look more carefully at the sentiments that sustain war, at how they are created and sustained. 'The war is so horribly exciting', one British supporter of the suffragette movement wrote of the First World War, 'but I can't *live* on it, it is like being drunk all day & I want some hot milk, clean and feeding'.[46] These words—usually cited without the second clause and without acknowledging their provenance—are sometimes taken today as a prime example of just how infectious the ecstasy of war can be. So infectious that it even excited the passions of a suffragette.[47] Yet that is not what the author, Jane Ellen Harrison, intended, as the second part of the quote attests. In fact, a closer look at Harrison tells us something important about the hypnotic allure of war.

Jane Harrison was an intellectual trailblazer, one of the first women to hold a research fellowship at Cambridge and a renowned authority on Greek religion and mythology. Her much-quoted quip was written in a letter to her friend and fellow classicist, Gilbert Murray, shortly after the outbreak of war. Harrison was confounded by the war, and distanced from Murray—a Liberal activist who supported the government's view that war was a necessary evil. Murray believed ardently that it was imperative that Liberals make the case for war, lest the political space come to be dominated by militarists. In a pamphlet entitled *How Can War Ever Be Right?* he argued not just that war was sometimes the lesser evil but that it also provided ordinary people rare opportunities for heroism. 'This', Murray wrote, no doubt casting his mind back to Homer, 'is the inward triumph which lies at the heart of the great tragedy'. War could make heroes of us all. Murray's contemporary, Rupert Brooke, marvelled at how the war had transformed intellectuals like him and Murray into warriors. 'It's all a terrible thing. And yet in its detail, it's great fun'.[48]

Harrison found herself surrounded by the sort of sentiment she was later credited with epitomizing. But in truth she was bewildered by it. An instinctive pacifist, she could not understand the logic of Murray's arguments and those of the many others like him. When read in full, the famous line in her letter to Murray stands as a critique of the social frenzy whipped up by war, not an endorsement. Harrison recognizes the excitement, expressed by Murray, Brookes, and others, yet cannot herself live on it. Life requires comforts—hot milk, warm blankets—not war.

In 1915, Harrison published a pamphlet on *Peace with Patriotism* to set out her view more fully. War, she argued, marked a return to savagery; a setback to civilization. Germany had caused it, she claimed, because it had become over-theoretical, over-intellectualized, and overly bureaucratic. Germans saw the world in abstractions—states, nations, interests, power—and sought to impose its will upon others, blindly unaware of the people caught in its wake. War fostered a 'herd mentality', a deadly collectivism that inhibited independent thought. In a later letter, Harrison observed with alarm how the audience at a political rally had complained that the speakers had not told them just what to think. In wartime, people felt proud to be given orders. These sentiments, she thought, drove further war. The antidote was to push back against collectivism, the herd mentality, and the sentiments that give rise to it. 'We must cleanse our hearts not only from hate in war, but from those subtler poisons that fester unto war—from all rivalry, jealousy, and from all spirit of competition ... we must live and let live, tolerating— nay fostering—in the life of individuals and of nations an infinite parti-coloured diversity, and so at least win *Peace with Patriotism*'.[49] War may be exciting, but one cannot live on it. Sentiments could, however, be re-educated, Harrison believed. The herd mentality need not predominate. It is a sad irony that Harrison's words have come to be taken as epithets of a mindset she so opposed, and tragic that her fuller perspective on war and peace seems to have been lost.

Harrison wrote those words in the autumn of 1914. Whilst certainly a distinct minority, she was not alone in her bewilderment. Her Cambridge colleague, the philosopher Bertrand Russell, expressed similar feelings. 'One by one', he observed, 'the people with whom one had been in the habit of agreeing politically went over to the side of the war'. The 'whole nation', he concluded, was in a state of 'violent collective excitement'.[50] Meanwhile, the editors of the *Cambridge Medieval History* set about removing German contributors from their project. Shortly after writing to her friend, Jane Harrison travelled to Paris—as she often did—to receive treatment for angina. That Christmas, barely 100 miles to the east of Paris, soldiers on the Western Front showed what a tantalizing possibility the cleansing of hearts and cherishing of diversity could be. For a brief moment, the guns fell silent as Christmas cheer was exchanged all along the frontline.

On Christmas Eve 1914, officers of the Royal Flying Corps carefully wrapped a plum pudding and dropped it on the German side of the front. The Germans reciprocated with a bottle of brandy, just as carefully wrapped. Near Armentieres, Rifleman A.J. Phillips was dispatched to meet five Germans who, after spending the day singing, had called out for the British to send someone to arrange a 'you no shoot, we no shoot' truce for Christmas. Phillips found the five Germans armed with nothing more than wine, cakes, chocolates, and cigarettes. Up and down the line that day, Germans posted messages with words to the effect of 'you no fight, we no fight'. The British responded with messages of 'Happy Christmas'. Near Poperinge, the Germans posted a 'Happy Christmas' message to the Belgian troops opposite. Then they climbed out of their trenches, unarmed, to offer greetings and gifts. As the afternoon mist turned into a clear but chilly night, even the embittered French began to take part. In the Aisne valley, German soldiers left their trenches signalling to the French. Further down the line, Bavarian soldiers—who had been refusing to fight for days—emerged from their trenches and exchanged bread, cognac, and post-cards with their French counterparts. In some places along the line, the deadlock was broken by Christmas trees, glowing with candles lifted aloft of the parapets. Elsewhere, it was traditional songs—famously *stille nacht*—that eased the tensions. Across the length of the whole frontline, gestures of peace became contagious. On Christmas Day itself, soldiers came out of their trenches, greeted one another, and shared gifts. They also reclaimed their dead from no-man's land. That day, more than one game of football was played in the ruined land between the frontlines.[51]

As many as 100,000 soldiers participated in the Christmas truce of 1914. Naturally, there was wariness on both sides. The first months of war had taken a million lives and the war had continued its bloody course throughout December. Soldiers on both sides knew that they took immense risks by coming out of their trenches unarmed. Yet they did so and in great numbers. 'We are having the most extraordinary time imaginable', wrote Captain Robert Miles:

> A sort of unarranged and quite unauthorized but perfectly understood and scrupulously observed truce exists between us and our friends in front...The thing started last night—a bitter cold night, with white frost—soon after dusk when the Germans started shouting 'Merry Christmas, Englishmen' to us. Of course our fellows shouted back and presently large numbers of both sides had left their trenches, unarmed, and met in the debatable, shot-riddled, no man's land between the lines. Here the agreement—all on their own—came to be made that we should not fire at each other until after midnight tonight. The men were all fraternizing in the middle (we naturally did not allow them too close to our line) and swapped cigarettes and lies in the utmost good fellowship. Not a shot was fired all night.[52]

From somewhere else on the line, Henry Williamson wrote to his mother:

> I am writing from the trenches. It is 11 o'clock in the morning. Beside me is a coke fire, opposite me a 'dug-out' (wet) with straw in it. The ground is sloppy in the actual trench, but frozen elsewhere. In my mouth is a pipe...In the pipe is

tobacco. Of course, you say. But wait. In the pipe is German tobacco. Haha, you say, from a prisoner or found in a captured trench. Oh dear, no! From a German soldier. Yes a live German soldier from his own trench. Yesterday the British & Germans met & shook hands in the Ground between the trenches, & exchanged souvenirs, & shook hands. Yes, all day Xmas day, & as I write. Marvellous, isn't it?.[53]

Not everyone approved. Commanders on both sides feared that fraternization would diminish the soldiers' 'fighting spirit' and encourage insubordination or even revolution. A young Bavarian corporal called Adolf Hitler was appalled.

The truce was barely reported in France and Germany, where the press was heavily censored. French newspapers claimed, for example, that it occurred only in British sections of the line. The German press insisted that the truce had been exaggerated. In Britain, by contrast, the truce was widely reported and celebrated. Popular newspapers the *Mirror* and *Sketch* published pictures of British and German troops mingling; *The Times* even published a letter from a German lieutenant and editorialized on 4 January that 'as the wonderful scenes in the trenches show, there is no malice on our side, and none in many of those who have been marshalled against us'.[54] It was the *Mirror*, the newspaper of the industrial working class, though, that perhaps best captured the significance of the moment, in what Sydney Weintraub describes as an 'almost treasonous' editorial:

> The soldier's heart rarely has any hatred in it. He goes out to fight because that is his job. What came before—the causes of the war and the why and where-fore—bother him little. He fights for his country and against his country's enemies. Collectively, they are to be condemned and blown to pieces. Individually, he knows they're not bad sorts...The soldier has other things to think about. He has to work and win. Consequently he has not time for rage, and blind furies only overwhelm him when the blood is up over fierce tussles in the heat of the thing. At other times the insane childishness is apparent to him...But now an end to the truce. The news, bad and good, begins again. 1915 darkens over. Again we who watch have to mourn many of our finest men. The lull is finished. The absurdity and the tragedy renew themselves.[55]

The following year, Allied commanders tried to prevent a repeat of the Christmas truce by launching a deadly December offensive. Britain's Commander, Douglas Haig, issued an order forbidding fraternization. The German army threatened to execute any who fraternized with the enemy. The soldiers themselves had also been hardened by the horrors of the preceding year: the use of poison gas, the bloody stalemate in the trenches, Zeppelin raids on British cities, and the disastrous landings at Gallipoli. Yet despite all that, on Christmas Day 1915, soldiers of the 15th Battalion Royal Welch shouted greetings to their German counterparts, who responded in kind. Once more, they left their trenches and gathered in no-man's land. Once more they exchanged greetings and gifts, and played football. The merriment was broken in mid-morning when Brigadier-General Lord Henry Seymour arrived at the front demanding that the truce end and threatening court-martials for all involved. British artillery opened up to underscore the point. But, by mid-afternoon, peace had returned and the soldiers were back in no-man's land, where they sang and talked together until nightfall.[56]

The Christmas truce is important in its own right but also because of what it tells us about the passions of war. It reminds us that these passions are neither impregnable nor immutable. Empathy (the soldiers could literally put themselves in each other's shoes), a sense of comradeship (as the *Mirror* observed, both sides comprised soldiers sent to do a job many of them did not understand), shared Christian values (and songs and traditions), and common interest (in burying their dead lost to no-man's land and in having a peaceful Christmas) overcame not just the differences of national identity and general enmity, but also the much more intimate animosities of frontline warfare and the commands of the military leadership of both sides. I observed earlier that nationalist or ideologically fuelled identities and sentiments can be powerful drivers of human behaviour. But because we are all simultaneously members of different groups, we have multiple identities and sometimes this plurality comes to the fore, dampening bellicosity. The Christmas truce—a series of spontaneous events—shows that this can happen even in the most unpropitious of circumstances. Christmas served as a shared cultural value that transcended the narrower identities and interests of the soldiers. This example highlights that peace efforts must be accompanied by efforts that reach out across boundaries to foster shared traditions and values.[57]

The Christmas truce shows that it is possible for shared identity, even mutual recognition of shared humanity, to extend beyond national or kin-groups and for this sentiment to be sufficiently powerful to influence behaviour. People are bound together by more than just self-interest and social contract, the philosophers of the Enlightenment told us. They are united by their feelings of common humanity. This way of thinking was pioneered by the seventeenth-century German jurist and philosopher, Samuel von Pufendorf. Von Pufendorf believed that it was not reason or self-interest alone that encouraged the formation of civil society out of the chaos of the state of nature, for neither of these could explain how individuals locked in a state of constant 'warre' could find sufficient trust to associate with others. The foundations for human society, Von Pufendorf argued, lay in *socialitas*, what we might call emotional recognition, and this arose not from reason but from the human imagination. From this mutual recognition stems the human capacities for empathy, compassion, and sympathy. As David Hume put it, 'no quality of human nature is more remarkable, both in itself and in its consequences, than that propensity we have to sympathize with others, and to receive by communication their inclinations and sentiments, however different from, or even contrary to, our own'.[58]

Our imagination can be extended to include the feelings of others, Hume argued, by 'some circumstances in the present which strikes us in a lively way'. From a singular experience, if our minds are sufficiently attuned, we may attain a 'lively notion of all the circumstances of that person whether past, present or future; possible, probable or certain'.[59] Once experienced in some form, and further cultivated through literature and the arts, the mere thought of a moral ill such as the cruelty faced by others or the suffering of war will leave a mark on the imagination that constructs how we think about morality and pursue moral lives.[60] For one of Hume's more famous collaborators, the economist Adam Smith, it was precisely this capacity to imagine the suffering of others that united humans. When 'our brother is on the rack', Smith observed, 'it is by imagination only that we can form any conception of what are his sensations'.

Smith opened his *Theory of Moral Sentiments* with a clear statement on the affective connections that bind humans:

> How selfish soever man may be supposed, there are evidently some principles in his nature, which interest him in the fortunes of others, and render their happiness necessary to him, though he derives nothing from it, except the pleasure of seeing it. Of this kind is pity or compassion, the emotion we feel for the misery of others, when we either see it, or are made to conceive it in a very lively manner. That we often derive sorrow from the sorrows of others, is a matter of fact too obvious to require any instances to prove it; for this sentiment, like all the other original passions of human nature, is by no means confined to the virtuous or the humane, though they perhaps may feel it with the most exquisite sensibility. The greatest ruffian, the most hardened violator of the laws of society, is not altogether without it.[61]

But Smith understood that sympathy is fleeting and thus unreliable as a guide to action. We tend, after all, to sympathize more with those more similar to us. Sentiment could also be transitory, limiting its capacity to drive public policy. Smith observed that a beggar's tears may elicit sympathy but that this might be countermanded by suspicion (is the beggar crying in order to elicit a response?) and, anyway, is likely only to induce a temporary state of concern. Reason, therefore, still had a part to play, working alongside not in place of sentiment. Sympathies, Smith argued, are activated to the full only when we understand *why* somebody is suffering. '[S]ympathy with the grief or joy of another, before we are informed of the cause of either is always extremely imperfect. More perfect compassion arises out of a fuller understanding of the circumstances which brought about the other person's agonies'.[62] Thus, understanding promoted by reason promotes the exercising of human sympathy.

In theory at least, to return to Hume, there are no a priori limits—beyond those of geography and technology—to the potential reach of human affection. Affection, after all, is rooted in membership of some common group and many groups—professional, religious, even familial—extend beyond the ethnic or national. There seemed, Hume thought, no inherent limit to the interest of humans in the lives of other humans. 'No passion if well understood can be entirely indifferent to us, because there is none, of which every man has no, within him at least the seeds and first principles'. Everywhere we look, we see evidence of human interest in the affairs of others. Why else, asked Hume, would we exhibit an interest in the affairs of distant provinces and states that have little bearing on our daily lives? Why else would we scour newspapers to learn tidings of people we do not know? Why else, we might ask today, would we spend so much of our time and energy conversing with near and distant strangers alike on social media? Although the affairs of distant strangers 'may not always be so strong and steady as to have great influence on our conduct and behavior', he pointed out, we are not indifferent to them. 'The interest of society', Hume concluded, 'appears to be the interest of every individual'.[63]

This shift from political theories based on self-interest and social contracts to ones that emphasize mutual recognition born of human affections and sentiments affords us a more complete concept of humanity: the idea that all humans are of fundamentally equal value and connected by emotional bonds. The barriers erected between humans—barriers of race, nation, ethnicity, class, and religion—are thus exposed as social artifices. They are no less powerful because of that fact, but this idea does suggest that humans have some degree of choice about how we organize ourselves and the meanings given to these organizational forms. That, in other words, the attachments that give rise to war are social inventions that can be rethought and re-practised. We already saw, in the writings of Jane Harrison and events of the Christmas truce, that even in the darkest of hours such re-imaginings are possible. Recall, too, that Darwin himself believed that there was no logical reason why the instincts and sympathies that bound humans together in nations could not be extended to all of humanity.[64]

It is a short leap from these ideas to more comprehensive theories about cosmopolitan world orders that bind all humans together in a single polity. Indeed, 'world government' has long been viewed by some, including one of the leading American strategic thinkers of the Cold War, Hans Morgenthau, as the only viable path to a permanent peace. Morgenthau insisted that permanent peace could be achieved only by a preponderance of power wielded by a global government. Yet Morgenthau realized that such government could be achieved only once a meaningful global community of humanity had been established— one that could lay claim to the allegiance and commitment of state leaders, armies, and civil societies.[65] In the absence of such a community, any attempt to construct a world state would be construed by much of the world as an imperial project and resisted as such, provoking only more war. So a world community must precede a world government. Yet a sense of community reaching across nations is possible only if there is peace in the first place. Thus, world peace may be as much a cause of world government as a consequence—another reason why the path to peace probably does not lie through world government.

How might we translate these ideas into practice? How is a community of humanity to be built? Certainly not through campaigns to force or persuade people to switch their identities. Grandiose schemes to build new communities and forge new identities have been responsible for great violence and terrible atrocities. As Amartya Sen points out, they create new animosities and sectarian divides. A community of humanity, therefore, is built not from the top down but from the bottom up, and not by replacing one dominant (national) identity within another (global). It arises instead through nurturing the plurality of our identities. We are all members of several different groups at the same time—family, city, region, religion, profession, ethnicity, nation. As such, we all have multiple identities. The emotions that give rise to war try to reduce this plurality and assert one ascendant identity—one so powerful that it overrides all other attachments. The key to resisting these trends, and to fostering bonds of sentimentality that cross dominant group boundaries, lies in recognizing and nurturing the plurality of our identities.

In practical terms, equitable trade, open commerce, freedom of movement, and open communications reduce the physical distance between individuals and groups, and enlarge the sphere of empathy and common interest, as I explained in Chapter 6. But we cannot assume that this would automatically reduce emotional distance. This can be done only by nurturing the different, overlapping, groups with which we identify and by using these connections to help educate the senses, building awareness, understanding, and appreciation of the lives of others. Through recognizing and celebrating the different things we have in common, the different sorts of groups to which we belong, we build a sense of common humanity based upon very basic principles of equality and fundamental human rights from the ground up.[66] It can be done by fostering the arts and literature in ways that encourage individuals and groups to expand their moral horizons and broaden their imaginations. By taking steps to privilege and emphasize the humanity of others. By embracing the movement of people and ideas across social and political boundaries. By celebrating the different groups to which we belong and resisting the urge to narrow our identities into singular types. Through this broadening of our sensibilities comes support for principles of human rights and human equality, since we come to understand all individuals as being basically equal and equally deserving of those rights that we would want to claim for ourselves.

Extending our horizons beyond the local and towards the global certainly requires a giant leap. Happily, it is not a leap we must attempt in one go. We can incrementally widen 'in-group' allegiance from individuals, to wider sets of groups, and finally to all of humanity. This was precisely what Darwin was intimating when he suggested that there was no theoretical limit to the boundaries of our communities. One starting place is the immediate community in which we live. As Sen points out, we all have multiple identities, born out of our membership of different groups, that we already have. Group conflicts arise when one dominant identity comes to the fore, pushing people into simple binary categories—'us–them', 'friend–foe'. The reality is that no group or society is homogeneous. All comprise people with different identity configurations. There are national, linguistic, religious, and familial differences. Differences born of place, profession, and preferences. When we look closely at any society, we find different identities. We find Greeks living in Galilee, Chinese amongst the earliest foreign settlers in Australia, Somalis in nineteenth-century Cardiff. We find thriving, longstanding, multiethnic centres such as Malacca, Istanbul, and Sarajevo whose flourishing over centuries was premised on accommodating differences. Yes, internal coherence often leads to external differentiation, but as these examples show, some human societies have thrived in contexts of difference. Identity is a constrained choice, of course. A Somali in Cardiff or Sarajevan Jew will always be marked out by the way others define and respond to them. But we do have the capacity to select which of our multiple identities or combinations of identities to emphasize and how to regard the identities of others. Celebrating and preserving that plurality, reaching out beyond restrictive identity norms, helps resist the all too easy categorization of peoples into binary groups, us and them.[67]

Another starting place could be the region in which we live. We can more easily extend our empathy to those closest to us. We trade, travel, and converse more with our nearest neighbours than we do with distant strangers. But when we do, we learn to extend our horizons and look beyond narrow prejudices. That is perhaps why groups of states and societies that form 'security communities'—networks of rules and institutions that make war between their members unthinkable—tend to spread their cultures of peace beyond their immediate boundaries. Cultivating these habits locally helps strengthen them globally.

If nothing else, seeing the enemy as a human, just like us, strengthens our inhibition against killing and makes it more difficult to justify war. A corollary of this is conflict resolution, for with heightened understanding of one another's positions and ambitions comes respect and a greater capacity to resolve disputes without violence. A sense of human equality also gives rise to humanitarianism—the notion that people in need, including those placed in need by war, should be given whatever assistance they need to sustain their life. Humanitarianism emerged in the nineteenth century from the visceral reaction of one man, Henry Dunant, to the brutality and inhumanity of the modern battlefield at Solferino.[68]

That Dunant's message was so widely accepted, giving rise to the Red Cross movement, suggests that many others felt a similar reaction to war's horrors or that they could relate to it. To leash the passions that give rise to war, not only must we strengthen the ties that bind humans together, we must also understand and *feel* the true horror of war. Feel the reality of war—not the sanitized and heroic Hollywood version that most us are exposed to today. 'War is not a polite recreation', Tolstoy's Prince Andrei observes in *War and Peace*, 'but the vilest thing in life, and we ought to understand that and not play at war. Our attitude towards the fearful necessity of war ought to be stern and serious. It boils down to this: we should have done with humbug, and let war be war and not a game'.[69] We must close the gap between popular perceptions of war and its far less glamorous reality. Many writers that have gone before have made this very point. H.G. Wells, for example, wrote that world government and with it lasting peace would arise only after catastrophic war; only when all was destroyed would people recognize the folly of war and come to accept what was necessary to eliminate it.[70] It is also the message of the passage from 'Locksley Hall' where we began.

It was precisely to encourage British society to adopt a sterner and more serious view of war that Virginia Woolf wrote *Three Guineas* in 1936–7. Woolf understood that war was possible only when those who waged it enjoyed sufficient support from society as a whole. To end war, therefore, one had to change society's attitude towards it. We must adopt a more realistic and less romantic view of what war was actually like. If people understood what war was really like, they would be less likely to support it, and the less people supported war, the less of a hypnotic effect it would exercise over society. When different people—in this case, Woolf and the male interlocutor introduced in the book—look at the images of a dead child, a body too mutilated to identify, and a house destroyed, the ruined ornaments of daily life now exposed to the elements, they have the same reaction:

> Those photographs are not an argument; they are simply a crude statement of fact addressed to the eye. But the eye is connected with the brain; the brain with the nervous system. That system sends its messages in a flash through every past memory and present feeling. When we look at those photographs some fusion takes place within us; however different the education, the traditions behind us, our sensations are the same; and they are violent. You, Sir, call them 'horror and disgust'. We also call them horror and disgust. And the same words rise to our lips. War, you say, is an abomination; a barbarity; war must be stopped at whatever cost. And we echo your words. War is an abomination; a barbarity; war must be stopped. For now at last we are looking at the same picture; we are seeing with you the same dead bodies, the same ruined houses.[71]

Shocking, upsetting, images of the reality of war are what it takes to embed its horrors in our imagination. Continued Woolf, 'Is it not possible that if we knew the truth about war, the glory of war would be scotched and crushed where it lies curled up in the rotten cabbage leaves of our prostituted fact-purveyors?' If, instead of peddling a heroic and highly sanitized vision of war, newspapers portrayed war as it actually was, the whole endeavour would become much less appealing. And if those same newspapers promoted the virtues of art, 'instead of shuffling and shambling through the smeared and dejected pages of those who must live by prostituting culture, the enjoyment and practice of art would become so desirable that by comparison the pursuit of war would be a tedious game for elderly dilettantes in search of a mildly sanitary amusement— the tossing of bombs instead of balls over frontiers instead of nets?' In short, Woolf argued, 'if newspapers were written by people whose sole object in writing was to tell the truth about politics and the truth about art we should not believe in war, and we should believe in art'.[72] Peace is thus tied to intellectual liberty—the right, indeed the duty, to show things as they really are.

Woolf believed that if people better understood what war was really like, they would be less willing to support it. Women, she thought, had a particularly important role to play. If women took 'no share in patriotic demonstrations' and refused to endorse patriotic sentiment or encourage war and militarism, it would become more difficult for war to impose itself on society. 'Psychology', Woolf reminds us, 'warrants the belief that this use of indifference by the daughters of educated men would help materially to prevent war' because 'it is far harder for human beings to take action when other people are indifferent and allow them complete freedom of action, than when their actions are made the centre of excited emotion'.[73]

Between the wars, peace activists in Germany, France, the UK, and the US tried to convey war's horrors to the broader population. Ernst Friedrich's 1924 *Kreig dem Kriege!* featured pictures of war casualties, many deemed unpublishable by the government. Abel Gance's 1938 silent movie *J'accuse* included close-up shots of some of the war's disfigured survivors—those victims of war so often shunned and kept out of sight.[74] Even today, images have the power to crystallize sentiment and drive behaviour, as the response to the tragedy of Alan Kurdi, a refugee of the Syrian war, attests. Of course, for the truth of war to translate into meaningful judgements about it, individuals—including soldiers— must have the right to make up their own minds about war's legitimacy—and the legitimacy of individual wars, and to act accordingly. That means a broader effort to allow the expression of different views and permit individuals to opt out of participating in wars they believe to be objectionable, something I return to in greater detail in Chapter 8.

In the US, Jane Addams also understood the importance of cultivating compassion and establishing bonds of friendship across difference. Labelled 'the most dangerous woman in America' by President Theodore Roosevelt for her opposition to the First World War, hers was a bottom-up and decidedly practical path, which held that peace demanded that individuals and nations move in the 'direction of compassionate tending to citizens'.[75] By tending to the needs of one another, Addams argued, people would become estranged from war. Addams' approach to peace rested on an ultimately optimist account of the human condition. Our similarities, she believed, were greater and stronger than our differences and our natural condition tended towards friendship and hence peace. War was unnatural, she argued, sustained only by social forces that distorted human nature. Our natural sociability could be rekindled through acts of compassion and solidarity, establishing bonds of friendship. The possibility of peace lay within those very bonds. Through her work with immigrant communities in Chicago, Addams saw how cooperation and partnership on functional matters such as housing and heating could forge bonds of friendship that reached across ethnicity, nationality, race, and religion. Such cooperation could build a new 'internationalism' in which 'virile good will would be substituted for the spirit of warfare'.[76] An outpouring of compassion, friendship, and cooperation could make war unthinkable, Addams believed.

Leashing the passions of war requires that we extend the bonds of sentiment and sympathy to those beyond our immediate groups. It means recognizing and celebrating the plurality of our identities. It also requires us to implant the reality of war within our imagination. Our failure, Susan Sontag writes, 'is one of imagination, of empathy'. We must confront the realities of war face-on. We must learn again to fear war.[77] 'This is what war *does*. And *that*, that is what war does, too. War tears, rends. War rips open, eviscerates. War scorches. War dismembers. War *ruins*'.[78] We will almost certainly continue to organize ourselves into separate and distinct social and political groups in the future, but if we better understand the lives and pains of others, understand how our connections to them extend across political boundaries, these lines of division will become less harsh and less violent. And if, at the same time, we force ourselves to gaze at the reality of war and give ourselves the freedom to make up our own minds about war's legitimacy, we will become less likely to wish it upon ourselves or to inflict it on others.

CHAPTER 8

TOWARDS WORLD PEACE

*P*reliminary articles for world peace in our time:

1. No one may violate the rules of international law relating to the use of force and conduct of armed conflict. To ensure that the law is respected, no Permanent Member of the UN Security Council should use a veto to prevent collective action in response to armed aggression or the threat or commission of genocide, war crimes, and crimes against humanity.
2. Each state shall contribute its fair share to the full and prompt implementation of decisions taken by the United Nations and other international institutions.
3. No state or private corporation shall transfer armaments to state or non-state actors who may be reasonably expected to use them in violation of international law.
4. States shall establish and sustain security communities with their neighbours.
5. Individuals should enjoy a universal right of hospitality. No state shall inhibit the free and fair movement of goods, services, people, and ideas between them.
6. Individuals should be held criminally accountable for acts of genocide, war crimes, crimes against humanity, and aggression.

Definitive articles for world peace in our time:

1. Each state shall be a capable, responsible, and legitimate sovereign.
2. Each state and society should promote and protect gender equality.

3. No government should inhibit the capacity of individuals to opt out of war. The free reporting of war and all its effects, open debate and dissent, and the right to refuse military service should be protected.

Additional imperative article for world peace in our time:
1. Individuals should organize and do what they reasonably can to support world peace.

For as long as we have fought wars, humans have also dreamed of peace. Yet peace has proven elusive, mainly because war continues to commend itself to a sufficient number of us as an effective and efficient means of acquiring resources, protecting values, and settling disputes. Because we have no world government, it takes only one bellicose state or society to keep war in business, for whilst one retains the will and capacity, war remains a possibility for all.

But there is every indication that war is becoming less useful. Nowadays, wealth and wellbeing are better achieved by peaceful activities such as manufacturing, trade, and the provision of services than through the barrel of a gun. War is increasingly associated with economic decline and decay, with contemporary civil wars aptly described as 'development in reverse'. Even major powers struggle to make gains from war. As Andrew Bacevich shows, the US has spent much of the last three decades using military means to resolve political problems in the Middle East but it has produced nothing but poor political outcomes, a toll of lives lost and harmed, and a massive financial bill.[1]

Time and again, contemporary war has proven itself to be a blunt instrument. Peace, on the other hand, is associated with dramatic improvements in human welfare. It is no coincidence that since the 1960s, East Asia has experienced not one, but two miracles: the well-known economic miracle that helped lift 1 billion people out of grinding poverty and the much less well-known peace miracle through which one of the world's most war-ridden regions became one of its most peaceful. The two miracles aided one another.

But despite growing evidence of its inefficiency, war continues to beguile the human imagination. Enough of us continue to *believe* that war can be useful. Military leaders themselves have sometimes fallen victim to war's charms, deluding themselves into thinking that military instruments can solve political problems. The US and UK could have walked away from Afghanistan in 2002, satisfied that they had dealt a severe blow to al-Qaeda and the Taliban in response to the 9/11 terrorist attacks. But political leaders wanted to do more. They wanted to fashion a new society in Afghanistan and believed they could use military means to do so. Against the advice of experts, who counselled that foreign state-building in Afghanistan was a fool's errand, a literally unwinnable win because it would never command the support of Afghans themselves, the military commanders agreed with their political leaders and extended the mission. After more than a decade of effort, and thousands of lives lost, this extended mission withdrew from Afghanistan, leaving a government barely able to govern beyond its capital and the Taliban ruling supreme in much of the country.[2]

We have also created powerful institutions and myths that make war appear not just rational and moral, but heroic. War is sanitized in public discourse, its true nature and consequences often kept from view. This helps reinforce the myth of war's usefulness, encouraging those with no actual experience of it to think of it as a laudable and surgical instrument of national policy. The myth of war, writes Chris Hedges, allows us to find meaning in mayhem and violence, to embrace a higher purpose.[3] These powerful myths produce a 'rally round the flag effect' when war beckons. At those moments on the brink of war when critical reflection and open debate are most needed, the social pressures exerted by nationalism serve to close them down.[4] Sometimes the myth is shattered by reality. For example, over time, the simple and generous act by the villagers of Wootton Bassett of lining the street to pay respect to returning British soldiers killed in Afghanistan provided a focal point that served to highlight the scale of loss caused by that war. Puncturing the myth of war, Wootton Bassett encouraged an increasingly sceptical public mood towards British involvement in Afghanistan.[5] Defeat in the Falklands had a similarly sobering effect on millions of Argentines.[6]

World peace arises not out of a single blueprint but from myriad 'minor utopias'. There are practices and institutional arrangements that can support these efforts, just as there are other types of practices and arrangements that can inhibit them. In Chapters 1–7, I identified three critical building blocks, without which world peace would be unlikely.

The first is the modern state, the bedrock of everyday peace in most parts of the world.[7] For all its imperfections, we have yet to find a better way of maintaining peace at home. But the modern state only exacerbates the problem of human division by institutionalizing it. In resolving the problem of everyday 'warre', we have created the problem of interstate war. Yet certain types of state have proven more peaceful than others.

The second building block involves building peace in our minds. In Chapter 6, I showed that the balance book has tilted decisively in favour of peace; that modern war rarely pays whereas peace opens up significant opportunities for human advancement. Some of this change was deliberate—the outlawing of conquest, for example, was a self-conscious attempt to make war less attractive as a policy option—but some coincidental. The explosion of world trade, for example, so critical to increasing prosperity, was not undertaken with the goal of peace in mind. But it is also incomplete. Enough leaders to keep war in business still believe that the benefits outweigh the costs. In Syria, for example, Bashar al-Assad believed it was worth destroying a country and killing hundreds of thousands of its people in order to keep himself in power. Russia's Vladimir Putin believes war's costs are acceptable for the reward of teaching Ukrainians a lesson. But the costs and payoffs of war can be deliberately manipulated. There is much more we could do to make war less appealing still as a rational option and peace more appealing.

The third building block relates to the need to build peace in our hearts, to reshape our emotional sensibilities away from nationalism and war, and towards more cosmopolitan, compassionate, and peaceful inclinations. Influencing human emotions has proven much more difficult than reframing the material costs and benefits of war. So powerful are the emotions that drive us to war, they continue to impel large numbers of people to support wars and policies that are palpably contrary to their own self-interest.

In what follows, I offer some suggestions about how we might challenge the emotional impulses that give rise to war and forge more peaceful sensibilities.

Immanuel Kant organized his blueprint for perpetual peace into six preliminary articles, prohibitions that he believed could be implemented almost immediately and that would establish a basic absence of war, and three definitive articles, a set of more far-reaching demands that, if implemented, would make war unthinkable. I have organized my own thoughts in a similar way, though mine is less a blueprint and more a set of signposts that make no claims to being definitive or exhaustive. My 'preliminary articles' focus on the management of relations between states and on the need to implement and enforce the laws we already have, using institutions that already exist and building new ones where needed on existing models. My three 'definitive articles' go deeper and focus on the internal characteristics of groups that make them more peaceful and less disposed to war. We might use these signposts to guide political projects and evaluate whether individual policies and action help move us in a more, or less, peaceful direction. I have taken the liberty of adding an additional 'imperative article' that emphasizes the importance of individual responsibility and collective activism for peace. The reforms outlined in the preliminary and definitive articles and the far wider range of minor utopias necessary for world peace will be realized only if individuals and groups work hard to achieve them. Building world peace starts with individual and collective action that reaches from local communities to beyond national boundaries.

These articles for world peace are meant to serve as a prompt for further research, debate, and activism. They do not pretend to be comprehensive. They do not exhaust the realm of possibility. Some, especially the more ambitious goals, are vague on the detail of how they might be achieved. That is deliberate and reflects the fact that world peace will be advanced not by grand schemas but by the steady accumulation of minor utopias built as much in communities as in parliaments and the world's great debating halls. Precisely *how* specific goals are best realized will be for individuals, communities, and governments to determine, taking into consideration the contexts and opportunities they confront. I have chosen to focus here on how we can build on some of the rules, institutions, and practices we already have to make the world more peaceful. When it comes to world peace, we don't need to reinvent the wheel; we need to make sure that it turns.

Preliminary articles for world peace in our time:

1. No one may violate the rules of international law relating to the use of force and conduct of armed conflict. To ensure that the law is respected, no Permanent Member of the UN Security Council should use a veto to prevent collective action in response to armed aggression or the threat or commission of genocide, war crimes, and crimes against humanity.

International order rests on mutually agreed laws that regulate relations between states. These laws help establish basic conditions of trust that allow states to interact peacefully with one another. Chief among them are laws prohibiting and regulating the use of force. We must stop seeing war as a normal part of politics or an inherent right bestowed upon states or those who claim the mantle of justice, and regard it as the legally prohibited action that it now is. Perhaps more than any other single initiative, the outlawing of war in the twentieth century tipped the balance of likely consequences sharply in the direction of peace. As the historian Mark Mazower observed, 'if the history of the past century shows anything, it is clear that legal norms, the empowering of states and the security of international stability more generally can also serve human welfare'.[8] The legal prohibition of war makes it possible for states to coexist peacefully. It also limits the conditions that might give rise to legitimate and political objectives for which war might be waged. What is more, by demarcating community expectations about the legitimate and illegitimate use of force, the legal prohibition increases the material and reputational costs of war and creates the possibility of collective enforcement action against aggressors, limiting war's contagiousness. To realize this ambition, we need to reinforce legal benchmarks outlawing aggressive war, strengthen parameters on how wars might be fought, and do more to ensure that those who break rules are held to account—on which more later.

Happily, as I pointed out in Chapter 3, when it comes to the prohibition of war—at least war between states—we have no shortage of international law. This first article is thus a simple demand for actors to abide by, and enforce, the laws we already have. In 1928, dozens of states—including major powers such as France, the US, and the UK—agreed to renounce war as an instrument of policy. Although the Kellogg–Briand Pact, as the articles of renunciation were known, failed to stem the tide of fascist and communist aggression in the 1930s, the idea that states did not have an automatic right to wage war took hold.[9] After the carnage of the Second World War, a war sparked by German and Japanese aggression, states agreed a comprehensive ban on aggressive war. Article 2(4) of the UN Charter prohibited the use or threat of force in international politics with only two exceptions: the use of force in self-defence and the UN Security Council's authority to mandate the use of force for the maintenance of international peace and security.

The outlawing of war played a significant role in reducing the incidence of war between states after the Second World War by raising its costs and reducing its capacity to deliver the desired political outcomes. But there are limits to what international law alone can achieve. It can shape and influence action by affecting the costs and payoffs associated with different behaviours, but it cannot compel action. Powerful states, or states with powerful friends, can use their material power to absorb material costs and their political influence to mitigate political costs. The problem we confront today is thus not a shortage of law, but a shortage of compliance. Force, and the threat of force, may well have been outlawed, but states still employ them regularly. Sometimes, the international community stands resolute in defence of the law as in its response to North

Korea's invasion of the South in 1950 and Iraq's invasion of Kuwait four decades later. But more often, as with Iraq's invasion of Iran in 1980, the US invasion of Iraq in 2003, and Russia's invasion of Ukraine in 2014, its response is underwhelming, undermining law's capacity to change behaviour. As a result, whenever they have felt the need to resort to war, states have generally continued to do so. They have become quite adept at skirting the law by claiming to be acting in self-defence or on behalf of some 'implied' authorization from the Security Council. Sometimes, as with Russia's 2014 intervention in eastern Ukraine and the US bombing of Cambodia and Laos during the 1970s, they simply deny—against all evidence—that they are using force in another country. Fake news is not new news. Diplomacy itself, Ambrose Bierce reminds us, is sometimes seen as the 'patriotic art of lying for one's country'. What is more, the implied *threat* of force remains a core part of many states' national security policies and underlies the whole strategy of nuclear deterrence.

Our first task, then, is to nudge governments towards greater compliance with the laws we already have. That involves persuading parliaments and peoples to inform themselves about what the law says about war and to hold their governments accountable. It requires building war and its laws into education curricula, university courses, and public discourse. It means that courts ought to scrutinize and pass judgement on the justifications offered by governments and hold decision-makers accountable. It means that individuals should be free to form, and act upon, their own judgements about the legality of war. That is why social goods such as the rule of law, individual accountability, a free and open civil society, and a universal right of conscientious objection feature prominently in my other articles for world peace; they are essential for advancing this first article.

By itself, however, the outlawing of aggressive war does nothing to inhibit civil war—the most common form of war in the twenty-first century thus far—or to limit the conduct of otherwise lawful war. The UN Charter system grants rights and responsibilities only to states. For the foreseeable future, any efforts to extend these rules to non-state actors, even if intended to constrain these actors, would be rejected by governments on the grounds that this could confer backhanded legitimacy upon them. For that reason, the best avenue we have to constrain non-state armed groups is international humanitarian law—the law governing the conduct of war, law which of course applies to states as well. Here again, we have no shortage of law. The Geneva Convention (1948), its subsequent protocols (1977), the Convention on the Prevention and Punishment of Genocide (1947), a raft of treaties governing specific aspects of war such as the Land Mines Convention, and the Rome Statute of the International Criminal Court offer a comprehensive set of regulations governing the use of force.

International humanitarian law imposes legal obligations on all armed actors irrespective of the legality or legitimacy of their cause. It is what prevents actors justifying the commission of great harm in the name of world peace. Amongst other things, it requires that armed groups not target non-combatants, civilian infrastructure, or protected sites such as schools and hospitals, as well as medical workers. It requires that armed actors take positive steps to discriminate between combatants and non-combatants. It requires that they permit humanitarian access, treat prisoners with full respect for their human rights, refrain from the forcible displacement of civilians, and refrain from otherwise discriminate military actions that may have a disproportionate effect on the civilian population. It requires that soldiers refrain from torture, sexual violence, or other forms of misconduct. It prohibits the use of certain weapons, such as land mines, chemical weapons, and biological weapons, and limits the use of weapons that cannot be precisely targeted to battlespaces away from civilian residences. It demands that actors take positive steps to ensure compliance with the law and prevent violations. Commanders are responsible in law for the actions of their subordinates; subordinates are responsible for their own actions and cannot claim that they were simply 'following orders'.[10]

Once again, the problem today is not one of insufficient law but of insufficient application. Sometimes, part of the problem is that publics are insufficiently informed about what the law requires and why it matters. They place insufficient pressure on their governments and parliaments to uphold the law, and are insufficiently outraged when it is violated. Of course, this is less relevant in authoritarian states where governments are less responsive to their people's demands—which is again why only some types of state are conducive to world peace, a theme I will return to later. Another part of the problem is that international institutions established to maintain the peace and enforce international law are often inhibited from doing so by political disagreements or the simple lack of will to commit the necessary resources—my next two preliminary articles address these issues directly. There are also gaps in individual legal accountability—more often than not, the actual perpetrators of aggression, atrocity crimes, and other violations of the law never face prosecution. They most often commit their crimes in a context of impunity. States are often unwilling to prosecute their own, non-state armed groups are even more of a closed shop; peace agreements regularly protect perpetrators, and the International Criminal

Court does not have universal jurisdiction and has not yet been able to assert its authority effectively even when it does have jurisdiction. Until laws are enforced, and individuals held accountable for their actions, the laws governing the use and conduct of force will have limited influence on armed groups. If actors complied with the laws we already have, however, the world would be a significantly more peaceful place.

Sometimes, when states or other armed groups commit genocide or employ mass killing, the use of force is necessary to protect populations from them. Only by defeating the Nazis in war could the Holocaust be ended; only through Vietnam's invasion was the Khmer Rouge's reign of terror in Cambodia ended; only by the defeat of the Rwandan government and its allies by the Rwandan Patriotic Front was the 1994 genocide ended. Conversely, no amount of non-coercive pressure succeeded in persuading the Syrian government to stop bombing, gassing, and torturing its own population in the 2010s. The UN system creates a pathway, through the UN Security Council, for lawful armed and other forms of intervention to protect populations from such grave violations of their human rights. Ideally, the Council should shoulder its responsibilities and enforce the law, an issue I will come to next. But for now we are left sometimes having to make judgements about whether it is sometimes legitimate to violate the anti-aggression rule in order to protect people from genocide and mass atrocities.

Using force in such circumstances without Security Council authorization would be unlawful and could undermine the legal prohibition of force. But failing to act would imperil civilians (and violate their human rights), breed impunity, and undermine international humanitarian law. To help us navigate the dilemma, we need an approach sensitive to each particular context. Here, we can import another legal principle—mitigation—into our discussion. Mitigation recognizes that there is not a perfect fit between law and morality. Mitigation does not make otherwise unlawful actions lawful, but it does mean that violations of law may be excused given the exceptional circumstances of the case at hand. Sometimes, for example, morality may dictate that laws be broken. Other times, it may be necessary to commit a crime in order to prevent or halt a greater crime. Until all the preliminary articles described here are implemented, we will need to accept that sometimes morality may require states to use force even though doing so would be unlawful.

To avoid undermining the legal prohibition on war, states compelled to act in that way should acknowledge the unlawfulness of their actions but present arguments in mitigation. They must also be placed in the position of not knowing, in advance, how their law-breaking treatment will be regarded by others and thus forced to confront the possibility that their actions will be condemned and punished, for to do otherwise would be to undermine the violated rule. This does create the possibility for a slippery slope in which states and others exploit the loophole for their own ends, undermining the prohibition on the use of force. That is why the exception can never become the rule, and why those who act on it can never be sure they will not face condemnation and punishment. That is also why the possibility for mitigation would end as soon as those institutions vested with responsibility for international peace and security began to fulfil their responsibilities on a consistent basis.

To fully overcome this problem, we must ensure that the laws we have are enforced consistently. If the institutions vested with responsibility for international peace and security, including the protection of populations from genocide and mass atrocities, discharged their responsibility faithfully and consistently, the problem of mitigation would not arise. Hans Morgenthau wrote in 1960 that peace within states was made possible by three conditions— the state's capacity for overwhelming force, national loyalties that superseded other identities, and citizens' reliable expectations of justice.[11] These elements of peace, he argued, were closely connected to one another but there could be no peace without overwhelming power at its centre. Overwhelming power was necessary, he argued, for keeping conflicts between individuals and groups within peaceful limits. World peace would remain illusory, Morgenthau believed, because the international domain lacked such a power. Only a world government could rectify this problem, but this was unattainable. That may be no bad thing. I argued earlier that although world government remains a mainstay of arguments for world peace, grandiose visions for world order have tended to lack legitimacy, arouse opposition, demand the use of violence to instantiate, and ultimately fail.[12] Thankfully, world government may not be needed to ensure world governance. In fact, the UN Security Council has all the authority it needs to maintain the peace and enforce international law. The problem lies in the fact that it is so often incapable or unwilling to do so.

In 1945, the UN Charter conferred on the Council primary responsibility for the maintenance of international peace and security and gave it wide authority to utilize whatever measures it thought were necessary to achieve that goal, including war. But the Charter did not give the Council or its five permanent members (China, France, the UK, the US, and Russia) free rein to use the body however they saw fit to satisfy their own interests. The Charter plainly requires that the Council act in accordance with the UN's purposes and principles (Article 24). These are:

1. Maintaining international peace and security by taking effective collective action to prevent and remove threats to the peace and suppressing acts of aggression or other breaches of the peace;
2. Developing friendly relations between states based on the principles of equal rights and self-determination;
3. Achieving cooperation in solving economic, social, cultural, and humanitarian problems and in promoting and encouraging respect for human rights;
4. Harmonizing the actions of states towards these goals.

Nowhere does the Charter say that the Council should pay more heed to sovereignty than to the pursuit of peace, security, and human rights. Nor does it say that the Council should define its role narrowly to include only interstate war or acts of aggression. Nor does it say that the Council must impose measures only as a last resort—indeed, quite the opposite: the Charter expressly permits use of the full range of measures to *prevent* breaches of the peace.

At its best, the Council has sometimes taken swift action to roll back armed aggression. It has also imposed enormous costs on transgressors and facilitated negotiated transitions from war to peace. It has deployed peacekeepers to oversee peace agreements, protect civilians, support the delivery of humanitarian aid, and support states to recover and rebuild. But its performance remains uneven and selective. International laws are therefore imperfectly enforced.

There are two parts to this problem. The first is that states are often unwilling to commit the material and political resources needed to maintain the peace and achieve the purposes of the UN. The second is that the Security Council is often unable to take measures because it is deadlocked by division and because the Council's permanent members use their power of veto to protect not just their own interests, but also those of their allies.

As a result of vetoes or threatened vetoes, the Council has often failed in the face of major challenges to world peace. Nearly two decades of war in Vietnam did not even make it to the Council's agenda. The Cold War, the Iran–Iraq war, the Soviet invasion of Afghanistan, civil wars in Sudan, Myanmar, and Lebanon, and Khmer Rouge tyranny in Cambodia all failed to elicit any kind of response from the Council. Things improved after the Cold War, but the Council's capacity to fulfil its responsibility remained stymied by the self-interest of its permanent members and their capacity to veto collective action. For example, in the 2010s China and Russia blocked collective action on the Syrian civil war that began in 2011 and collective responses to atrocities in Myanmar and North Korea; the US and its allies did likewise on the Yemen civil war and on Palestine; Russian aggression in Ukraine and US aggression in Iraq went unpunished for the same reason. They all chose to look the other way in 2009 when the Sri Lankan government unleashed hell on Tamil civilians, killing thousands. This selectivity, the price that global governance had to pay to power politics, is a fundamental flaw in the international security architecture. Peace will remain partial and selective until it is addressed and the Council allowed to fulfil the responsibility bestowed upon it by the UN Charter.

The challenge before us, therefore, is not to reinvent the institutional architecture but to make it work better. Amongst other things, that means unshackling the Security Council from the sometimes pernicious self-interest of the five permanent Great Power members that exercise a right of veto over collective decision-making so that it can become a more effective and less partial protector of the peace. For all its many problems in terms of blocking collective action, this system has ensured the continuing cooperation of the Great Powers, allowing the Council to respond to issues when consensus among them has been possible.

We need to find a way of remedying this system's selectivity and inconsistency, whilst preserving its basic integrity. The most obvious and straightforward way of doing that would be for the Security Council's permanent members to voluntarily refrain from using the veto on matters relating to armed aggression or protecting populations from genocide and mass atrocities in situations where a proposed resolution would otherwise pass (i.e. had the required nine affirmative votes). This might be done in the first instance by an agreed statement of principles, then followed incrementally by binding resolution. The purpose would not be to immediately strip permanent members of their legal right to use a veto (which they would not agree to, and would likely have the effect of distancing them from the UN), but to increase the political costs associated with casting a veto to block collective action. With sustained pressure, vetoes could be made so politically expensive that the permanent members would consider employing them only when absolutely necessary, putting the Security Council to better use as an instrument for international peace and security.

It is unlikely that, left to their own devices, the permanent members would voluntarily elect to limit their prerogatives in this fashion. So we must look to how pressure might be brought to bear upon them. The Security Council exercises authority on behalf of the UN membership as a whole. The most representative body in the UN is the General Assembly. The Assembly elects the Council's ten non-permanent members, and is entitled to consider and make recommendations on any matters (including peace and security) and to refer situations to the Security Council. For example, in recent years the Assembly referred the human rights situation to the Council and passed a resolution deploring the Council's failures on Syria. To push the Council to fulfil its responsibilities, and encourage the permanent members to refrain from employing the veto, the Assembly could do a number of things to strengthen accountability: it could demand that Council members explain their positions to the Assembly, it could use its authority to recommend measures when the Council fails to do so, it could refer situations to the Council, and it could revive an obscure resolution—known as 'Uniting for Peace'—to circumvent, or threaten to circumvent, a blocked Council.

Formally referred to as General Assembly Resolution 377, 'Uniting for Peace' was passed at the start of the Korean crisis in 1950, when a Soviet veto threatened to block a collective response to North Korean aggression. It states that should the Council fail to adopt measures in response to a breach of the peace, the General Assembly could step in and—with a two-thirds majority—recommend measures including the use of force to states. It is not hard to see how the Assembly might use 'Uniting for Peace' to encourage the permanent members to restrain their use of the veto. It could, for example, signal its intent to use the resolution in future and in specific cases indicate its preferred measures to the Council. And it could, of course, employ the mechanism. Fear of being sidelined would undoubtedly encourage the permanent members to rethink their positions. The precise mechanics of how to restrain the veto is a matter for further research and debate. The key, for world peace, is that the veto is restrained. This is not an idle hope. More than 120 states have already demanded it.

2. Each state shall contribute its fair share to the full and prompt implementation of decisions taken by the United Nations and other international institutions.

States should provide their fair share of support for the full and prompt implementation of the decisions taken by the institutions that they have consented to join. Primarily, I have in mind—and will focus on—decisions taken by the various organs of the United Nations, but this article also applies to regional organizations, international trade bodies, and other institutions of global governance. This is a broad-ranging recommendation and yet quite narrow since it requires nothing more than ensuring that governments actually do those things they have committed to do, or are obligated to do by law.

Two aspects of this article warrant particular emphasis: the implementation of decisions relating specifically to international peace and security (including conflict prevention, peace enforcement and peacekeeping operations, peace-building, action against chemical weapons, anti- and counter-proliferation, state-building, human protection, humanitarian relief, women, peace, and security, transitional justice, countering terrorism, and violent extremism) and the provision of support to collectively agreed endeavours or obligations that impact upon world peace (for example, human rights decisions taken by the UN Human Rights Council and recommendations under the UN's 'Universal Periodic Review' process, economic development, and national capacity-building).

In relation to the first, there is a significant body of evidence showing that concerted collective action helps to prevent wars, shorten wars, limit civilian casualties, and reduce the likelihood of recurrence.[13] Yet it is equally clear that the international community falls well short of providing the UN or other organizations with the resources they need to fully implement agreed policies, mandates, and laws. No matter which of the long list of relevant policy areas we look at, a significant gap exists between the agreed objectives and the resources committed to achieving them.

To take just one example, most, if not all, UN peacekeeping operations lack the capabilities needed to fulfil their mandates. There is a mountain of research confirming that this is a significant and persistent problem, intimately connected to peace-building's patchy track record. But we can grasp the scale of the problem by applying two simple rules of thumb commonly used to calculate the necessary force size for complex military operations.[14] The first assumes that 2–10 troops are required for every 1,000 inhabitants within an area of deployment. The second method is based on the idea that the intervention force be at least the size of the largest indigenous armed force. By these rules of thumb, all the UN's missions seem to be under-staffed, some of them massively so.

The UN's mission in South Sudan (UNMISS), for example, should have either between 16,000 and 80,000 troops (ranging from the bare minimum needed to hold things together, to the capacity needed to implement the mandate) or (by rule two) more than 40,000. In 2018, UNMISS had 13,000 troops—well below even the minimum threshold. The scales were even more skewed in the Democratic Republic of Congo. In a country the size of Western Europe, rule one would demand a force of somewhere between 30,000 and 150,000, depending on how much of the country was deemed to be conflict affected, whilst rule two would require a force of at least 50,000. In early 2018, the UN's mission in the Congo (MONUSCO) had just 15,000 troops. The UN fares somewhat better in southern Lebanon, where operations attract more Great Power interest, but appearances may be deceptive since they depend on population estimates which are difficult to verify. By rule one, the UN forces (UNIFIL) should have between 2,400 and 12,000 troops, and by rule two more than 25,000 troops. The UN mission there actually has 10,000 troops; well stocked by UN standards, but still less than half the deployable forces available to the Hezbollah force it is meant to be helping disarm.

Shortfalls in the resources committed to supporting peace can be seen across the board. The situation has deteriorated in the wake of the 2009 global financial crisis. Austerity measures have resulted in shrinking aid and international development budgets. The UN has also made cuts to its budget. Since 2014, each annual budget has been around 1 per cent smaller than the previous year's, despite growing demands and rising costs.[15] Budget cuts impact on programmes and activities that support the implementation of collective decisions and agreed laws. For instance, diplomacy and mediation at the UN are chronically underfunded, with 20 per cent of the UN's Department of Political Affairs' budget, including all of its Mediation Support Unit's funds, acquired through voluntary contributions. Humanitarian action and the growing crisis of displacement are two other areas where global action falls far short of needs and obligations. In 2016, only 25 per cent of the Humanitarian Response Plan presented by the UN was funded. In monetary terms, this amounted to just $5.5 billion out of $21.6 billion of the identified financial requirements.[16] Meanwhile, global displacement levels reached 65.3 million in 2015, which is the highest they have been since the Second World War. Of this number, only 107,100 were resettled in 2015.[17]

Even when it has the mandates, agreements, and laws necessary to support world peace, the international community still falls well short more often than not—for the simple reason that states do not do enough to implement their decisions or fulfil their obligations. Doing more to ensure that all states contribute their fair share to the collective quest for peace is therefore imperative.

It bears mentioning that states already have a legal obligation to 'accept and carry out the decisions of the Security Council' thanks to Article 25 of the UN Charter. But although the Council enjoys far-reaching authority, the effectiveness of its resolutions depends to a great extent on its capacity to *persuade* states to implement and sometimes enforce its resolutions. As the editors of Oxford's handbook on *The United Nations Security Council and War* noted, because it 'does not in practice command the automatic obedience of states', the Council must persuade others to implement its decisions.[18] The Council has few material resources under its command and therefore relies almost entirely on the goodwill of states to provide the (sometimes extensive) resources required to implement its decisions. What is needed is a full and proper accounting of the responsibilities that ought to fall upon states as a result not only of their Article 25 responsibilities (albeit these being the most clearly articulated), but also the full range of responsibilities they have undertaken. This includes responsibilities to support peace-building, transitional justice, and human protection. States need to hold one another to account, and publics and parliaments ought to act too.

Global governance extends well beyond the management of armed conflict and this is the second area where more needs to be done to ensure that international commitments that support peace are translated into action. The United Nations alone has mandates covering human rights, supporting states to build the capacities they need for sustainable peace, and through its Sustainable Development Goals for marshalling international cooperation to eradicate poverty, build core services such as primary education and healthcare, and even to reduce all forms of injustice and violence. None of these are goals idly dreamed up by academics. All are political commitments made by the world's governments that, if fulfilled, would make a significant difference to world peace. We know that concerted, well-resourced, and carefully thought through efforts to implement peace agreements, build sustainable peace, and support state capacity can deliver good effects. All other things being equal, countries that receive support tend to do better than those that do not. Sustained and well-targeted development assistance can help states and societies achieve significant progress in alleviating poverty and establishing public goods. Among other things, economic advances and improvements in state capacity and the rule of law significantly reduce the likelihood of civil war. In theory at least, peace-building, state-building, and economic development help states establish the basic building blocks of domestic peace: a monopoly of legitimate force, accountability, respect for basic rights, and secure livelihoods.

It stands to reason that if legitimate and effective states are among the building blocks of world peace, the community of states as a whole should support one another to become legitimate and effective. That means supporting capacity-building and the rule of law, the promotion and protection of human rights, and economic development, among other things. Sometimes, states are reluctant to commit the necessary resources to help others, or are driven by political or ideological reasons to privilege particular approaches that might not be well suited. For these and other reasons, despite their overall utility, collective action on state capacity, human rights, and development have a patchy track record. Doing more to support other states to forge peace after war, improve their capacity to deliver basic services, and achieve secure livelihoods for their populations would help reinforce the foundation of world peace—the stable and legitimate state.

3. No state or private corporation shall transfer armaments to state or non-state actors who may be reasonably expected to use them in violation of international law.

Armaments do not cause wars, but they do facilitate them. The simple fact is that actors with insufficient arms are less likely to begin or sustain wars than those with a surplus of arms. Not for nothing did the victorious powers impose severe arms restrictions on post-Napoleonic France, post-Wilhelm and Nazi Germany, and post-imperial Japan. There are few better ways of curtailing a state's expansive ambitions or of inhibiting a non-state group from taking up arms than by curtailing their access to weaponry. Had the First World War Allies acted more resolutely against the first signs of German rearmament in the 1930s, the course of history might have been very different.

The same is true for civil wars. Access to arms is one of the factors distinguishing a peaceful revolt from a civil war. All other things being equal, access to arms also helps explain the duration and lethality of civil wars. The capacity of non-state armed groups to sustain the fight is shaped to a great extent by their access to arms. This may relate to their capacity to translate the resources they have access to into weapons or it may mean their capacity to secure the allegiance of foreign states willing to keep open the supply of arms.[19] Whatever it may be, the willingness of outsiders to sell or supply arms to non-state armed groups has a critical impact on their capacity to wage war. Non-state groups starved of such support seldom survive for long, and feel the need to negotiate earlier.

International law prohibits the transfer of arms to non-state armed groups. As a result, much of it occurs through 'grey' channels. Occasionally, dealers in illicit armaments are apprehended but this is the exception, not the rule. The practice continues in large part because it is often convenient to powerful states to maintain it and highly lucrative for individuals to pursue it. For example, contemporary conflicts in the Middle East were fuelled by an inflow of arms from states such as the US, Russia, Qatar, Saudi Arabia, Iran, and Turkey, private actors based in Kuwait, and non-state armed groups such as Hezbollah. To stem the tide of war, much more needs to be done to curtail these illicit flows of arms.

But this is only part of the problem, because in most cases the first transfer of arms from the manufacturer is perfectly legal—going to a state. Until recently there have been few restrictions on the state's right to purchase arms and few, if any, checks on what happens to those arms once delivered. Thus, not only did states intent on waging armed aggression or launching genocide have a perfect right to buy the means with which to commit these crimes, there was also very little to stop them transferring weapons to third parties. Such states often manufacture arms themselves and so we need to recognize that efforts to address the trade in arms will do little to address that particular problem.

The need to regulate the manufacture and flow of arms is a longstanding concern of peace movements. Its importance was recognized in the UN Charter. Article 26 required that the Security Council develop plans 'for the establishment of a system for the regulation of armaments' to ensure 'the least diversion for armaments of the world's human and economic resources'. That idea came to naught, but in the twilight years of the Cold War, states did begin to negotiate and accept mutually agreed limitations on certain types of armaments. But 'arms control', as these agreements were called, was as much a reflection of the accumulation of surplus military capacity as a reflection of genuine commitment to reducing the threats posed by armaments. It also paid little heed to the *purposes* for which arms were acquired. Manufacturers were still entitled to supply states with arms, even if they had grounds for believing they would be used in aggressive wars or campaigns of terror. That is the challenge: to find a way of ending the supply of arms to those who would use them to breach the peace.

There has been progress, albeit tentative, towards this goal. In December 2014, the Arms Trade Treaty (ATT) came into force. The ATT recognizes that states have a right to purchase arms for their self-defence and to contribute to collective security. But, for the first time, it imposed restraints on both the purchase and transfer of arms. State parties are required to establish their own national system to control the flow of arms. They must ensure that arms are not transferred to another actor if doing so would violate a Security Council resolution (especially an arms embargo) or any other international convention or treaty obligation (such as in relation to illicit trafficking), or if the weapons might be used to commit genocide, crimes against humanity, war crimes, or any other violation of the 1949 Geneva Conventions. The treaty also requires that states consider the following when deciding whether to allow transfers: whether the transfer would undermine international peace and security, whether it could facilitate violations of international humanitarian and human rights law, whether it would violate obligations to counter terrorism, and whether it would contribute to the commission of sexual and gender-based violence and violations against children. In each case, state parties are required to assess the risks associated with the transfer and are legally obliged to not permit the transfer should a risk be identified. They are also required to take the necessary steps to enforce their decisions.

There is one glaring substantive and a host of procedural gaps in the ATT, which reflect its negotiating history and the need to make tradeoffs to secure consensus. The substantive gap, one that needs to be urgently filled, is exclusion of armed aggression from the list of risks which should inhibit the supply of arms. World peace demands that arms not be supplied to those who would use them to wage aggressive war. Of the procedural gaps, three stand out. First, sixty-three states are still not a party to the ATT. That needs to change. Second, enforcement of the treaty is left entirely to states themselves and there is no external oversight. Third, there are no criminal penalties for violating the ATT by transferring arms or by deliberately or negligently approving transfers that ought not to be approved. These three concerns need to be addressed if we are to move towards a situation where arms are not transferred to those who would use them to breach the peace. The ATT was a significant if tentative first step that shows that advances in the control of arms are possible in the here and now, even if there remains a long way to go.

4. States shall establish and sustain security communities with their neighbours.

Some groups of states can, and do, overcome—or at least manage—the underlying sustainers of war (humanity's division into groups, war's productivity, and war's contagion) by establishing regional communities in which war becomes unthinkable. These are 'security communities' and they have proven highly effective. Having more of them, and making them deeper and more institutionalized, will help make the world more peaceful. Building peace from the ground up means that governments should contribute to peace in their own neighbourhoods by consciously striving to establish security communities.

Both the concept and the practice of the security community can be traced to the early years of the Cold War. A security community is a group of states 'in which there is a real assurance that the members of that community will not fight each other physically, but will settle their disputes in some other way'. The concept was first articulated by the US-based Czech political scientist Karl Deutsch in 1957.[20] Deutsch and his collaborators identified two types of security community, which they described as 'amalgamated' and 'pluralistic'. 'Amalgamated' security communities were created by the 'formal merger of two or more previously independent units into a single larger unit'. This is rare, but there are examples including the ill-fated union between Egypt and Syria and the much more successful unions of colonial states in the US and Australia. 'Pluralistic' security communities are much more common. Indeed, they are surprisingly common and—given the limited attention they receive—surprisingly effective as builders of peace. In this type of security community, the individual members retain their legal independence but take conscious steps to create a sense of community between them that over time creates reliable expectations that their political disputes will be resolved non-violently.[21] Not only do members of a security community not actually wage war against one another, they do not fear war between them either.

How is this achieved? At the most basic level, members of security communities agree not just to stop fighting wars against other, or supporting others who fight wars against other members. They also have to stop *preparing* to wage war on each other. This is how the perpetual fear of war is converted, over time, into a reliable expectation of peace. Beyond that, Deutsch insisted that communities required some form of institutionalization to promote cooperation, coordination, and trust-building, and to provide a trusted means of resolving disputes. The precise degree of institutionalization can vary, though, from a very loose accommodation (such as ASEAN in Southeast Asia which is a community only modestly institutionalized) to highly developed sets of institutions and integration (such as the EU today). Beyond institutions, however, security communities are bound together by compatible core values, shared languages and institutions, and a degree of shared identity.

Security communities offer us a way of rethinking how we get from global war to world peace without the need for giant leaps of imagination and practice. Historical experience provides compelling evidence that it works.

Conceptually, security communities offer a viable way of thinking about 'community' beyond national boundaries within the international space. Communities arise out of interaction and cooperation—precisely the things required to establish reliable expectations that disputes will be resolved peacefully. To establish a security community, states first have to demonstrate goodwill by consistently refraining from even the preparation for war with each other over a period of time. Within a security community, *si vi pacem, para bellum* becomes *si vi pacem, para pacem*. Members have to not just end practising or preparing for war, they also have to *say* that this is what they are doing; that is, they have to consistently and truthfully communicate their peaceful intent.

Over time, consistent peaceful action combined with expressions of peaceful intent build the trust needed to establish a community. It does so by rigging the game. Literally. 'Prisoner's dilemma' is a game used by theorists to explore how self-interest and limited information determines the limits of cooperation. There are two players, X and Y. Each is a prisoner presented with two options: keep silent or betray the other. The players are not allowed to communicate. If they betray each other each will serve five years in jail. If neither betrays the other, both go free. But if X betrays Y, whilst Y stays silent, X will be set free and Y will serve ten years. Although the optimal solution is achieved by both remaining silent, the fear of betrayal by the other will push them both to betray the other, providing a sub-optimal outcome for both. This is usually how things transpire when you play the game once. It shows how fear and uncertainty tend to produce outcomes that do not suit anyone.

When they join a security community, X and Y cheat the game. First, they communicate with one another. They can tell each other that they intend not to betray the other. This significantly increases the likelihood of cooperation. But more than that, they don't talk—or play—only once. They talk and play over and over again. As they do, they learn to trust one another. Eventually, betrayal becomes not just unlikely, but unthinkable. And just as X and Y learn how to act in order to optimize their outcome in the 'prisoner's dilemma' game, so security communities help states learn how to act in the real world.

In 'nascent' security communities, states begin to consider coordinating their activities to increase mutual security, reduce transaction costs, and create the potential for further interaction in the future. Sometimes, Deutsch argued, this might occur if community members are threatened by a common enemy. In Southeast Asia, the ASEAN security community was propelled into being by a common fear of communist expansion. 'Ascendant' security communities display 'increasingly dense networks; new institutions and organizations that reflect either tighter military coordination and cooperation and/or decreased fear that the other represents a threat'. There is a deepening of trust and as inter-action increases, new collective identities are created. Building institutions further increases social interaction, accelerating the creation of shared identities and mutual interests. This can lead to the formation of a 'mature' security community. 'At this point', Emmanuel Adler and Michael Barnett explain, 'regional actors share an identity and, therefore, entertain dependable expectations of peaceful change'.[22] When a security community matures, peaceful interaction, mutual aid, and cooperation become habitual; war unthinkable.

Security communities are more than simply memberships of regional organizations. They are patterns of relationship, often supported by institutions. Greece and Turkey, for example, are members of NATO but do prepare for war with each other. That is because Turkey is not part of Western Europe's security community. Similarly, non-membership of an institution does not necessarily preclude membership of the community. During the Cold War, Austria was a member neither of NATO nor the EU, yet it was part of the Western European security community as it developed.

Security communities are not just nice concepts. They have proliferated since the 1950s, almost uniformly bringing greater peacefulness. The most obvious example is the already mentioned case of Western Europe. The most deeply integrated and institutionalized political union of independent states, the European project began as a self-conscious effort to rethink international relations and make them more peaceful. It proved spectacularly successful. In Southeast Asia, security cooperation fostered around ASEAN deepened into a regional security community that helped eliminate interstate war. It remains the case that no two ASEAN members have fought a war with one another, although border disputes and other fissures remain. In North America, the US, Canada, and Mexico have established peaceful relations. There are signs of an emergent security community in South America too as cooperation between governments grows. And in the fractious Persian Gulf, the countries of the Gulf Cooperation Council may not have progressed far in establishing a security community—and may well have gone backwards in the past decade—but they have taken some steps in this direction. In Central Asia, West Africa, and perhaps southern Africa, there are also signs of emergent security communities. And everywhere where conscious steps are taken by states to build security communities, regions experience greater peace.

But, as I mentioned briefly in Chapter 7, the benefits of security communities extend beyond the particular region in which they are established. There is clear evidence that as a security community develops and matures, the peaceful habits it fosters—and the rules and institutions they give rise to—tend to spread beyond the community's border. Indeed, the very notion of a boundary becomes blurry as identities and institutional arrangements multiply.

There are two main reasons why that happens.[23] The first is ideational pull. Because they are effective at reinforcing peace and cooperation, the community's habits and ways of doing business become attractive to outsiders. For example, multilateral dialogue and cooperation across the wider East Asian region is now prefaced on the rules and practices of the 'ASEAN way'. That was partly because those rules proved so effective in helping a region once ravaged by war move towards much greater peacefulness. And, as a result, the ASEAN peace has spread to the wider region.

The second reason is institutional enmeshment. Remember, security communities are defined not by institutional membership but by something more amorphous—trusting relationships. In fact, as security communities mature, they tend to give rise to more and more institutional frameworks. Some of these extend beyond the community's core membership and thus entangle non-members in some of the rules and relationships of the community itself. For example, in East Asia, ASEAN sits at the heart of a web of institutional arrangements, including the ASEAN Regional Forum, the East Asia Summit, and the ASEAN Plus Three initiatives, that extend beyond the Southeast Asian security community into the wider region. Thus, the stuff that binds the security community together is transmitted to non-members and the boundaries between members and non-members become blurry. As that happens, the community's pacifying effects are diffused. These effects seem to become stronger as security communities mature.

Security communities are thus an important part of the campaign for world peace not just because they bring greater peacefulness to their own regions (which they do, and which in itself is significant), but also because they provide a transmission belt through which the peaceful habits learned in our own backyards can be gradually spread. They therefore provide an important bridge between the local and national (on which more later) and the global.

5. Individuals should enjoy a universal right of hospitality. No state shall inhibit the free and fair movement of goods, services, people, and ideas between them.

To resist the emotional sentiments that lead societies to war, we need to nurture the plurality of our identities.[24] Those identities relate to our membership of different sorts of groups within civil society. Kant and Bentham both recognized that the improvement of international relations would come about through 'civilized public opinion'. That is, governments would act to institute world peace only once civil society demanded and facilitated it. Bentham thought that the business sector alone could be the driving force of change, whereas Kant always understood peace as a primarily political project.[25] What both were clear on, however, was that civil society has a particular property that was imperative for world peace: it is *transnational*. Civil society connects individuals and groups in lots of different ways that reach beyond national boundaries. As such, it provides the vehicle for the pluralization of identity that is so crucial to the project of peace. But it is precisely transnational characteristics that state regulation and nationalist ideology look to close down. It is imperative therefore that the physical transmission belts of interaction that facilitate the pluralization of identity are kept open. That means ensuring that people, goods, and ideas are allowed to travel freely across borders.

Peace has always been internationalist, if not cosmopolitan, in identity and outlook. Kant included among his definitive articles for *Perpetual Peace* one which called on governments to recognize a principle of universal hospitality—understood as an individual's right to enter the territory of another state and engage in conversation with the inhabitants. By this, Kant simply meant that people should have a right to travel and stay in other countries. The principle of hospitality is what makes all the other connections between groups, so fundamental to the pluralization of our identities and thus to world peace itself, possible. Hospitality facilitates interaction and exchange. It creates the very possibility of groups whose membership extends beyond national or ethnic or religious boundaries. It provides the basis for peaceful relations and mutual cooperation between distant peoples.

Exchange is important not just for the immediate goods it delivers, but also for the longer-term relationships it fosters and the habits it promotes. For instance, movement across borders allows the emergence of domestic coalitions of entrepreneurs, government officials, civil society activists, ordinary citizens, and others (often supported by the international networks they create) that adopt internationalist identities and mindsets. These networks, which might be professional or values-based or focused on specific issues of shared concern (e.g. climate change), challenge the insider–outsider logic of nationalism that can drive differences between groups and establish domestic constituencies that support international cooperation. These internationalist coalitions constrain governments and embed internationalist ideals within domestic political contexts. Most obviously, they encourage outward-looking postures and policies, trade and engagement, and increased foreign investment, and they tend to oppose militarism, particularism, and stances that close off opportunities for collaboration. They also encourage governments to adopt internationalist perspectives in foreign policy, pushing them to commit support to multilateral efforts to support peace. In practice, internationalist-minded coalitions often find themselves confronted by nationalist coalitions at home, but they have the added advantage of being able to connect with the like-minded in other countries, forging transnational networks. The proliferation of civil society networks, and the flows across borders they create, help to build trust between communities. It also establishes and reinforces community bonds that extend across the national or ethnic—bonds of class, gender, profession, interest, and belief that are transnational. It strengthens the pluralization of identity and constrains homogenization. So, when states run into disputes with one another, there will be constituencies on either side promoting mutual understanding and a shared interest in stability.[26] Bonds that cut across dominant identity groups soften the boundaries between them and challenge the insider–outsider dynamics that fuel the passions of war.

Hospitality can also drive material changes conducive to peace. From these bonds spring trade, a bedrock of world peace. 'I defy you to agitate any fellow with a full stomach', William Cobbett (1763–1835), one of the great English reformers, is reported to have complained. He had a point. Economics and war are connected in innumerable ways. As GDP per capita increases, the risk of civil war decreases significantly; communities with more profound horizontal inequalities are at greater risk than those with less profound inequalities; societies with pronounced income inequality are more susceptible to revolutionary violence than those that are more equal; states that trade together tend not to fight wars with one another; societies that have stable economies are less war-prone than those that have endured economic shocks. Indeed, so pronounced is the relationship between economics and war that contemporary thinking suggests that the decline of war in the past few decades is not so much the result of a democratic peace as of a capitalist peace. Hospitality feeds trade. Free and fair trade builds connections and improves livelihoods. It also further strengthens transnational groups and shared identities. These societies become less prone to war. (Of course, trade that is exploitative creates more grounds for war than peace, which is why trade should be both free *and* fair.)

There are multiple ways in which wealth and war are connected. Trade patterns matter, for instance, since free and fair trade builds mutual interdependence between states, which in turn increases the costs and reduces the payoffs of war. Economic modernization increases the economic value of individuals, making humans a more expensive asset to lose than they once were. Trade helps drive this effect. Governments focused on improving the economic wellbeing of their populations are forced to divert resources from the military to the civilian sector. This imposes restraints on behaviour since states have to be stable and predictable to attract inwards investment, have to foster trade and travel across borders, and have to practise fiscal discipline. Trading states tend to be smaller than communist, fascist, or other authoritarian states, and need to raise additional capital to fund wars, making it more difficult for them to support war than it is for other types of state.[27]

Whilst proponents of these different explanations jostle over which is most persuasive, the reality is that all have some effect, though to differing degrees in different times and places. Trade and peace are mutually dependent on one another. Both rely on relations of reciprocity between individuals, groups, and governments. But for trade to prosper, behaviours need to be conditioned. The behaviours that support trade also support peace. Stability is needed to guarantee the safe and timely passage of physical goods, to create confidence in contracts and currencies. Partners must have confidence in one another over the long-term. Reciprocity and trust are vital here—trade requires buyers, sellers, and a marketplace that both have confidence in. It requires rules, mutually satisfying taxation and tariff regimes, and a system of arbitration and conflict resolution that commands mutual respect. For trade to flourish, the parties must conceive their relationship as a positive-sum game—a relationship from which they both benefit.

All this stems from the mutual recognition of hospitality. Hospitality encourages flows between groups, including trade which in turn helps drive improvements to the economic wellbeing of people and relations between different groups. Not only should states respect a general principle of hospitality; governments, corporations, and other economic actors should refrain from inhibiting free and fair trade and from actions that could undermine the economic wellbeing of others.

6. Individuals should be held criminally accountable for acts of genocide, war crimes, crimes against humanity, and aggression.

One of the principal reasons why states and other armed groups so regularly flout the international laws governing war is that, more often than not, violations are treated with impunity. Only a small fraction of the leaders, commanders, and soldiers that commit crimes of aggression or atrocity crimes ever face justice. So the prospect of future prosecution rarely enters their calculation. Not until political leaders, military commanders, and individual soldiers—both state and non-state—face the consistent and real possibility of criminal prosecution for aggressive war and atrocity crimes will the full potential of the law be realized.

This ambition is far from being a utopian pipe dream, though it will be monumentally difficult to achieve. We already have an international court (the International Criminal Court) and legal charter (the Rome Statute) empowered to investigate allegations concerning genocide, war crimes, and crimes against humanity levelled against any of its more than 120 state parties or any other party (state or non-state) referred to it by the Security Council, and bring forward prosecutions. Yet the court faces serious challenges from those concerned about its judicial reach and the risk that it may one day prosecute them, or their friends. One challenge, therefore, is to strengthen support for the Court, to extend its reach so that it may become a universal and permanent court, and to ensure that it receives the material and political support it needs.

Another route is through the application of universal jurisdiction. Genocide, war crimes, and crimes against humanity are just that—crimes that offend against all of humanity. It stands to reason that states should prosecute individuals under their jurisdiction for committing these crimes, no matter where in the world the crimes themselves were committed. Some states, including Spain, Belgium, and Germany, have already introduced the principle of universal jurisdiction for atrocity crimes into national legislation. Germany, for example, indicted more than fifty individuals found on its territory for crimes committed in Syria. In the famous Pinochet case, in the late 1990s, the British House of Lords ruled that certain crimes were so grave as to warrant universal jurisdiction and that sovereign immunity constituted no defence. Pinochet, Chile's President between 1973 and 1990, eventually escaped prosecution, but on health grounds, not legal grounds. More states should extend the principle of universal jurisdiction for atrocity crimes, to improve the chances of individual legal accountability.

But what of the crime of aggression? That too is closer to hand than we might think. The idea that armed aggression may constitute an international 'crime against peace' was advanced by the British and French governments after the First World War. It featured among the crimes for which Nazis were prosecuted at Nuremberg after the Second World War.[28] In the 1990s, states agreed that the 'crime of aggression' should sit alongside crimes against humanity and war crimes in the Rome Statute. But they could not agree on what 'aggression' was.

Activists continued to push, however, and in 2010 parties to the Rome Statute finally agreed to extend the Court's jurisdiction. As noted earlier, the 2010 Kampala agreement defined the crime of aggression as any act of force which constitutes by its 'character, gravity, and scale' a grave violation of the UN Charter. What we need now is for states to accept this extension. Then, it will be for the Court and its state parties to begin enforcing the law against armed aggression.

Political and military leaders that confront a realistic chance of prosecution should they launch aggressive wars or permit their forces to commit atrocity crimes are leaders much less likely to choose these paths. This is precisely why many still refuse to accept the International Criminal Court's jurisdiction. But the less powerful can play an important role by changing the moral ground and making it more difficult for the recalcitrant to stand against the international rule of law. If not 123 but 180 states were parties to the International Criminal Court, and if all of those states faithfully discharged their legal responsibilities, over time the Great Powers would find it more difficult, both politically and materially, to shun the law. That may seem a long way off (and it may well be), but for the first time in history we have both the laws and the institutions necessary to make the outlawing of aggressive war and atrocity crimes and the principle of individual criminal accountability a reality.

The six preliminary articles take features of world politics as we have it and show how they can be extended to make the world more peaceful. In the most part, these articles rely on governments doing what they have already committed themselves to do: obeying and enforcing international law, acting in good faith to fulfil legal responsibilities, doing their fair share to uphold collective responsibilities, and respecting basic civil and political rights. Only three go beyond what all states have already agreed to do—the idea of individual criminal accountability for aggressive war, the idea that permanent members of the UN Security Council should show restraint in exercising their right to veto, and the prohibition of arms sales to those who would use it for aggression—yet each of these has found support among dozens of states (more than thirty have already accepted the crime of aggression; more than 110 support veto restraint). It is not a great leap from the world we have today to the world envisaged by these six articles.

Yet that would be a world where war was greatly diminished. In this world, where the six preliminary articles are fulfilled, weak states would receive the support they need to build institutions, deliver services, and improve the livelihoods of their populations—reinforcing the basic building blocks of peace and the sovereign state, and putting downwards pressure on civil war. By criminalizing aggressive war and enforcing the law more consistently, making arms more difficult to acquire, building security communities, increasing the prospect of individual legal accountability for crimes of aggression and atrocity, and heightening the opportunity costs of lost trade, war would become even more expensive, and peace still more profitable. The heightened prospect of collective action to support the peace would weaken war's contagiousness. Stronger flows of goods, people, and ideas across borders would pluralize identities and build resistance to some of the emotional forces that give rise to war.

These measures would, therefore, reduce the incidence of war. They may even achieve a fleeting world peace. But they would not, by themselves, establish a sustainable long-term peace because, even with the best of help from outside, societies might still fragment into civil war, and even with the burdens of rationality and passion against them, leaders might still decide to embark on what they hoped would be productive wars of aggression. Over the long-term, as Kant himself recognized, sustainable peace can be achieved only if the basic building blocks of our societies are reorganized to better support it. The definitive articles offer some guidance as to how this might be done.

1. Each state shall be a capable, responsible, and legitimate sovereign.

The basic building block of world peace is the state. But with the state comes a terrible paradox: that the arrangements we make to sustain peace at home (the state) create the possibility of war abroad. As Kant understood better than most, unless changes are made to the way we organize ourselves—to the fundamental nature of states—no amount of legal, economic, or institutional tinkering at the global level will deliver world peace. Tinkering might make the world more peaceful—and that is the purpose of my preliminary articles—but sustained world peace is impossible without fundamental reform to the state itself.

It is not any kind of state that can lay the foundations for world peace. Legitimate and capable states are unlikely to implode into civil war and are less likely than other types to engage in aggressive war. Kant was on the right lines when he argued that states with republican constitutions were needed, but today we know more about the characteristics that make states more, and less, peaceful. Peaceful states are built on more than just a republican constitution. States that are least prone to war have several characteristics.

First, they hold a monopoly of legitimate violence. That is, they have the physical capacity to enforce the law across their entire territory and, thanks to their legitimacy, do not confront armed challengers from within.

Second, they are accountable to their people. Accountability ties a state to the people it governs and prevents it from acting rashly or in ways that benefit only particular sectors of society. Decisions to wage war and about how to conduct war must be subjected to public debate and scrutiny. Democracy is the most obvious way in which accountability is achieved, and ideally decision-making about war should be overseen by parliaments, but this is not the only available model. Accountability demands not just that the political system create and protect the free flow of information between state and society, and possibility for the legal and political scrutiny of government action, it also places a burden of responsibility upon individuals, journalists, and other groups in civil society. They must take positive steps to ensure that decisions are scrutinized, evaluated, and debated.

Third, they protect the fundamental human rights of their populations, including individual rights to life, liberty, citizenship, and rights to non-discrimination on the grounds of race, religion, ethnicity, gender, disability, and political affiliation, among others.

Fourth, they ensure that their populations have secure livelihoods and fair access to public goods. Legitimate and capable states prioritize the living conditions of their populations above all else.

A fifth element discussed in Chapter 5, gender equality, is so significant and far-reaching that it warrants its own definitive article.

States that achieve these conditions—and I have drawn them broadly and quite vaguely to emphasize that there is no single pathway by which to achieve them; each state and society must craft its own approach, taking account of its own history, culture, and context—tend to be more peaceful than those that do not. They are unlikely to succumb to civil war because they respond to the conflicts and grievances that give rise to such conflicts (usually rooted in human rights problems, entrenched discrimination, or economic inequalities) as a matter of routine business. Individuals and groups are protected, they have decent livelihoods, they can access legitimate and transparent legal processes for resolving differences, they can express themselves, and they can play an active part in national decision-making. Combined with the reforms proposed in the preliminary articles, such states are also less likely than others to engage in aggressive foreign wars for conquest or enrichment. Accountability and the rule of law inhibit rash decision-making and the requirement of secure livelihoods would inhibit actions that would harm the national economy.

The actors primarily responsible for achieving these goals reside within each country. The principal role for external actors—such as the UN, regional organizations, development agencies, and foreign governments, or international civil society groups—lies in helping support locally and nationally driven activism. Typically, when thinking about national reforms and economic development, we have tended to assume that outsiders know what is best. But as decades of inefficient aid programmes attest, they often do not. Change starts with national institutions, groups, and individuals. The role of outsiders is to support and nurture them, keeping in mind the five broad goals (including gender equality), and to commit sufficient resources to help states and societies achieve them—a requirement of the third preliminary article.

2. Each state and society should promote and protect gender equality.

Greater levels of gender equality support greater levels of peace. If we can make progress towards gender equality, we necessarily make progress towards peace.[29] That we should be striving towards gender equality as a good in its own right is beyond doubt. In fact, the world's governments unanimously committed themselves, in unambiguous terms, to 'achieve gender equality and empower women and girls' by 2030 as part of the Sustainable Development Goals. More specifically, they promised to achieve nine things, each of which would help make the world more peaceful. They are: (1) end all forms of discrimination against women and girls everywhere; (2) eliminate all forms of violence against women and girls; (3) eliminate all harmful practices, such as child and forced marriage and female genital mutilation; (4) recognize the unpaid work undertaken by women and girls; (5) ensure women's full participation and equal opportunities for leadership in all levels of decision-making; (6) ensure full and equal access to sexual and reproductive health and reproductive rights; (7) ensure equal access to economic resources; (8) enhance the use of enabling technologies; and (9) strengthen national legislation to enforce gender equality.

Every government has made a commitment to strive to achieve all of these things, and will be held accountable through public reporting of their performance. Each government must work with its own civil society to understand the challenges they confront that might prevent them achieving these goals and to develop pathways to move beyond them. They must also dedicate the political support and resources needed. If they find that resources are stretched, most could redirect funds from their military to support the advancement of gender equality. They should also seek the help of others. Those with the capacity to help, meanwhile, have an obligation to do so. All governments have a responsibility to assist one another to achieve these goals through the investment of resources, sharing of expertise, and offering of encouragement.

Achieving these goals will be complex and difficult. Each country will have to develop its own suite of policies and pathways to address each of the nine priority areas. Five cross-cutting priorities seem particularly significant, however. The first is simply to acknowledge that we are not yet close to parity when it comes to recognizing the basic human rights of women and girls. Many states still fail to recognize basic equality or grant women and girls the same rights that are afforded to men and boys. This is human rights' greatest piece of unfinished business. The second is to prioritize the prevention of all forms of violence against women and girls. All forms of violence must be prohibited by law (nearly fifty states still have no laws against domestic violence; a far greater number do not rigorously enforce those laws), and those laws rigorously enforced. This means, among other things, confronting cultural, religious, and legal systems that discriminate on the basis of gender when it comes to marriage, land, housing, clothing, and much else. The third is to achieve equality in participation in decision-making. That involves everything from equal opportunities to achieve the highest political positions to parity of representation in national parliaments, to equality in leadership in community organizations and workplaces. The fourth is equality in educational opportunities. Access to education at every level, from primary to postgraduate, is one of the keys to making progress on every other front. The fifth is economic equality. Economics is one of the major barriers to equality. Achieving equality in pay and conditions, properly valuing the work that women are disproportionately encumbered with, and recognizing unpaid work are key here.

No society has yet achieved gender equality, though some Scandinavian societies have got quite close, but it is a commitment that all governments have made and something to which significant energy and resource should be dedicated. Gender equality is a good in itself, but it is also one of the foundations of world peace.

3. No government should inhibit the capacity of individuals to opt out of war. The free reporting of war and all its effects, open debate and dissent, and the right to refuse military service should be protected.

War is a fiercely collective endeavour. It demands that individual rights, interests, values, and perspectives be set aside in favour of the collective interest. War therefore tends to restrict, and sometimes squash, the individual. Powerful institutions and social forces, such as states and nationalism and group pressure, exert pressure on individuals. Typically, these forces make it far easier to support killing in war than to resist it. Those who resist are pilloried, coerced, punished, sometimes killed. Those who accept war are not. If we are to have any hope of building a more peaceful world, this needs to change. Peace demands that, as far as possible, individuals be allowed to determine and voice their own mind about war and—just as importantly—be allowed to follow their own conscience.

To have reasonable debates about war, individuals must be able to access reliable information about what war is really like. But 'before conflicts begin', writes journalist Chris Hedges, 'the dissidents are silenced'.[30] A theme that runs right through this book is that there is a wide gap between what most of us *imagine* war to be like and what it actually *is* like, and that this gap is essential for keeping war in business. If more of us knew what war was actually like, and if we were free to form—and act upon—our own judgements about war in general as well as particular wars, societies would become less eager to fight, less capable of fighting, and more inclined towards resolving disputes peacefully.

War in the public imagination is heavily sanitized. The 'we', who do not fully understand war, Susan Sontag writes, 'is everyone who has never experienced anything like what they went through—don't understand. We don't get it. We truly can't imagine what it was like. We can't imagine how dreadful, how terrifying war is'.[31] In part that is due to the valorization of war and the militarization of everyday life that writers such as A.C. Grayling and Joanna Bourke have railed against.[32] In part, it is because images of war are heavily censored, whether to safeguard national morale or limit public distress. In part, it is because some of war's sensations—the persistent fear, the terrible smell—cannot be accurately conveyed. In part, it is because once the shooting stops, those left with lasting wounds are often hidden from view and memory. And in part, it is because once the shooting starts, dissenting voices are closed down and 'rarely heeded'.[33]

Most of the leaders who commit soldiers to war or the publics that cheer them on from the sidelines have little comprehension of what war is really like. What is more, soldiers themselves—be they volunteers or forced conscripts—are not permitted to make up and act upon their own mind about the legitimacy of war in general or of the specific wars they are instructed to fight. A first and important step to leashing the passions of war must be to let these realities—the many tragedies and brutalities—of war be known and to protect dissenting voices. The second is to allow individuals to make up their own minds about its virtues and to act upon their judgements. That is, there should be a universal right of conscientious objection.

One who learned of the costs of war too late was the English poet Rudyard Kipling. An ardent champion of the British empire, his writings often the emblem of jingoism, Kipling was a cheerleader for war in 1914, leading public efforts to vilify Germany and the German people. When his own son, John, then aged seventeen, had his application for military enrolment rejected on medical grounds, Kipling pulled some high-level strings to have the decision reversed. He delighted at the sight of his son in uniform, committed to doing his patriotic duty. Second Lieutenant John Kipling of the Royal Irish Guards took part in the disastrous assault on Loos on 27 September 1915. He was declared missing, presumed dead. His family never discovered his final resting place. Although this terrible loss failed to drive jingoism entirely out of Kipling's writings, and his profound love of empire never wavered, his later writings were tinged with melancholy. Kipling dedicated himself to an exhaustive and dispassionate account of the Irish Guards at war and a series of couplets, 'Epigraphs of War', that spoke to the tragedies of loss. One, in particular, stands out for its contrast with the author's earlier belligerence:

> If any question why we died,
> Tell them, because our fathers lied.

One of his final stories, 'The Gardener', was described as being 'utterly bereft of his usual jingoism'. In it, a woman visits a graveyard searching for the remains of her illegitimate son. There, she is greeted by the cemetery gardener, who is actually Christ resurrected. The gardener looks upon her with compassion and forgiveness before revealing where her son lies. The realities of war, Kipling had discovered, were far removed from its fantasies.[34]

We can achieve more honest deliberations on war by allowing the realities to be seen, as Susan Sontag demanded. 'Let the atrocious images haunt us', for even though they cannot reveal the full horror, they still perform a vital function. 'The images say: This is what human beings are capable of doing—may volunteer to do, enthusiastically, self-righteously. Don't forget'.[35] They also send a chilling warning to would-be Kiplings: be wary of the war you wish for, lest it be visited upon you and yours.

Honest debate about war is possible only if dissent is protected. Those who fervently believe in the justice of their war should have nothing to fear from those who think differently, yet history records that dissent is vilified and dissenters persecuted. War is too important a matter to be excluded from scrutiny, criticism, and debate. In fact, there is every reason to think that open reflection leads to better decision-making. So much so that the need for open debate figured prominently in the 'just war' theory advanced by professor of theology in sixteenth-century Salamanca, Francisco de Vitoria (1486–1546). But, as Vitoria himself recognized, it is not enough to simply permit open debate. Everyone should scrutinize the moral case for war within their own conscience. And if they find that case lacking, they should refuse to fight or support it. They should, in other words, become conscientious objectors. But conscientious objectors face legal, political, and social persecution. We have created societies that make it much easier to support killing in unjust wars than to object to it. That needs to change, which is why alongside free and open debate about war we also need a universal right to conscientious objection.

To understand why, we can go back to Vitoria. Indeed, his account of the ethics of war continues to shape moral reasoning and Catholic doctrine today. Vitoria maintained that 'any [single] man's opinion was not sufficient to make it good'. Princes should consult widely before deciding to wage war and those consulted are 'duty bound' to examine the just causes. Even once a decision to fight was made, our human fallibility—what Vitoria called our 'invincible ignorance'—meant that there was every chance that we acted in error and that our cause was not, in fact, just. For that reason, Vitoria maintained, we should conduct ourselves morally, ever mindful of the possibility that God's justice lay with our opponent. And because it was possible that war be entered into unjustly, individuals had not just a right, but an *obligation*, to evaluate the morality of their cause and to refuse to fight if they thought it unjust. At the time he wrote, espousing such views could land oneself in prison, or worse. Yet Vitoria argued that 'if the war seems patently unjust to the subject, he must not fight, even if he is ordered to do so by the prince'. One should follow one's conscience, even if it is mistaken.[36] If conscientious objection is indeed a moral obligation, and I think Vitoria was right about that, then it must also be a right, one closely related to the need to protect truth-telling and dissent in war.

This is not to demand universal pacifism (mine is not a pacifist path to world peace, for reasons I have already set out) or to say that we must necessarily agree with those opposed to war (for example, I find the arguments of the UK's 'Stop the War' movement on Syria to be immoral, imprudent, and ill-informed).

It is, however, to demand that pacifists and dissenters be heard, and that the right to dissent, object, and refuse to serve be everywhere protected. It is vital that people 'speak with their own' voice about war, and learn to hear and engage with the voices of others.[37] The protection of truth-telling, dissent, and conscientious objection is necessary to prevent states and societies from sleepwalking into war, deluded by fantasies about its nature and its effects. War should be entered into with full knowledge of the costs and its stakes.

The protection of dissent and conscientious objection is an ambitious objective, no easier to achieve than legitimate and effective statehood and gender equality, because of the forces ranged against it. Yet, just like the other definitive articles, these prescriptions are not wildly utopian either. These principles can be found in existing laws and have been realized, to a decent extent, in some times and places. If they can be achieved somewhere, then—in principle at least—they can be achieved everywhere. Open reporting and the protection of dissent (though not conscientious objection) demand only that individuals be granted rights that every government has already committed itself to, rights set out in the Universal Declaration of Human Rights. Everyone has the right to freedom of thought and conscience, and a right to manifest that belief in practice (Article 18). We all have a right to freedom of opinion and expression—including the right to hold and express opinions without interference and without regard to frontiers (Article 19).

Whether freedom of conscience entails a right to conscientious objection is another thing entirely, however. But if we are to move the world towards peace, then it should. Neither the Universal Declaration nor subsequent conventions on civil and political rights are clear on the matter. The UN's Human Rights bodies have adopted several resolutions (though not unanimously) that define forced military service as a violation of freedom of conscience, but governments legislate differently on the matter with a majority not yet recognizing the right to object. Yet for the reasons Vitoria set out nearly four centuries ago, the right to refuse military service ought to be protected alongside the right to tell the truth about war and to voice dissent. Truth, dissent, and refusal help close the gap between the image and reality of war and create the space we all need to make and act upon our own judgements about the legitimacy of war and of particular wars.

Additional imperative article for world peace in our time:

1. Individuals should organize and do what they reasonably can to support peace.

Peace, like war, is a human artifice. It can be built. It can be torn down. My preliminary and definitive articles identified some of the main ways in which our world can be made more peaceful. But they say less about *how* these goals might be achieved. *How*, for instance, will governments be persuaded to obey the law, contribute more to peace efforts, and guarantee human rights? *How* will the emotional forces that give rise to war be countered with more constructive ways of managing differences and resolving conflicts? Inspirational leaders and individual activists can, and have, made an important difference over the years. But if we are serious about achieving world peace, each of us needs to take some responsibility for it. World peace, after all, is everybody's business.

The principal vehicles for change are the political and moral sentiments of peoples and governments. Governments of all stripes can be moved to make quite fundamental changes when their publics demand it. Repressive governments can sometimes be toppled altogether by non-violent resistance. Civil society can organize locally and reach out across national boundaries, not only creating transnational movements for change but also challenging the forces that divide us by forging overlapping and cosmopolitan identities and interests, such as those pioneered by Monnet and others in Europe after the Second World War. Some of the different roles that can be played by individuals and groups acting outside the state have already been mentioned, but it is worth emphasizing five clusters of activity that individuals and groups need to become actively engaged in if world peace is to become more than just an ideal.

First, fostering open and honest public deliberation about war. I have already argued that individuals should have the right to speak openly and frankly about war and to opt out of war should they so choose. But they also have a *duty* to do so. It is imperative that individuals scrutinize the grounds given for wars waged in their name, deliberate and debate those grounds, and reach—and act upon—informed decisions. This is a basic responsibility endowed upon all whose governments use force in their name. It is the responsibility of schools and universities to ensure that people have the moral, analytical, and discursive skills they need to perform this core function of citizenship.

Second, holding public institutions accountable. Public accountability is crucial to closing the all too evident gap between the legal and moral responsibilities of governments and other political groupings and their actual behaviour.

Civil societies must mobilize to understand what political actors ought to be doing to support world peace, scrutinize what they are doing, and employ encouragement, rewards, and sanctions as needed to close the gap between the two. Organizations such as United Nations Associations, the Women's International League for Peace and Freedom, and Amnesty International—amongst many others—already do this, but they remain too few to consistently persuade decision-makers to fulfil their responsibilities. They must become mass movements, their efforts supplemented with reinvigorated mass movements for peace, such as those seen across Europe at the start of the twentieth century, so that a government's persistent failure to match its words with deeds on matters of international peace and security carries tangible political consequences.

Third, organizing and mobilizing to support peace. Individuals and groups must organize within and between countries to campaign for progress in strengthening the pillars of peace described earlier. Transnational advocacy by groups can be incredibly effective. The International Criminal Court, for example, exists in large part because of the efforts of the global 'Coalition for the ICC'—a civil society movement coordinated by Canada's World Federalist Movement. Likewise, land mines and cluster munitions were prohibited only because a transnational movement of activists pushed governments to do so. Individual advocacy can make a significant difference too. Genocide is an international crime largely because of the tireless activism of Raphael Lemkin. Without Hersch Lauterpacht, we might not today have such a thing as 'crimes against humanity'. Public transnational activism to address specific parts of the puzzle of peace is absolutely crucial.

Fourth, embodying peace in the everyday. I have argued that peace entails more than just the absence of war; that it also involves a civic order in which conflicts are resolved without violence. Whilst states have a crucial role to play in creating the conditions that make that possible, it is left to individuals and groups to embody that peace. This they can do by fostering mutual respect and compassion for one another, establishing ways of resolving differences peacefully, respecting the fundamental rights of others and demanding that others do likewise, and much more besides. Like the Filipino bibingka coconut rice-cake, peace needs to be cooked on both sides—from the top down through the responsibilities of sovereignty described earlier, but also from the bottom up through the daily actions of individuals and communities.[38]

Fifth, fostering a transnational public sphere. In 2003, Mary Kaldor published a book on *Global Civil Society*, whose subtitle declared it to be an 'answer to war'. That was not meant to imply that civil society necessarily had all the answers, she pointed out, just that it offered a way of arguing about and exploring the alternatives to war. Indeed, as she makes clear, the very idea of civil society has always been linked to the minimization of violence in social relations.[39] Civil society—social relations outside the state that include formal non-governmental organizations, the business sector, the arts, professional communities, and much else besides—characteristically reaches across national boundaries and is therefore comfortable with a transnational ethos. The fostering of transnational public spaces—a global civil society—is important to world peace both for what it is and for what it enables. Global civil society is a way of countering the social forces that give rise to war. In both Western Europe and East Asia, we saw in Chapter 7, increased economic interaction encouraged increased social interaction and created constituencies of people not only less inured to atavistic nationalism and xenophobia, but also willing to challenge it. In both regions, this was associated with dramatic declines in warfare. Global civil society also provides a transmission belt for the free flow of ideas between countries, the provision of mutual support to individuals and groups, and the coordination of global activism for peace.

All this depends upon one thing: that each and every one of us assumes some responsibility for world peace. World peace is possible. But it has to be strived for by each generation. Even if it were achieved for a moment, it could easily be lost. World peace cannot be achieved by following a single path.[40] There is no single route to gender equality, or to accountable government, or to the freedom of expression about war. We should be deeply sceptical of those who claim otherwise. If these goods are to be achieved at all, they will be achieved by individuals, communities, groups, and governments finding their own paths and achieving their own minor utopias. World peace has to be actualized by many different types of actors, in lots of different ways. As the then UN Secretary-General, Ban Ki-moon, explained on International Peace Day, 2016, 'peace is not an accident. Peace is not a gift. Peace is something we must all work for, every day, in every country'. We all have a role to play in building the minor utopias in our own times and places that contribute to greater peacefulness. That, when multiplied time and time again, can nudge us towards world peace. That is the imperative article.

NOTES

Preface

1. Alfred Zimmern, 'Organize the Peace World!', *The Political Quarterly*, 5 (2) 1934, p. 156.

Chapter 1

1. Exceptions include John Horgan, *The End of War* (San Francisco, CA: McSweeney's, 2012), John Gittens, *The Glorious Art of Peace* (Oxford: Oxford University Press, 2012), and John Mueller, *The Remnants of War* (Ithaca, NY: Cornell University Press, 2007), all of which have influenced the ideas put forth in this book.
2. John Keegan, *A History of Warfare* (New York: Vintage, 1994), p. 56 and p. 59.
3. A point demonstrated—exhaustively—by Steven Pinker, *The Better Angels of Our Nature: A History of Violence and Humanity* (London: Penguin, 2012).
4. As I showed in Alex J. Bellamy, *East Asia's Other Miracle: Explaining the Decline of Mass Atrocities* (Oxford: Oxford University Press, 2017).
5. This is Pinker's central thesis. See Pinker, *Better Angels*.
6. UCDP/PRIO Armed Conflict Dataset version 4, 2016.
7. Sebastian von Einseidel, 'Civil War Trends and the Changing Nature of Armed Conflict', United Nations University Centre for Policy Research, Occasional Paper No. 10, March 2017, p. 2.
8. Erik Melander, Therese Pettersson, and Lotta Themner, 'Organised Violence, 1989–2015', *Journal of Peace Research*, 53 (5) 2016. Also see Monty G. Marshall and Benjamin R. Cole, *Global Report 2014: Conflict, Governance and State Fragility* (Vienna, VA: Center for Systemic Peace, 2014), pp. 18–19.
9. For example, Fareed Zakaria and Niall Ferguson, *The End of the Liberal Order?* (London: Oneworld, 2017) and Richard Haas, *World in Disarray: American Foreign Policy and the Crisis of the Old Order* (New York: Penguin, 2017).
10. Martin Ceadel, *Thinking about Peace and War* (Oxford: Oxford University Press, 1989).
11. Michael Mandelbaum, *The Rise and Fall of Peace on Earth* (Oxford: Oxford University Press, 2019).
12. Jennifer Welsh, *The Return of History: Conflict, Migration and Geopolitics in the Twenty-First Century* (Toronto: House of Anansi Press, 2017).
13. 'A Just and Lasting Peace', Nobel Lecture delivered by President Barack Obama, Oslo, 10 December 2009.
14. Maurice R. Davie, *The Evolution of War: A Study of Its Role in Early Societies* (New Haven, CT: Yale University Press, 1929), p. 1.
15. Keegan, *A History of Warfare*, p. xvi.

16. Pinker, *Better Angels*, pp. xxi and 1.

17. Christopher Coker, *Can War Be Eliminated?* (Cambridge: Polity, 2014), p. 5.

18. William James, 'The Moral Equivalent of War [1910]', in Leon Branson and George W. Goethals (eds.), *War: Studies from Psychology, Sociology, Anthropology* (New York: Basic Books, 1964), p. 21.

19. Its arrival dated to the nineteenth century, according to Michael Howard. Michael Howard, *The Invention of Peace* (New Haven, CT: Yale University Press, 2000).

20. Martin Van Creveld, *More on War* (Oxford: Oxford University Press, 2017), p. 17.

21. Susan Sontag, *Regarding the Pain of Others* (London: Picador, 2004).

22. For instance, Nigel Biggar, *In Defence of War* (Oxford: Oxford University Press, 2014), p. 1 and Coker, *Can War Be Eliminated?*, p. 97.

23. Christopher Clark, *The Sleepwalkers: How Europe Went to War in 2014* (London: Penguin, 2014).

24. Rodney Castleden, *Minoans: Life in Bronze Age Crete* (London: Routledge, 1994).

25. See Jane R. McIntosh, *A Peaceful Realm: The Rise and Fall of the Indus Civilization* (Boulder, CO: Westview, 2002).

26. Cited by Romila Thapar, *Asoka and the Decline of the Mauryas* (Oxford: Oxford University Press, 1961), pp. 255–6.

27. Charles Allen, *Ashoka: The Search for India's Lost Emperor* (London: Abacus, 2012).

28. A point made by Van Creveld, *More on War*, p. 29.

29. One of the principal messages delivered by Margaret MacMillan in her 2018 series of Reith Lectures, broadcast on BBC Radio 4. Also see Margaret MacMillan, 'It Would Be Stupid to Think We Have Moved on From War: Look Around', *The Guardian*, 24 June 2018.

30. John Dewey, *Human Nature and Conduct: An Introduction to Social Psychology* (New York: Cosimo, 2007 [1922]).

31. Mueller, *The Remnants of War*.

32. Van Creveld, *More on War*, p. 42.

33. Cathal J. Nolan, *The Allure of Battle: A History of How Wars Have Been Won and Lost* (Oxford: Oxford University Press, 2017).

34. Paul Collier, *The Bottom Billion: Why the Poorest Countries Are Failing and What Can Be Done About It* (Oxford: Oxford University Press, 2007).

35. This quote, and the broader story, can be found in Steven Watts, *The People's Tycoon: Henry Ford and the American Century* (New York: Alfred Knopf, 2014), pp. 228–40.

36. Albert Einstein, letter to Sigmund Freud, 30 July 1932. The letter, and Freud's reply, was published by the International Institute for Intellectual Cooperation under the title 'Why War?' in 1933.

37. John F. Kennedy, 'Commencement Address at the American University', 10 June 1963, John F. Kennedy Presidential Library and Museum, accession no. TNC: 319.

38. Lawrence H. Keeley, *War Before Civilization: The Myth of the Peaceful Savage* (New York: Oxford University Press, 1997), pp. 143–7.

39. Some of these are cited in Horgan, *End to War*, p. 57.

40. Detailed in Joanna Bourke, *An Intimate History of Killing: Face to Face Killing in Twentieth Century Warfare* (New York: Basic Books, 1999) and Chris Hedges, *War Is a Force That Gives Us Meaning* (London: Anchor, 2002).

41. Gary Sheffield, *Douglas Haig: From the Somme to Victory* (London: Aurum Press, 2016), which explains how the lack of aggressive spirit was a perpetual concern of the British high command in the First World War.

42. On which see John Ferejohn and Frances McCall Rosenbluth, *Forged Through Fire: War, Peace and the Democratic Bargain* (New York: W. W. Norton, 2017).

43. A point emphasized by Hannah Arendt, *On Violence* (London: Harcourt, 1970), p. 5.

44. On which see Johnson, *Quest for Peace*.

45. Oliver P. Richmond, *Peace: A Very Short Introduction* (Oxford: Oxford University Press, 2014), p. 7. On Galtung's theory see Johan Galtung, 'Violence, Peace, and Peace Research', *Journal of Peace Research*, 6 (3) 1974, pp. 167–91 and Johan Galtung and Dietrich Fischer, *Galtung: Pioneer of Peace Studies*, Springer Briefs Vol. 5, 2013.

46. For example, Johan Galtung, 'Peace: Negative and Positive', in Nigel Young (ed.), *The Oxford International Encyclopedia of Peace* (Oxford: Oxford University Press, 2010) and 'Security and Positive Peace', in Furio Cerrutti and Rodolfo Ragionieri (eds.), *Rethinking European Security* (London: Crane Russak, 1990), pp. 29–36.

47. See www.visionofhumanity.org.

48. Cited in Jean Bethke Elshtain, *Jane Addams and the Dream of American Democracy: A Life* (New York: Basic Books, 2002), p. 219.

49. See Thomas Hippler, *Governing From the Skies: A Global History of Aerial Bombing* (London: Verso, 2017), pp. 9 and 62.

50. Michael Banks, 'Four Conceptions of Peace', in Dennis J.D. Sandole and Ingrid Sandole-Saroste (eds.), *Conflict Management and Problem Solving: Interpersonal to International Applications* (New York: New York University Press, 1987), p. 269.

51. Peter Wallensteen, *Quality Peace: Peacebuilding, Victory and World Order* (Oxford: Oxford University Press, 2015), pp. 3–6.

52. A.J.P. Taylor is cited by Geoffrey Best, *Humanity in War* (New York: Columbia University Press, 1980), pp. 6–7.

53. Cited by Lawrence Freedman, *The Future of War: A History* (London: Allen Lane, 2017), pp. 43–4.

54. Glover, *Humanity*, p. 313.

55. A point made by Keegan, *A History of Warfare*, p. 50.

56. I'm grateful to John Gledhill for this formulation.

57. Michael Ignatieff, *The Ordinary Virtues: Moral Order in a Divided World* (Cambridge, MA: Harvard University Press, 2017), p. 22.

58. My thinking here draws upon Isaiah Berlin's point that some principles of justice cannot be held simultaneously. See Isaiah Berlin, 'Two Concepts of Liberty', in Isaiah Berlin, *Liberty* (Oxford: Oxford University Press, 2004).

59. We should be 'learning to live with conflict' rather than peddling myths about human unity, writes John Gray. John Gray, *Heresies: Against Progress and Other Illusions* (London: Granta, 2005), pp. 103–4.

60. Susan Sontag, *At the Same Time* (London: Penguin, 2007), p. 145.

61. Lassa Oppenheim, *International Law: A Treatise*, Vol. 2, *War and Neutrality* (London: Longmans, Green and Co., 1906), p. 56. Emphasis added.

62. Here, I am following Jay Winter's illuminating description. Jay Winter, *Dreams of Peace and Freedom: Utopian Moments in the 20th Century* (New Haven, CT: Yale University Press, 2006), pp. 4–5.

63. Cited by Glenn R. Wilkinson, *Depictions and Images of War in Edwardian Newspapers, 1899–1914* (London: Palgrave, 2003), p. 57.

64. Friedrich Nietzsche, *Thus Spoke Zarathustra*, chapter 2.

65. Friedrich Nietzsche, *On the Genealogy of Morals*, Keith Ansell-Pearson (ed.), Carol Diethe (trans.) (Cambridge: Cambridge University Press, 1997 [1887]), II: 6.

66. Joshua S. Goldstein, *Winning the War on War: The Decline of Armed Conflict Worldwide* (New York: Dutton, 2011).

67. As David Rieff observed, none of the most solid states that exist today will likely exist 3,000 years from now, a blink of the eye in geological time. David Rieff, *In Praise of Forgetting: Historical Memory and Its Ironies* (New Haven, CT: Yale University Press, 2017), p. 7.

68. The apt title of the 2017 Cyril Foster lecture delivered by Lawrence Freedman at the University of Oxford.

69. Margaret MacMillan, *The War That Ended Peace: How Europe Abandoned Peace for the First World War* (London: Profile Books, 2013) and Margaret MacMillan, '1914 and 2014: Should We Be Worried?', *International Affairs*, 90 (1) 2014, pp. 59–70.

Chapter 2

1. Michael Howard, *The Invention of Peace* (New Haven, CT: Yale University Press, 2000), pp. 1–2.

2. Much of it elegantly recounted by A.C.F. Beales, *The History of Peace: A Short Account of the Organised Movements for International Peace* (New York: The Dial Press, 1931). More recent accounts include Antony Adolf, *Peace: A World History* (Cambridge: Polity, 2009) and Peter N. Stearns, *Peace in World History* (London: Routledge, 2014).

3. *Iliad*, 5, 890–1.

4. Described in detail by John Gittens, *The Glorious Art of Peace: From the Iliad to Iraq* (Oxford: Oxford University Press, 2012), pp. 44–6.

5. *Odyssey*, 24, 485–6.

6. Gerardo Zampaglione, *The Idea of Peace in Antiquity*, trans. Richard Dunne (Notre Dame, IN: University of Notre Dame Press, 1967), pp. 35–7.

7. Thucydides, *History of the Peloponnesian War*, trans. Rex Warner (London: Penguin, 1974).

8. See Kurt A. Raaflaub, 'Greek Concepts and Theories of Peace', in Kurt A. Raaflaub (ed.), *Peace in the Ancient World: Concepts and Theories* (Oxford: John Wiley, 2016), pp. 140–1.

9. Karen Armstrong, *Fields of Blood: Religion and the History of Violence* (New York: Anchor Books, 2014), pp. 66–7.

10. Armstrong, *Fields of Blood*, p. 102.

11. Adrian Goldsworthy, *Pax Romana: War, Peace and Conquest in the Roman World* (London: Weidenfeld & Nicolson, 2017).

12. Augustine, *Contra Julianum*, cited by G.A. Harrer, 'Cicero on Peace and War', *The Classical Journal*, 14 (1) 1918, p. 30.

13. This was not the only justification Cicero offered for war; others included the glory of empire and the increasing of its power—justifications that aligned more closely with the reasons behind Roman war-fighting.

14. Ovid, *Fasti*, I. 711–22.
15. See Peter Brock, *Pacifism in Europe to 1914* (Princeton, NJ: Princeton University Press, 1972), pp. 10–12.
16. Augustine, *City of God*, cited by James Turner Johnson, *The Quest for Peace: Three Moral Traditions in Western Cultural History* (Princeton, NJ: Princeton University Press, 1987), p. 63.
17. Augustine, *City of God*, cited by Johnson, *The Quest for Peace*, p. 64.
18. Beales, *The History of Peace*, p. 23.
19. Alan Gerwith, *Marsilius of Padua: The Defender of Peace* (New York: Columbia University Press, 1956), vol. 1, p. 97.
20. Fred R. Dallmayr, 'A War Against the Turks? Erasmus on War and Peace', *Asian Journal of Social Science*, 34 (1) 2006, p. 69.
21. Brock, *Pacifism*, pp. 63–5.
22. Cited by Johnson, *Quest for Peace*, p. 178.
23. See Céline Spector, 'Who Is the Author of the Abstract of Monsieur l'Abbé de Saint-Pierre's "Plan for Perpetual Peace"? From Saint-Pierre to Rousseau', *History of European Ideas*, 39 (3) 2013, pp. 371–93.
24. Cited by F.H. Hinsley, *Power and the Pursuit of Peace: Theory and Practice in the History of Relations Between States* (Cambridge: Cambridge University Press, 1962), p. 45.
25. Both cited by Hinsley, *Power and the Pursuit of Peace*, p. 25.
26. W.B. Gallie, *Philosophers of Peace and War: Kant, Clausewitz, Marx, Engels and Tolstoy* (Cambridge: Cambridge University Press, 1978), p. 24.
27. Gallie, *Philosophers*, p. 27.
28. For an excellent and more comprehensive account than is possible here see Bela Kapossy, Isaac Nakhimovsky, and Richard Whatmore, *Commerce and Peace in the Enlightenment* (Cambridge: Cambridge University Press, 2017).
29. Thomas Paine, 'Rights of Man', in Philip S. Foner (ed.), *Complete Writings of Thomas Paine* (New York: Citadel Press, 1945), vol. 1, p. 449.
30. A.C. Grayling, *War: An Enquiry* (New Haven, CT: Yale University Press, 2017), p. 149.
31. Jeremy Bentham, 'A Plan for an Universal and Perpetual Peace', available at http://www.laits.utexas.edu/poltheory/bentham/pil/pil.e04.html.
32. See Patrick J. McDonald, *The Invisible Hand of Peace: Capitalism, the War Machine and International Relations Theory* (Cambridge: Cambridge University Press, 2009).
33. Katherine Barbieri, *The Liberal Illusion: Does Trade Promote Peace?* (Ann Arbor, MI: University of Michigan Press, 2002), p. 127.
34. It is now commonly argued that the ethics and laws of war did as much to legitimize as to regulate war. This view rests on both a mistaken account of their evolution and a misunderstanding of the motives that lay behind efforts to regulate war, motives ably explained here by Moynier. For a detailed explanation see Johnson, *The Quest for Peace*.
35. Cited in Best, *Humanity in War*, p. 10.
36. See Anthony Pagden's *The Enlightenment and Why It Still Matters* (Oxford: Oxford University Press, 2015).
37. An encyclopedic and wonderfully illuminating account of British peace movements is offered by Martin Ceadel's *The Origins of War Prevention: The British Peace Movement and International Relations, 1730–1854* (Oxford: Clarendon Press, 1996) and *Semi-Detached*

Idealists: The British Peace Movement and International Relations, 1854–1945 (Oxford: Oxford University Press, 2000).

38. 'The Peace Endowment of Mr Carnegie', *American Journal of International Law*, 5 (1) 1911, p. 211.

39. Michael Howard, *War and the Liberal Conscience* (London: Temple Smith, 1978), p. 53.

40. Keegan, *History of Warfare*, p. 364.

41. Cited by Neil Hollander, *Elusive Dove: The Search for Peace in World War I* (Jefferson, NC: McFarland and Co., 2013), p. 51.

42. Not entirely fatuously. See William Mulligan, *The Great War for Peace* (New Haven, CT: Yale University Press, 2014).

43. Oona Hathaway and Scott J. Shapiro, *The Internationalists: And Their Plan to Outlaw War* (London: Penguin, 2017).

44. Hans J. Morgenthau, *Politics Among Nations: The Struggle for Power and Peace* (New York: Knopf, 1985 [first published 1948]), p. 47.

45. Bernard Brodie (ed.), *The Absolute Weapon: Atomic Power and World Order* (New York: Harcourt, 1946), p. 76.

46. Hedley Bull, 'The Great Irresponsibles? The United States, the Soviet Union and World Order', *International Journal*, 35 (3) 1980, p. 437.

47. Gil Loescher, Alexander Betts, and James Milner, *The United Nations High Commissioner for Refugees (UNHCR): The Politics and Practice of Refugee Protection into the Twenty-First Century* (London: Routledge, 2008), pp. 2–3.

48. See Thomas G. Weiss, *What's Wrong with the UN and How to Fix It?* (Cambridge: Polity, 2013), chapter 3.

49. William Schabas, *Unimaginable Atrocities: Justice, Politics and Rights at the War Crimes Tribunals* (Oxford: Oxford University Press, 2012), p. 57.

50. David Mitrany, *A Working Peace System* (New York: Quadrangle, 1966 [1943]), p. 98.

51. Thomas L. Friedman, *The Lexus and the Olive Tree: Understanding Globalization* (New York: Farrar, Straus & Giroux, 1999).

52. Etel Solingen, 'Internationalization, Coalitions and Regional Conflict and Cooperation', in Edward D. Mansfield and Brian M. Pollins (eds.), *Economic Interdependence and International Conflict: New Perspectives on an Enduring Debate* (Ann Arbor, MI: University of Michigan Press, 2003), p. 65.

53. Etel Solingen, *Regional Orders: At Century's Dawn: Global and Domestic Influences on Grand Strategy* (Princeton, NJ: Princeton University Press, 1998), p. 65.

54. Richard Rosecrance, *The Rise of the Trading State: Commerce and Conquest in the Modern World* (New York: Basic Books, 1986).

55. This is one of the central messages of John Keegan, *War and Our World* (London: Pimlico, 1999).

56. Gary Goertz, Paul F. Diehl, and Alexandru Balas, *The Puzzle of Peace: The Evolution of Peace in the International System* (Oxford: Oxford University Press, 2016).

57. Core argument of Coker, *Can War Be Eliminated?*.

Chapter 3

1. Michael Ghiglieri, *The Dark Side of Man: Tracing the Origins of Male Violence* (Reading, MA: Perseus, 1999), pp. 161–3.

2. Mike Martin, *Why We Fight* (London: Hurst, 2018).

3. Thomas Hobbes, *Leviathan*, trans. C.B. Macpherson (London: Penguin, 1982), book XII.

4. William Sumner, *Folkways: A Study of the Sociological Importance of Usages, Manners, Customs, Mores, and Morals* (Boston, MA: Gin and Co., 1906), p. 2.

5. Thomas Henry Huxley, 'The Struggle for Existence: A Programme', *Popular Science Monthly*, 32, April 1888.

6. Raymond Dart, 'The Predatory Transition from Ape to Man', *International Anthropological and Linguistic Review*, 1, 1953, pp. 207–8. See also Raymond Dart, 'The Predatory Implemental Technique of Australopithecines', *American Journal of Physical Anthropology*, 7, 1949, pp. 1–38. For more details see Ashley Montagu (ed.), *Men and Aggression* (New York: Oxford University Press, 1973).

7. Dart, 'Predatory Transition', p. 208.

8. Raymond Dart, *Adventures with the Missing Link* (New York: Harper, 1959), p. 113.

9. Robert Ardrey, *African Genesis* (New York: Dell, 1961), p. 316. Also see Robert Ardrey, *The Territorial Imperative* (New York: Atheneum, 1966).

10. Konrad Lorenz, *On Aggression*, trans. M. Wilson (London: Methuen and Co., 1966).

11. Lorenz, *On Aggression*, pp. 233–4.

12. Lorenz, *On Aggression*, p. 270.

13. See Jane Goodall, *Through a Window: My Thirty Years with the Chimpanzees of Gombe* (London: Houghton Mifflin, 2010) and *The Chimpanzees of Gombe: Patterns of Behavior* (Cambridge, MA: Harvard University Press, 1986).

14. Richard Wrangham and Dale Peterson, *Demonic Males: Apes and the Origin of Human Violence* (Boston, MA: Houghton Mifflin, 1996), p. 235.

15. R.P. Shaw and Yuwa Wong, *Genetic Seeds of Warfare: Evolution, Nationalism and Patriotism* (Boston, MA: Unwin Hyman, 1989), p. 17.

16. A. Leroi-Gourhan, *Le Geste et la Parole, Vol. 2: La Mémoire et les Rythmes* (Paris: Albin Michel, 1965), pp. 236–7.

17. Barbara Ehrenreich, *Blood Rites* (London: Granta, 2011), p. 89.

18. Sigmund Freud, 'Why War?', in Leon Bramson and George W. Goethals (eds.), *War: Studies from Psychology, Sociology, Anthropology* (New York: Basic Books, 1968), pp. 75–7. For an earlier exposition of this destruction instinct see Sigmund Freud, *Civilization and Its Discontents* (London: Hogarth Press, 1930), p. 86.

19. Roland Stromberg, *Redemption by War: The Intellectuals and 1914* (Lawrence, KS: University of Kansas Press, 1982), p. 82.

20. Francis Fukuyama, 'Women and the Evolution of World Politics', *Foreign Affairs*, September/October 1998.

21. Lawrence Keeley, 'Giving War a Chance', in S. Rice and S. LeBlanc (eds.), *Deadly Landscapes: Case Studies in Prehistoric Southwestern Warfare* (Salt Lake City, UT: University of Utah Press, 2001), pp. 331–42.

22. Goldstein, *Winning the War*, p. 38.

23. See C.K. Brain, 'New Finds at the Swartkrans Australopithecine Site', *Nature*, 225, 1970, pp. 1112–19.

24. Giambattista Vico, 'New Science', in Giambattista Vico, *Vico: Selected Writings*, edited and trans. Leon Pompa (Cambridge: Cambridge University Press, 1982), pp. 113–14.

25. Samuel Von Pufendorf, *Of the Law of Nature and Nations*, trans. Basil Kennet (London: Carew, 1729), I.I.viii.

26. Matt Ridley, *The Origins of Virtue* (London: Viking, 1996), p. 6.

27. One of the central arguments of Yuval Noah Harari, *Sapiens: A Brief History of Humankind* (New York: Harper, 2014).

28. Frans de Waal, *Primates and Philosophers: How Morality Evolved* (Princeton, NJ: Princeton University Press, 2006), p. 4.

29. Frans de Waal, *Our Inner Ape: A Leading Primatologist Explains Why We Are Who We Are* (New York: Penguin, 2005).

30. Charles Darwin, *The Descent of Man* (London: John Murray, 1871), p. 83.

31. Darwin, *Descent of Man*, p. 83.

32. Yuval Noah Harari, *Homo Deus: A Brief History of Tomorrow* (London: Vintage, 2015), p. 154.

33. Keeley, *War Before Civilization*, p. 38.

34. Evan Hadingham, *Secrets of the Ice Age: The World of the Cave Artists* (New York: Walker, 1979), pp. 255–8.

35. Robert L. O'Connell, *Ride of the Second Horseman: The Birth and Death of War* (Oxford: Oxford University Press, 1999), pp. 50–1.

36. Keeley, *War Before Civilization*, p. 37 and Ehrenreich, *Blood Rites*, p. 122. The questions are raised by Douglas P. Fry, *Beyond War: The Human Potential for Peace* (Oxford: Oxford University Press, 2006), p. 53. We should be careful to distinguish evidence of war and evidence of violence. There is plenty of evidence of interpersonal violence before this date, but little evidence that it was *collective* violence—the hallmark of war.

37. Fred Wendorf, *The Prehistory of Nubia* (Dallas, TX: Southern Methodist University Press, 1968), p. 993.

38. Arthur Ferrill, *The Origins of War: From the Stone Age to Alexander the Great* (New York: Thames and Hudson, 1985), p. 30.

39. James C. Scott, *Against the Grain: A Deep History of the Earliest States* (New Haven, CT: Yale University Press, 2017). On the emergence of inequality as dominant form of living (and the subsequent struggle to promote equality), see Larry Siedentop, *Inventing the Individual: The Origins of Western Liberalism* (London: Penguin, 2014).

40. For example, there is evidence that some early Australian aboriginal groups developed agriculture without totally sacrificing hunter-gathering techniques. See Bruce Pascoe, *Dark Emu: Aboriginal Australia and the Birth of Agriculture* (Melbourne: Scribe, 2018). I am grateful to Stephen Mcloughlin for this point.

41. Margaret Mead, *Coming of Age in Samoa* (New York: William Morrow and Co., 1928).

42. Margaret Mead, 'War Is Only an Invention—Not a Biological Necessity', 1940; reprinted in Richard K. Betts (ed.), *Conflict after the Cold War: Arguments on the Causes of War and Peace* (Boston, MA: Pearson, 4th edition, 2013), pp. 402–5.

43. The charge was led by Derek Freeman, *Margaret Mead and Samoa* (Cambridge, MA: Harvard University Press, 1983). Freeman's critique has been widely criticized on the grounds that he misrepresented evidence, did not marshal sufficient evidence to disprove Mead's thesis, and did not take account of change over time. See, for example, Paul Shankman, *The Trashing of Margaret Mead: Anatomy of an Anthropological Controversy* (Madison, WI: University of Wisconsin Press, 2009) and Alice Dreger,

Galileo's Middle Finger: Heretics, Activists and the Search for Justice in Science (New York: Penguin, 2015).

44. Napoleon Chagnon, *Yanomamo: The Fierce People*, 3rd edition (New York: Holt, Rinehart and Winston, 1983), p. 214.

45. Keeley, *War Before Civilization*, pp. 36–8 and Azar Gat, *War in Human Civilization* (Oxford: Oxford University Press, 2006), pp. 17–25.

46. See Carol Ember and Mervin Ember, 'Warfare, Aggression and Recourse Problems: Cross-Cultural Codes', *Behaviour Science Research*, 26, 1992, pp. 169–226; Carol Ember and Mervin Ember, 'Resource Unpredictability, Mistrust and War', *Journal of Conflict Resolution*, 36 (2) 1992, pp. 242–62; and Carol Ember and Mervin Ember, 'War, Socialization and Interpersonal Violence: A Cross-Cultural Study', *Journal of Conflict Resolution*, 38 (4) 1994, pp. 620–46.

47. Keith Otterbein and Charlotte Otterbein, 'An Eye for an Eye, a Tooth for a Tooth: A Cross-Cultural Study of Feuding', *American Anthropologist*, 70, 1968, pp. 277–89.

48. Quincy Wright, *Study of War* (Chicago, IL: University of Chicago Press, 1964), p. 546.

49. Robert C. Kelly, 'From the Peaceful to the Warlike: Ethnographic and Archaeological Insights into Hunter-Gatherer Warfare and Homicide', in Douglas P. Fry (ed.), *War, Peace, and Human Nature: The Convergence of Evolutionary and Cultural Views* (Oxford: Oxford University Press, 2013), p. 156.

50. Raymond C. Kelly, *Warless Societies and the Origin of War* (Ann Arbor, MI: University of Michigan Press, 2000), p. 125.

51. Kelly, *Warless Societies*, p. 125.

52. Which is also why archaeological finds of fossils bearing the marks of violence cannot be automatically taken as evidence of war. Kelly, *Warless Societies*, p. 103 and Fry, *Beyond War*, pp. 62–3.

53. O'Connell, *Ride of the Second Horseman*, pp. 29–30.

54. Marvin Harris, *Our Kind: Who We Are, Where We Came From, Where We Are Going* (New York: Harper, 1990), p. 344.

55. Bruce Bonta, 'Conflict Resolution Among Peaceful Societies: The Culture of Peacefulness', *Journal of Peace Research*, 33 (4) 1996, pp. 403–20.

56. David Rieff (*In Praise of Forgetting*) notes the capacity of societies to remember, and forget, histories and identities with remarkable rapidity, changing how they understand themselves, their histories, and their futures.

57. Fry, *Beyond War*, pp. 142, 144.

58. Robert Axelrod, *The Evolution of Cooperation* (New York: Basic Books, 1984).

59. Horgan, *The End of War*, pp. 30–1 and David Barash, 'Evolution and Peace', in Fry (ed.), *War, Peace, and Human Nature*, p. 35.

60. Kelly, *Warless Societies*, pp. 118–19.

61. See Joam Evans Pim, 'Man the Singer: Song Duels as an Aggression Restraint Mechanism for Nonkilling Conflict Management', in Fry (ed.), *War, Peace, and Human Nature*, pp. 514–40.

62. Davie, *Evolution of War*, pp. 188–91.

63. Kelly, *Warless Societies*, p. 107.

64. Kelly, *Warless Societies*, p. 38 and Robert K. Dentan, *The Semai: A Nonviolent People of Malaysia*, 2nd edition (New York: Holt, Rinehart and Winston, 1979), p. 57.

65. Fry, *Beyond War*, p. 83.

66. Fry, *Beyond War*, p. 88.

67. See Ronald Berndt and Catherine Berndt, *The World of the First Australians*, 5th edition (Canberra: Aboriginal Studies Press, 1996).

68. Mervyn Meggitt, *Desert People: A Study of the Walbiri Aboriginals of Central Australia* (Chicago, IL: University of Chicago Press, 1965), pp. 245–6.

69. Gerald Wheeler, *The Tribe, and Intertribal Relations in Australia* (London: John Murray, 1910), pp. 147–9.

70. Berndt and Berndt, *World of the First Australians*, pp. 145–6; Meggitt, *Desert People*, p. 42; and Wheeler, *The Tribe*, p. 65.

71. Tony Swain, *A Place for Strangers* (New York: Cambridge University Press, 1993), pp. 54–6.

72. Berndt and Berndt, *World of the First Australians*, ch. 10.

73. Robert Tomlinson, 'Social Control and Conflict Management Among Australian Aboriginal Desert People Before and After the Advent of Alcohol', in Fry (ed.), *War, Peace, and Human Nature*, pp. 268–9.

74. Keeley, *War Before Civilization*, p. 149.

75. Davie, *Evolution of War*, p. 177.

76. Berndt and Berndt, *World of the First Australians*, p. 358.

77. Keeley, *War Before Civilization*, p. 64.

78. Bruce M. Knauft, 'Culture and Cooperation in Human Evolution', in Leslie E. Sponsel and Thomas Gregor (eds.), *The Anthropology of Peace and Nonviolence* (Boulder, CO: Lynne Rienner, 1994), p. 45 and Signe Howell and Roy G. Willis, 'Introduction', in Signe Howell and Roy G. Willis (eds.), *Societies at Peace: Anthropological Perspectives* (New York: Routledge, 1989), p. 25.

79. Charles A. Kupchan, *How Enemies Become Friends: The Sources of Stable Peace* (Princeton, NJ: Princeton University Press, 2010), p. 320.

80. Davie, *Evolution of War*, pp. 181–5.

81. Davie, *Evolution of War*, p. 191.

82. Thomas Arnold, *Introductory Lectures on Modern History* (London: B. Fellowes, 1849), p. 175.

Chapter 4

1. Grayling, *War*, p. 160.

2. Keegan, *History of Warfare*, p. 386.

3. Keegan, *History of Warfare*, p. 386.

4. Cycles of violence, conflict traps, and a lack of imagination explain the dogged persistence of war, argues Jonathan Glover. See Jonathan Glover, *Humanity: A Moral History of the 20th Century* (New Haven, CT: Yale University Press, 1999), pp. ix–xv.

5. The idea of war's causes as ingredients is borrowed from Paul D. Williams' excellent study of contemporary African war, *War and Conflict in Africa*, 2nd edition (Cambridge: Polity, 2017).

6. Central argument of Armstrong, *Fields of Blood*, to which I will return later.

7. Christopher Coker, *Barbarous Philosophers: Reflections on the Nature of War from Heraclitus to Heisenberg* (London: Hurst and Co., 2010), pp. 12–13 and Azar Gat, *Military Thought in the Nineteenth Century* (Oxford: Oxford University Press, 1992), p. 67.

8. Ridley, *Origins of Virtue*, p. 6.

9. John Maynard Smith, *The Theory of Evolution*, 3rd edition (London: Penguin, 1975), p. 312.

10. Ridley, *Origins of Virtue*, p. 181.

11. Claude Lévi-Strauss, *Structural Anthropology* (New York: Doubleday, 1963), pp. 21–37.

12. David Sloan-Wilson, *Darwin's Cathedral: Evolution, Religion and the Nature of Society* (Chicago, IL: University of Chicago Press, 2007).

13. Peter Kropotkin, *Mutual Aid: A Factor of Evolution* (New York: Dover, 2009 [1902]), pp. 8–12.

14. Siep Stuurman, *The Invention of Humanity: Equality and Cultural Difference in World History* (Cambridge, MA: Harvard University Press, 2017).

15. De Waal, *Primates and Philosophers*, p. 54 and Ridley, *Origins of Virtue*, p. 174.

16. Sontag, *At the Same Time*, p. 145.

17. E.H. Carr, *The Twenty Years' Crisis 1919–1939: An Introduction to the Study of International Relations* (London: Palgrave, 2016 [1939]).

18. Gallie, *Philosophers of Peace and War*, p. 74.

19. David Hume, *An Inquiry Involving the Principle of Morals* (Cambridge, MA: Hackett Publishing, 1983 [1751]).

20. Amartya Sen, *The Idea of Justice* (New York: Allen Lane, 2009) and Ignatieff, *The Ordinary Virtues*.

21. Ridley, *Origins of Virtue*, p. 170.

22. Grayling, *War*, p. 123.

23. Amartya Sen, *Identity and Violence: The Illusion of Destiny* (London: Penguin, 2006).

24. Michael Walzer, *Just and Unjust Wars: A Moral Argument with Historical Illustrations* (New York: Basic Books, 1977), p. 44.

25. William Graham Sumner, 'War' [1903], in *War and Other Essays* (New Haven, CT: Yale University Press, 1919), pp. 3–20.

26. Something I explored in detail in Alex J. Bellamy, *Security Communities and their Neighbours* (London: Palgrave, 2002).

27. Arendt, *On Violence*, p. 5.

28. George Orwell, *The Lion and the Unicorn: Socialism and the English Genius* (London: Penguin, 1970 [1941]), p. 37.

29. Carl von Clausewitz, *On War*, trans. Michael Howard and Peter Paret (Princeton, NJ: Princeton University Press, 1976), p. 149.

30. 'The Peace Endowment of Mr Carnegie', *American Journal of International Law*, 5 (1) 1911, p. 211.

31. Donald Kagan, *On the Origins of War and the Preservation of Peace* (New York: Anchor, 1995), p. 8.

32. Norbert Elias, *The Civilizing Process*, trans. Edmund Jephcott (Oxford: Blackwell, 1982 [1939]). More recently, Ian Morris, *War: What Is It Good For?* (London: Profile Books, 2014).

33. Bertrand Russell, 'Has Religion Made Useful Contributions to Civilization?', 1930, available at http://www.update.uu.se/~fbendz/library/has_reli.htm.

34. Richard Dawkins, *An Appetite for Wonder: The Makings of a Scientist* (London: Transworld, 2014).

35. R. Scott Appleby, *The Ambivalence of the Sacred: Religion, Violence and Reconciliation* (Lanham, MD: Rowman & Littlefield, 1999).

36. Armstrong, *Fields of Blood*, p. 393.

37. Roland H. Bainton, *Christian Attitudes Toward War and Peace: A Historical Survey and Critical Re-Evaluation* (Nashville, TN: Abingdon Press, 1960).

38. This is the main argument of Marc Gopin, *Between Eden and Armageddon: The Future of World Religions, Violence and Peacemaking* (Oxford: Oxford University Press, 2002).

39. See William T. Cavanagh, *The Myth of Religious Violence: Secular Ideology and the Roots of Modern Conflict* (Oxford: Oxford University Press, 2009).

40. Clausewitz, *On War*.

41. Kagan, *On the Origins of War*.

42. John Hutchinson, *Nationalism and War* (Oxford: Oxford University Press, 2017), p. 50.

43. On how diplomacy went hand in hand with war in European expansion see J.C. Sharman, *A Global Military Revolution? War, European Expansion and the Making of the Modern International System* (Cambridge: Cambridge University Press, 2018).

44. Much of the real historical action of the time lay elsewhere. See Peter Frankopan, *Silk Roads: A New History of the World* (London: Bloomsbury, 2015).

45. Van Creveld, *More on War*, pp. 36 and ff.

46. Goldsworthy, *Pax Romana*, p. 411.

47. Frantz Fanon, *Wretched of the Earth* (London: Penguin, 2014 [1961]), p. 61 and Sartre's preface.

48. There is good empirical evidence to suggest that non-violent resistance was actually a more effective means of resistance than war. See Erica Chenoweth, *Why Civil Resistance Works: The Strategic Logic of Nonviolent Conflict* (New York: Columbia University Press, 2011).

49. Nick Mansfield, *Theorizing War: From Hobbes to Badiou* (London: Palgrave, 2008), p. 163.

50. Ferejohn and Rosenbluth, *Forged Through Fire*. This account draws a sharp link between war and citizenship that, however, tends to gloss over circumstances where states responded to war by retracting citizenship rights.

51. Walter Scheidel, *The Great Leveler: Violence and the History of Inequality from the Stone Age to the Twenty-First Century* (Princeton, NJ: Princeton University Press, 2017).

52. Azar Gat, *The Causes of War and the Spread of Peace* (Oxford: Oxford University Press, 2017), p. 158. I have made a similar argument in the context of East Asia. Bellamy, *East Asia's Other Miracle*.

53. See Frances Stewart (ed.), *Horizontal Inequalities and Conflict: Understanding Group Violence in Multiethnic Societies* (London: Palgrave, 2008).

54. Gerard Prunier, *Darfur: The Ambiguous Genocide* (London: Hirst, 2005), pp. 3–4; Julie Flint and Alex de Waal, *Darfur: A New History of a Long War* (London and New York: Zed Books, 2008), p. 19.

55. Barbara W. Tuchman, *The Proud Tower: A Portrait of the World Before the War: 1890–1914* (New York: Macmillan, 1966), p. 462.

56. Biggar, *In Defence of War*.

57. Quoted in Bourke, *An Intimate History of Killing*, p. 19.

58. Hedges, *War Is a Force*, p. 3.

59. Hutchinson, *Nationalism and War*, p. 3.

60. Shashi Tharoor, *Inglorious Empire: What the British Did to India* (London: C. Hurst and Co., 2017).

61. Grayling, *War*, p. 232.
62. Well explained by Philip Zimbardo, *The Lucifer Effect: How Good People Turn Evil* (London: Rider, 2007).
63. Christopher Browning, *Ordinary Men: Reserve Battalion 101 and the Final Solution in Poland* (New York: Harper Collins, 1992).
64. Sontag, *Regarding the Pain of Others*.
65. A thesis put forward by Jared Diamond, *Collapse: How Societies Choose to Fail or Succeed* (New York: Viking Press, 2005).
66. There have been many recent publications making this same point. See Terry Hunt and Carl Lippo, *The Statues That Walked: Unravelling the Mystery of Easter Island* (New York: Counterpoint, 2012).
67. John Stoessinger, *Why Nations Go to War* (New York: St. Martin's Press, 1997).
68. An idea advanced by Judith Butler, *Frames of War: When Is Life Grievable?* (London: Verso, 2009).
69. Reproduced in Emily Cooper Johnson (ed.), *Jane Addams: A Centennial Reader* (New York: Macmillan, 1960), pp. 4 and 259.
70. Cited by Bethke Elshtain, *Jane Addams*, p. 337 and pp. 203–4 respectively.
71. This vision of peace through grassroots social action to satisfy needs and build bonds between groups was what Addams meant by her newer—positive—ideals of peace. See Jane Addams, *Newer Ideals of Peace* (Urbana and Chicago, IL: University of Illinois Press, 2007).
72. Van Creveld, *More on War*, p. 2.
73. George Orwell, *Homage to Catalonia* (London: Penguin, 1962 [1938]), p. 138.
74. 'It is obvious who is likely to have the upper hand', writes A.C. Grayling, *War*, p. 15.
75. Hedley Bull, 'Disarmament and the International System', *Australian Journal of Politics and History*, 5 (1) 1959, pp. 41–50.
76. Max Weber, 'Politics as a Vocation', lecture given in Munich, 28 January 1919, available at http://anthropos-lab.net/wp/wp-content/uploads/2011/12/Weber-Politics-as-a-Vocation.pdf.
77. Jacob D. Kathman, 'Civil War Contagion and Neighboring Intervention', *International Studies Quarterly*, 54 (4) 2010, pp. 989–1012.
78. J.D. Bernal, *World Without War* (London: Routledge & Kegan Paul, 1961).
79. Edward Grey, *Twenty-Five Years, 1892–1916* (London: Frederick A. Stokes, 1922), vol. 2, p. 52.
80. Arendt, *On Violence*, p. 3.
81. As proposed by Ernie Regehr, *Disarming Conflict* (London: Zed, 2015).
82. See H.S. Reiss (ed.), *Kant: Political Writings* (Cambridge: Cambridge University Press, 1970), p. 47.
83. Sidney Hook, *The Hero in History: A Study in Limitation and Possibility* (New York: John Day, 1943), p. 256.

Chapter 5

1. Charles Tilly, *The Formation of National States in Western Europe* (Princeton, NJ: Princeton University Press, 1975), p. 42.

2. Charles Tilly, 'War Making and State Making as Organized Crime', in Peter Evans, Dietrich Reuschemeyer, and Theda Skocpol (eds.), *Bringing the State Back In* (Cambridge: Cambridge University Press, 1985), pp. 169–91.

3. Charles Tilly, *Coercion, Capital and European States, AD 990–1990* (Oxford: Blackwell, 1992).

4. Hedley Bull and Adam Watson (eds.), *The Expansion of International Society* (Oxford: Oxford University Press, 1984).

5. Michael Mann, *The Sources of Social Power: Volume 1* (Cambridge: Cambridge University Press, 1986).

6. Quotes taken from A.C. Armstrong, 'Hegel's Attitude on War and Peace', *Journal of Philosophy*, 30 (25) 1933, p. 686.

7. G.W.F. Hegel, *Elements of the Philosophy of Right*, trans. H.B. Nisbet (Cambridge: Cambridge University Press, 1991), p. 324.

8. Armstrong, 'Hegel's Attitude', p. 686.

9. Michael Howard, *War in European History*, updated edition (Oxford: Oxford University Press, 2009), p. 1.

10. Tim Marshall, *Worth Dying For: The Power and Politics of Flags* (London: Elliott and Thompson, 2016).

11. Hutchinson, *Nationalism and War*, p. 21.

12. Prompting more recent figures to write not of the 'expansion' of international society, but its 'globalization'. Tim Dunne and Christian Reus-Smit (eds.), *The Globalization of International Society* (Oxford: Oxford University Press, 2016).

13. Sharman, *Global Military Revolution?*.

14. Jean-Pierre Proudhon, *La Guerre et la Paix: Recherches sur la principe et la constitution du droit des gens* (Paris: Hachette Livre, 2016 [1861]).

15. Mark Levene, *Genocide in the Age of the Nation State, Vol. 2—The Rise of the West and the Coming of Genocide* (London: I. B. Tauris, 2005).

16. Zygmunt Bauman, *Modernity and the Holocaust* (Oxford: Polity, 1992).

17. Hannah Arendt, *Eichmann in Jerusalem: A Report on the Banality of Evil* (London: Penguin, 2011 [1963]).

18. Ken Booth, *Theory of World Security* (Cambridge: Cambridge University Press, 2007), p. 24.

19. Morris, *War: What Is It Good For?*, p. 18.

20. Pinker, *Better Angels*, pp. 50–1.

21. Ted Robert Gurr, 'Historical Trends in Violent Crime: A Critical Review of the Evidence', in Michael Tonry and Norval Morris (eds.), *Crime and Justice: An Annual Review of Research*, vol. 3 (Chicago, IL: University of Chicago Press, 1981), pp. 295–353.

22. Robert Muchembled, *A History of Violence* (Oxford: Polity, 2012), p. 39.

23. Thomas Nagel, 'The Problem of Global Justice', *Philosophy and Public Affairs*, 33 (2) 2005, pp. 113–47.

24. A point demonstrated ably by Ben Kiernan's epic history of genocide. Ben Kiernan, *Blood and Soil: A World History of Genocide and Extermination from Sparta to Darfur* (New Haven, CT: Yale University Press, 2007).

25. All brilliantly documented by Bettina Stagneth, *Eichmann Before Jerusalem* (New York: Alfred Knopf, 2014).

26. Precisely how is expertly set out by Daron Acemoglu and James A. Robinson, *Why Nations Fail: The Origins of Power, Prosperity, and Poverty* (London: Profile, 2013).

27. Kurt A. Raaflaub, 'Introduction: Searching for Peace in the Ancient World', in Kurt A. Raaflaub (ed.), *War and Peace in the Ancient World* (Oxford: Blackwell, 2007), p. 1.

28. Hobbes, *Leviathan*, chapter 30.

29. For an excellent history of sovereign responsibilities, from which this point is derived, see Luke Glanville, *Sovereignty and the Responsibility to Protect: A New History* (Chicago, IL: University of Chicago Press, 2013).

30. John Locke, *Two Treatises on Government* 2nd treatise (1690), reproduced in Michael L. Morgan (ed.), *Classics of Moral and Political Theory* (Indianapolis, IN: Hackett, 2011, fifth edition), p. 713.

31. Discussed in detail by David Armitage, *Foundations of Modern International Thought* (Cambridge: Cambridge University Press, 2013), pp. 75–89.

32. Lynn T. Hunt, *Inventing Human Rights: A History* (London: W. W. Norton and Co., 2007), p. 20.

33. It is reproduced on the website of the US National Archives. See https://www.archives.gov/founding-docs/declaration-transcript.

34. The full text can be found at https://www.open.edu/openlearn/ocw/pluginfile.php/612270/mod_resource/content/1/rightsofman.pdf.

35. In Peter Balakian, *The Burning Tigris: The Armenian Genocide and America's Response* (New York: Perennial, 2004), pp. 307–8.

36. Atlantic Charter, 12 August 1941. See Elizabeth Borgwardt, *A New Deal for the World: America's Vision for Human Rights* (Cambridge, MA: Harvard University Press, 2005).

37. Hunt, *Inventing Human Rights*, p. 203.

38. Gat, *Causes of War*, pp. 153 ff.

39. Indeed, it remains one of the most significant determinants. See D. Scott Bennett and Allan C. Stam, *The Behavioural Origins of War* (Ann Arbor, MI: University of Michigan Press, 2004), pp. 202–3.

40. Immanuel Kant, *Perpetual Peace* (Cambridge, MA: Hackett, 2003), first definitive article.

41. Carnegie Commission on Preventing Deadly Conflict, *Preventing Deadly Conflict* (New York: Carnegie Corporation, 1997), p. xviii.

42. These attributes are described and listed differently by different studies, but there is broad agreement backed by statistical and other types of evidence to support their significance. See, for example, Acemoglu and Robinson, *Why Nations Fail* and David Cortright, Conor Seyle, and Kristen Wall, *Governance for Peace: How Inclusive, Participatory and Accountable Institutions Promote Peace and Prosperity* (Cambridge: Cambridge University Press, 2017).

43. See Robert H. Bates, *Prosperity and Violence: The Political Economy of Development* (New York: W. W. Norton, 2009).

44. Coker, *Barbarous Philosophers*, p. 32.

45. For an example of the perils of transition and the remedies see John Gledhill, 'Assessing (In)security After the Arab Spring', *PS: Political Science and Politics*, 46 (4) 2013, pp. 709–15 and John Gledhill, 'Conclusion: Managing (In)security in Post-Arab Spring Transitions', *PS: Political Science and Politics*, 46 (4) 2013, pp. 736–9.

46. Michael Mann, *The Dark Side of Democracy: Explaining Ethnic Cleansing* (Cambridge: Cambridge University Press, 2009).

47. An argument I have made at length in the context of East Asia. See Bellamy, *East Asia's Other Miracle*.

48. See Leo Kuper, *Genocide: Its Political Use in the Twentieth Century* (New Haven, CT: Yale University Press, 1982), p. 57; Helen Fein, *Accounting for Genocide: National Response and Jewish Victimization During the Holocaust* (New York: Free Press), p. 9.

49. Henry Shue, *Basic Rights: Subsistence, Affluence and US Foreign Policy*, 2nd edition (Princeton, NJ: Princeton University Press, 1996). The fair provision of public goods and economic opportunities is a cornerstone of peace-supporting governance, argues David Cortright and his colleagues. See Cortright, Seyle, and Wall, *Governance for Peace*.

50. Mary Caprioli, 'Gender Equality and State Aggression: The Impact of Domestic Gender Equality on State First Use of Force', *International Interactions*, 29 (3) 2003, pp. 195–214.

51. See Valerie Hudson, Bonnie Ballif-Spanvill, Mary Caprioli, and Chad F. Emmett, *Sex and World Peace* (New York: Columbia University Press, 2014).

52. Ole R. Holsti and James Rosenau, 'Gender and the Political Beliefs of American Opinion Leaders', *Journal of Conflict Resolution*, 32 (2) 1988, pp. 248–94.

53. Erik Melander, 'Gender Equality and Intrastate Armed Conflict', *International Studies Quarterly*, 49 (4) 2005, pp. 695–714.

54. Hudson et al., *Sex and World Peace*.

55. Victor Asal, Richard Legault, Ora Szekely, and Jonathan Wilkenfeld, 'Gender Ideologies and Forms of Contentious Mobilization in the Middle East', *Journal of Peace Research*, 50 (3) 2013, pp. 305–18. Thanks to John Gledhill for this point.

56. Thanks to Sara E. Davies for this point.

57. Deborah Jordan Brooks and Benjamin A. Valentino, 'A War of One's Own: Understanding the Gender Gap in Support for War', *Public Opinion Quarterly*, 75 (2) 2011, pp. 270–86.

58. Betty A. Reardon, *Sexism and the War System* (Syracuse, NY: Syracuse University Press, 1996), p. 4.

59. Carol Cohn and Sara Ruddick, 'A Feminist Ethical Perspective on Weapons of Mass Destruction', in Sohail H. Hashmi and Steven Lee (eds.), *Ethics and Weapons of Mass Destruction: Religious and Secular Perspectives* (Cambridge: Cambridge University Press, 2004), p. 410.

60. Caron E. Gentry and Laura Sjoberg, *Beyond Mothers, Monsters, Whores: Thinking About Women's Violence in Global Politics* (London: Zed Books, 2016).

61. On that relationship, see Joshua S. Goldstein, *War and Gender: How Gender Shapes the War System and Vice-Versa* (Cambridge: Cambridge University Press, 2003).

62. R.J. Rummel, 'Is Collective Violence Correlated with Social Pluralism?', *Journal of Peace Research*, 34 (1) 1997, p. 170.

63. Scott, *Against the Grain*.

64. The central thesis of Morris, *War*.

65. O'Connell, *Ride of the Second Horseman*, p. 231.

66. Sinisa Malesevic disagrees and argues that the accumulation of state power has increased violence. Ultimately, though, this thesis rests on a broad definition of

violence that stretches beyond physical violence. See Sinisa Malesevic, *The Rise of Organized Brutality: A Historical Sociology of Violence* (Cambridge: Cambridge University Press, 2017).

67. Ignatieff, *The Ordinary Virtues*, p. 17.
68. Mueller, *Remnants of War*.
69. Russell Jacoby, *Bloodlust: On the Roots of Violence from Cain and Abel to the Present* (New York: Free Press, 2011), p. 44.
70. David Armitage, *Civil Wars: A History in Ideas* (New Haven, CT: Yale University Press, 2017), pp. 39, 46, and 88.
71. Armitage, *Civil Wars*, p. 75.
72. Thucydides, *Peloponnesian War*, book III, 82–5.
73. Thucydides, *Peloponnesian War*, book III, 84–5.
74. Armitage, *Civil Wars*, p. 106.
75. Pankaj Mishra, *Age of Anger: A History of the Present* (New York: Farrar, Straus & Giroux, 2017).
76. John Leader Maynard, 'Rethinking the Role of Ideology in Mass Atrocities', *Terrorism and Political Violence*, 26 (5) 2014, pp. 821–41.

Chapter 6

1. John Slessor, *The Central Blue: Recollections and Reflections* (London: Cassell, 1956).
2. Van Creveld, *More on War*, p. 201.
3. Kagan, *On the Origins of War*.
4. Ivan Stanislavovich Bloch, *Is War Now Impossible? Being an Abridgment of the War of the Future in Its Technical, Economic, and Political Relations* (London: Grant Richards, 1899), p. 9.
5. Bloch, *Is War Now Impossible?*, p. 5.
6. Bloch, *Is War Now Impossible?*, p. 11.
7. Bloch, *Is War Now Impossible?*, p. 294.
8. See Freedman, *The Future of War*.
9. Norman Angell, *The Great Illusion: A Study in the Relation of Military Power in Nations and Their Economic and Social Advantage* (London: Putnam's Sons, 1911), p. 295. The book was first published by Simpkin, Marshall, Hamilton, and Kent in 1909 under the title *Europe's Optical Illusion*.
10. Angell, *Great Illusion*, p. 361.
11. Niall Ferguson, *The Pity of War 1914–1918* (London: Penguin, 1998), p. 10.
12. Phillip Supino, 'The Norman Angell Peace Campaign in Germany', *Journal of Peace Research*, 9 (9) 1972, p. 164.
13. General Friedreich von Bernhardi, *Germany and the Next War* (London: Edward Arnold, 1912).
14. Barbara Tuchman writes sarcastically that Angell 'proved that war had become vain...By impressive examples and incontrovertible argument'. Barbara W. Tuchman, *The Guns of August* (New York: Ballantine, 1962), p. 12.
15. Orwell, *Homage to Catalonia*, p. 24.
16. Bloch, *Is War Now Impossible?*, p. xxxi.
17. Cited by James Joll and Gordon Martell, *Origins of the First World War* (London: Routledge, 2006), p. 16.

18. Emphasis added. Winston Churchill, *The World Crisis Volume V: The Unknown War: The Eastern Front* (London: Bloomsbury, 1931), p. 1.

19. Cited by Adam Hochschild, *To End All Wars: A Story of Protest and Patriotism in the First World War* (London: Macmillan, 2011), p. xv.

20. Clark, *The Sleepwalkers*, p. 562.

21. MacMillan, *The War That Ended Peace*, p. xxii.

22. *Global Peace Index 2017*, Institute of Economics and Peace, p. 53.

23. As cited by John Mueller, *Atomic Obsession: Nuclear Alarmism from Hiroshima to Al Qaeda* (Oxford: Oxford University Press, 2010), p. 30.

24. Carl Kaysen, 'Is War Obsolete?', *International Security*, 14 (4) 1990, pp. 42–64.

25. One of the principal arguments advanced by Ferejohn and McCall Rosenbluth, *Forged Through Fire*.

26. See Paul Collier et al., *Breaking the Conflict Trap: Civil War and Development Policy* (Oxford: Oxford University Press, 2003).

27. Douglas Lemke, *Regions of War and Peace* (Cambridge: Cambridge University Press, 2002).

28. *Global Peace Index 2017*, pp. 65–9.

29. For example, Nazli Choucri and Robert North, *Nations in Conflict: National Growth and International Violence* (New York: Freeman, 1975) and Tilly, 'War Making and State Making as Organized Crime'.

30. Jeffrey Dixon, 'What Causes Civil Wars? Integrating Quantitative Research Findings', *International Studies Review*, 11 (4) 2009, p. 708.

31. Collier, *The Bottom Billion*.

32. Jean Monnet cited by Ernest Wistrich, *After 1992: The United States of Europe* (London: Routledge, 1991), p. 24.

33. Ole Wæver, 'Insecurity, Security and Asecurity in the West European Non-War Community', in Emanuel Adler and Michael Barnett (eds.), *Security Communities* (Cambridge: Cambridge University Press, 1998), p. 90.

34. Cited by R.C. Mowat, *Creating the European Community* (New York: Barnes and Noble, 1973), p. 59.

35. Etel Solingen, 'Pax Asiatica versus Belli Levantina: The Foundations of War and Peace in East Asia and the Middle East', *American Political Science Review*, 101 (4) 2007, p. 758.

36. Rosemary Foot, 'Social Boundaries in Flux: Secondary Regional Organizations as a Reflection of Regional International Society', in Barry Buzan and Yongjin Zhang (eds.), *Contesting International Society in East Asia* (Cambridge: Cambridge University Press, 2014), p. 196.

37. On which see Stephen Brooks, *Producing Security: Multinational Corporations, Globalization, and the Changing Calculus of Combat* (Princeton, NJ: Princeton University Press, 2005).

38. John Ravenhill, 'Production Networks in Asia', in Saadia Pekkanen, John Ravenhill, and Rosemary Foot (eds.), *The Oxford Handbook of the International Relations of Asia* (Oxford: Oxford University Press, 2014), pp. 358–9.

39. Arendt, *On Violence*, p. 10.

40. Mueller, *The Remnants of War*.

41. Gat, *Causes of War*.

42. Howard, *Invention of Peace*, p. 100.
43. See Gallie, *Philosophers of Peace and War*, pp. 19–20.
44. Christopher Greenwood, 'The Concept of War in Modern International Law', *International and Comparative Law Quarterly*, 36 (2) 1987, p. 305.
45. This list is partly derived from Goertz, Diehl, and Balas, *Puzzle of Peace*.
46. On the importance of the changing politics of conquest, see Tanisha Fazal, *State Death: The Politics and Geography of Conquest, Occupation and Annexation* (Princeton, NJ: Princeton University Press, 2007).
47. Tanisha Fazal and Ryan Griffiths, 'Membership Has Its Privileges: The Changing Benefits of Statehood', *International Studies Review*, 16 (1) 2014, pp. 79–106.
48. Goertz, Diehl, and Balas, *Puzzle of Peace*, pp. 144–5.
49. See Karma Nabulsi's excellent *Traditions of War: Occupation, Resistance, and the Law* (Oxford: Oxford University Press, 1999).
50. Hew Strachan, *The Direction of War: Contemporary Strategy in Historical Perspective* (Cambridge: Cambridge University Press, 2013), p. 16.
51. Theo Farrell, *Unwinnable: Britain's War in Afghanistan: 2001–2014* (London: Bodley Head, 2017).
52. Larry May, *Contingent Pacifism: Revisiting Just War Theory* (Cambridge: Cambridge University Press, 2015), p. 1.
53. David Bosco, *Five to Rule Them All: The UN Security Council and the Making of the Modern World* (New York: Oxford University Press, 2009), p. 22.
54. Edward C. Luck, *United Nations Security Council: Practice and Promise* (London: Routledge, 2008), p. 63.
55. Rupert Smith, *The Utility of Force: The Art of War in the Modern World* (London: Penguin, 2006).
56. See Nolan, *The Allure of Battle*.
57. Pierre Hassner, 'Beyond the Three Traditions: The Philosophy of War and Peace in Historical Perspective', *International Affairs*, 70 (4) 1994, p. 754.

Chapter 7

1. Von Clausewitz, *On War*, pp. 20–1.
2. Cited by Mike Rossiter, *Sink the Belgrano* (London: Corgi, 2008), p. 157.
3. Their story is told in Ralph Gibson and Paul Oldfield, *Sheffield City Battalion* (Barnsley: Pen and Sword Books, 2009).
4. Ferguson, *The Pity of War*, p. 364.
5. Daniel Chirot and Clark McCauley, *Why Not Kill Them All? The Logic and Prevention of Political Mass Murder* (Princeton, NJ: Princeton University Press, 2006), p. 77.
6. Chirot and McCauley, *Why Not*, p. 77.
7. Stromberg, *Redemption by War*, p. 190.
8. Paul Bloom, *Against Empathy: The Case for Rational Compassion* (London: Bodley Head, 2017).
9. Cited in Stuurman, *The Invention of Humanity*, p. 275.
10. J.G. Fichte, *The Science of Rights*, trans. A.E. Kroeger (London: Trubnor and Co., 1889), p. 228.

11. Ehrenreich, *Blood Rites*, p. 13.

12. Orwell, *The Lion and the Unicorn*, p. 3.

13. Central argument advanced by Amartya's Sen's excellent *Identity and Violence*.

14. Christopher Coker, '(Ir)rational Actors: Why Great Powers Can Still Go to War', in Andreas Herberg-Rothe (ed.), *Lessons from World War I for the Rise of Asia* (Stuttgart: Idiben, 2015), p. 23.

15. George Mosse, *Fallen Soldiers: Reshaping the Memory of the World Wars* (Oxford: Oxford University Press, 1990), p. 7 and throughout.

16. Cited in Mosse, *Fallen Soldiers*, p. 65.

17. Cited by June Purvis, *Emmeline Pankhurst: A Biography* (London: Routledge, 2002), p. 272.

18. Christabel Pankhurst, 'No Compromise Peace', *Britannia*, 3 August 1917, p. 72.

19. Stefan Zweig, *The World of Yesterday* (Lincoln, NE: University of Nebraska Press, 1964), pp. 222–4.

20. See Stromberg, *Redemption by War*.

21. Michael Howard, *The Causes of War* (Cambridge, MA: Harvard University Press, 1983), pp. 26–7.

22. Cited by Ehrenreich, *Blood Rites*, p. 202.

23. Ehrenreich, *Blood Rites*, p. 16.

24. As David Rieff reminds us. Rieff, *In Praise of Forgetting*.

25. Sen, *Identity and Violence*.

26. Cited by Jens Bartelson, *War in International Thought* (Cambridge: Cambridge University Press, 2018), p. 39.

27. Benedict Anderson, *Imagined Communities: Reflections on the Origin and Spread of Nationalism* (London: Verso, 1983), p. 9.

28. James, 'The Moral Equivalent of War', p. 19.

29. Martin Van Creveld, *The Transformation of War* (New York: Free Press, 1991), pp. 218–33.

30. Ernst Junger, *Storm of Steel* (London: Penguin, 2004 [1920]). Quotes come from different parts, including pp. 55, 171, and 207.

31. All quoted in Bourke, *An Intimate History of Killing*, p. 19.

32. Cited in Mosse, *Fallen Soldiers*, p. 64.

33. Lt. Col. Dave Grossman, *On Killing: The Psychological Cost of Learning to Kill in War and Society*, revised and updated edition (New York: Back Bay Books, 2009), pp. 18–29.

34. Hedges, *War Is a Force That Gives Us Meaning*.

35. Glover, *Humanity*, p. xviii.

36. Hedges, *War Is a Force That Gives Us Meaning*, p. 38.

37. Orwell, *Homage to Catalonia*, p. 15.

38. Mosse, *Fallen Soldiers*, pp. 266–7. Mosse provides numerous examples to demonstrate how this narrative is consciously developed.

39. Hedges, *War Is a Force That Gives Us Meaning*, pp. 83–4.

40. John Weaver, *A Sadly Troubled History: The Meanings of Suicide in the Modern Age* (Montreal-Kingston: McGill-Queen's University Press, 2009).

41. Jay M. Winter, 'Notes on the Memory Boom: War Remembrance and the Use of the Past', in Duncan Bell (ed.), *Memory, Trauma and World Politics: Reflections on the Relationship Between Past and Present* (London: Palgrave, 2006), pp. 54–73.

42. Richard Holmes, *Acts of War: The Behaviour of Men in Battle* (New York: Simon & Schuster, 1989), p. 361.

43. Cited by Stanley Weintraub, *Silent Night: The Remarkable Christmas Truce of 1914* (London: Simon & Schuster, 2001), p. 197.

44. Leo Tolstoy, *The Kingdom of God Is Within You* (London: Dover, 2006 [1894]), pp. 68–9.

45. Gallie, *Philosophers*, p. 123.

46. Cited by Annabel Robinson, *The Life and Work of Jane Ellen Harrison* (Oxford: Oxford University Press, 2002), p. 261.

47. See Ehrenreich, *Blood Rites*; Johanna Alberti, *Beyond Suffrage: Feminists in War and Peace, 1914–1928* (New York: St. Martin's Press, 1989), p. 50; Adam Jones, *Genocide: A Comprehensive Introduction* (London: Routledge, 2017), n. 67.

48. All cited in Robinson, *Life and Work*, p. 261.

49. Cited in Robinson, *Life and Work*, p. 263.

50. Bertrand Russell, 'Some Psychological Difficulties of Pacifism in Wartime', in Julian Bell (ed.), *We Did Not Fight: 1914–1918 Experiences of War Resisters* (London: Cobden-Sanderson, 1935), p. 327.

51. All these come from Weintraub, *Silent Night*.

52. Cited by Toby Neal, 'Seasons Over the Decades, 1914', *Shropshire Star*, 26 December 2014.

53. A photo of Williamson's original letter can be found at https://www.henrywilliamson. co.uk/biography/firstworldwar/57-uncategorised/158-henry-williamson-and-the-christmas-truce.

54. Weintraub, *Silent Night*, pp. 179–81.

55. Weintraub, *Silent Night*, p. 180.

56. John Shute, 'The Forgotten Christmas Truce the British Tried to Suppress', *The Telegraph*, 26 December 2016.

57. With thanks to John Gledhill for this point.

58. David Hume, 'Of National Characters', in Eugene F. Miller (ed.), *Essays Moral, Political and Literary* (Indianapolis, IN: Liberty Fund, 1985), p. 202.

59. David Hume, *A Treatise on Human Nature*, edited by Ernest Mossner (London: Penguin, 1986 [1740]), p. 386.

60. Pagden, *The Enlightenment and Why It Still Matters*, p. 73.

61. Adam Smith, *The Theory of Moral Sentiments* (London: Penguin, 2010 [1759]), p. 9.

62. Smith, *Theory of Moral Sentiments*, pp. 9–12.

63. David Hume, *An Enquiry Concerning the Principle of Morals* (Cambridge, MA: Hackett Publishing, 1983 [1751]), p. 22.

64. Darwin, *Descent of Man*, p. 83.

65. Hans J. Morgenthau, *Peace, Security, and the United Nations* (Chicago, IL: University of Chicago Press, 1946), p. 6.

66. Sen, *Identity and Violence*.

67. Sen, *Identity and Violence*.

68. Henry Dunant, *A Memory of Solferino* (Geneva: International Committee of the Red Cross, 1939 [1862]).

69. Leo Tolstoy, *War and Peace* (London: Penguin, 2008 [1869]), pp. 921–2.

70. H.G. Wells, *Anticipations of the Reaction of Mechanical and Scientific Progress upon Human Life and Thought* (London: Chapman and Hall, 1902).

71. Virginia Woolf, *Three Guineas* (San Diego, CA: Mariner, 1963 [1938]), p. 32.

72. Woolf, *Three Guineas*, p. 36.

73. Woolf, *Three Guineas*, p. 130.

74. Sontag, *Regarding the Pain of Others*, pp. 13–14.

75. Jean Bethke Elshtain, *Jane Addams and the Dream of American Democracy: A Life* (New York: Basic Books, 2002), pp. 217–19.

76. Quoted in Elshtain, *Addams*, p. 218.

77. Joanna Bourke, *Wounding the World: How Military Violence and War-Play Invade Our Lives* (London: Virago, 2014), p. 248.

78. Sontag, *Regarding the Pain of Others*, p. 7.

Chapter 8

1. Andrew J. Bacevich, *America's War for the Greater Middle East: A Military History* (New York: Random House, 2016).

2. Farrell, *Unwinnable*.

3. Hedges, *War Is a Force That Gives Us Meaning*, p. 23.

4. And the symbols themselves become fodder for the fight. See Marshall, *Worth Dying For*.

5. On which see K. Neil Jenkins, Nick Megoran, Rachel Woodward, and Daniel Bos, 'Wootton Bassett and the Political Spaces of Remembrance and Mourning', *Areas*, 44 (3) 2012, pp. 356–63.

6. Hedges, *War Is a Force That Gives Us Meaning*, p. 44.

7. This phrase is borrowed from Roger Mac Ginty, who develops the concept 'everyday peace' to refer to a more specific set of issues. See Roger Mac Ginty, 'Everyday Peace: Bottom-Up and Local Agency in Conflict-Affected Societies', *Security Dialogue*, 45 (6) 2014, pp. 548–64.

8. Mark Mazower, *Governing the World: The History of an Idea* (New York: Allen Lane, 2012).

9. Hathaway and Shapiro, *The Internationalists*.

10. For an excellent introduction, produced in conjunction with the International Committee of the Red Cross, see Liesbeth Zegveld and Frits Kalshoven, *Constraints on the Waging of War: An Introduction to International Humanitarian Law*, 4th edition (Cambridge: Cambridge University Press, 2015).

11. Morgenthau, *Politics Among Nations*, pp. 502–8.

12. A solution commonly proposed by peace activists and more hard-minded realists alike. More recently by Mike Martin, who maintains that since larger political groups are more peaceful than smaller ones, the only way of achieving world peace would be to establish a world government. Martin, *Why We Fight*.

13. For example, Virginia Page Fortna, *Does Peacekeeping Work? Shaping Belligerents' Choices After Civil War* (Princeton, NJ: Princeton University Press, 2008) and Lisa Hultman, 'UN Peace Operations and Protection of Civilians: Cheap Talk or Norm Implementation?', *Journal of Peace Research*, 50 (1) 2013, pp. 59–73.

14. Michael O'Hanlon and Peter W. Singer, 'The Humanitarian Transformation: Expanding Global Intervention Capacity', *Survival*, 46 (1) 2004, p. 97, n. 7.

15. 'UN General Assembly Approves \$5.5 Billion Budget for 2014/2015' by Michele Nichols, 27 December 2013, *Reuters*, available at www.reuters.com/article/2013/12/27/us-un-budget-idUSBRE9BQoJX20131227; 'Fifth Committee Recommends \$5.4 Billion Budget for 2016–2017 Biennium as It Concludes Main Part of Seventieth Session', *United Nations Meetings Coverage and Press Releases*, available at http://www.un.org/press/en/2015/gaab4185.doc.htm.

16. OCHA, *Global Humanitarian Overview 2016* (Geneva: OCHA, 2016).

17. UNHCR, *Global Trends: Forced Displacement in 2014* (Geneva: UNHCR, 2016).

18. Vaughn Lowe, Adam Roberts, Jennifer Welsh, and Dominik Zaum, 'Introduction', in Vaughn Lowe, Adam Roberts, Jennifer Welsh, and Dominik Zaum (eds.), *The United Nations Security Council and War: The Evolution of Thought and Practice since 1945* (Oxford: Oxford University Press, 2008), p. 30.

19. Marie Olsen Lounsbery and Frederic Pearson, *Civil Wars: Internal Struggles, Global Consequences* (Toronto: University of Toronto Press, 2009), p. 148.

20. Karl Deutsch et al., *Political Community and the North Atlantic Area: International Organizations in the Light of Historical Experiences* (Princeton, NJ: Princeton University Press, 1957), p. 5.

21. To draw on a more recent definition of the term. Emmanuel Adler and Michael Barnett (eds.), *Security Communities* (Cambridge: Cambridge University Press, 1998).

22. Emmanuel Adler and Michael Barnett, 'A Framework for the Study of Security Communities', in Adler and Barnett (eds.), *Security Communities*, pp. 53–5.

23. I have set out how both operate in the East Asian context in Bellamy, *East Asia's Other Miracle*.

24. Sen, *Identity and Violence*.

25. Gallie, *Philosophers*, p. 35.

26. Solingen, *Regional Orders at Century's Dawn*, p. 65.

27. See Azar Gat, *Causes of War*; McDonald, *The Invisible Hand of Peace*; and Erik Gartzke, 'The Capitalist Peace', *American Journal of Political Science*, 51, 2007, pp. 66–191.

28. For an excellent history see Kirsten Sellars, *'Crimes Against Peace' and International Law* (Cambridge: Cambridge University Press, 2013).

29. I am grateful to Sara E. Davies for this formulation.

30. Hedges, *War Is a Force That Gives Us Meaning*, p. 15.

31. Sontag, *Regarding the Pain of Others*, p. 113.

32. Grayling, *War* and Bourke, *Wounding the World*.

33. Hedges, *War Is a Force That Gives Us Meaning*, p. 15.

34. Drawn from Hochschild, *To End All Wars*, pp. 48–9, 336, 363–4.

35. Sontag, *Regarding the Pain of Others*, p. 102.

36. Francisco de Vitoria, 'On the Law of War', in Anthony Pagden and Jeremy Lawrence (eds.), *Vitoria: Political Writings* (Cambridge: Cambridge University Press, 1991), question 2 article 2, and question 2 article 3, pp. 306–11.
37. Hedges, *War Is a Force That Gives Us Meaning*, p. 15.
38. See Roger Mac Ginty and Pamina Firchow, 'Top-Down and Bottom-Up Narratives of Peace and Conflict', *Politics*, 36 (3) 2016, pp. 308–23.
39. Mary Kaldor, *Global Civil Society: An Answer to War* (Cambridge: Polity, 2003), p. 3.
40. An idea that has guided my argument throughout. It resembles the position taken by Michael Ignatieff on the idea of a common morality. See Ignatieff, *The Ordinary Virtues*, p. 11.

BIBLIOGRAPHY

Acemoglu, Daron and James A. Robinson, *Why Nations Fail: The Origins of Power, Prosperity, and Poverty* (London: Profile, 2013).

Addams, Jane, *Newer Ideals of Peace* (Urbana and Chicago, IL: University of Illinois Press, 2007).

Adler, Emmanuel and Michael Barnett, 'A Framework for the Study of Security Communities', in Adler and Barnett (eds.), *Security Communities* (Cambridge: Cambridge University Press, 1998).

Adler, Emmanuel and Michael Barnett (eds.), *Security Communities* (Cambridge: Cambridge University Press, 1998).

Adolf, Antony, *Peace: A World History* (Cambridge: Polity, 2009).

Alberti, Johanna, *Beyond Suffrage: Feminists in War and Peace, 1914–1928* (New York: St. Martin's Press, 1989).

Allen, Charles, *Ashoka: The Search for India's Lost Emperor* (London: Abacus, 2012).

Anderson, Benedict, *Imagined Communities: Reflections on the Origin and Spread of Nationalism* (London: Verso, 1983).

Angell, Norman, *The Great Illusion: A Study in the Relation of Military Power in Nations and Their Economic and Social Advantage* (London: Putnam's Sons, 1911).

Ardrey, Robert, *African Genesis* (New York: Dell, 1961).

Ardrey, Robert, *The Territorial Imperative* (New York: Atheneum, 1966).

Arendt, Hannah, *On Violence* (London: Harcourt, 1970).

Arendt, Hannah, *Eichmann in Jerusalem: A Report on the Banality of Evil* (London: Penguin, 2011 [1963]).

Armitage, David, *Foundations of Modern International Thought* (Cambridge: Cambridge University Press, 2013).

Armitage, David, *Civil Wars: A History in Ideas* (New Haven, CT: Yale University Press, 2017).

Armstrong, A.C., 'Hegel's Attitude on War and Peace', *Journal of Philosophy*, 30 (25) 1933, pp. 684–9.

Armstrong, Karen, *Fields of Blood: Religion and the History of Violence* (New York: Anchor Books, 2014).

Arnold, Thomas, *Introductory Lectures on Modern History* (London: B. Fellowes, 1849).

Asal, Victor, Richard Legault, Ora Szekely, and Jonathan Wilkenfeld, 'Gender Ideologies and Forms of Contentious Mobilization in the Middle East', *Journal of Peace Research*, 50 (3) 2013, pp. 305–18.

Axelrod, Robert, *The Evolution of Cooperation* (New York: Basic Books, 1984).

Bacevich, Andrew J., *America's War for the Greater Middle East: A Military History* (New York: Random House, 2016).

Bainton, Roland H., *Christian Attitudes Toward War and Peace: A Historical Survey and Critical Re-Evaluation* (Nashville, TN: Abingdon Press, 1960).

Balakian, Peter, *The Burning Tigris: The Armenian Genocide and America's Response* (New York: Perennial, 2004).

Banks, Michael, 'Four Conceptions of Peace', in Dennis J.D. Sandole and Ingrid Sandole-Saroste (eds.), *Conflict Management and Problem Solving: Interpersonal to International Applications* (New York: New York University Press, 1987).

Barash, David, 'Evolution and Peace', in Douglas P. Fry (ed.), *War, Peace, and Human Nature: The Convergence of Evolutionary and Cultural Views* (Oxford: Oxford University Press, 2013).

Barbieri, Katherine, *The Liberal Illusion: Does Trade Promote Peace?* (Ann Arbor, MI: University of Michigan Press, 2002).

Bartelson, Jens, *War in International Thought* (Cambridge: Cambridge University Press, 2018).

Bates, Robert H., *Prosperity and Violence: The Political Economy of Development* (New York: W. W. Norton, 2009).

Bauman, Zygmunt, *Modernity and the Holocaust* (Oxford: Polity, 1992).

Beales, A.C.F., *The History of Peace: A Short Account of the Organised Movements for International Peace* (New York: The Dial Press, 1931).

Bellamy, Alex J., *Security Communities and Their Neighbours* (London: Palgrave, 2002).

Bellamy, Alex J., *East Asia's Other Miracle: Explaining the Decline of Mass Atrocities* (Oxford: Oxford University Press, 2017).

Bentham, Jeremy, 'A Plan for an Universal and Perpetual Peace', available at http://www.laits.utexas.edu/poltheory/bentham/pil/pil.e04.html.

Berlin, Isaiah, 'Two Concepts of Liberty', in Isaiah Berlin, *Liberty* (Oxford: Oxford University Press, 2004).

Bernal, J.D., *World Without War* (London: Routledge & Kegan Paul, 1961).

Berndt, Ronald and Catherine Berndt, *The World of the First Australians*, 5th edition (Canberra: Aboriginal Studies Press, 1996).

Best, Geoffrey, *Humanity in War* (New York: Columbia University Press, 1980).

Biggar, Nigel, *In Defence of War* (Oxford: Oxford University Press, 2014).

Bloch, Ivan Stanislavovich, *Is War Now Impossible? Being an Abridgment of the War of the Future in Its Technical, Economic, and Political Relations* (London: Grant Richards, 1899).

Bloom, Paul, *Against Empathy: The Case for Rational Compassion* (London: Bodley Head, 2017).

Bonta, Bruce, 'Conflict Resolution Among Peaceful Societies: The Culture of Peacefulness', *Journal of Peace Research*, 33 (4) 1996, pp. 403–20.

Booth, Ken, *Theory of World Security* (Cambridge: Cambridge University Press, 2007).

Borgwardt, Elizabeth, *A New Deal for the World: America's Vision for Human Rights* (Cambridge, MA: Harvard University Press, 2005).

Bosco, David, *Five to Rule Them All: The UN Security Council and the Making of the Modern World* (New York: Oxford University Press, 2009).

Bourke, Joanna, *An Intimate History of Killing: Face to Face Killing in Twentieth Century Warfare* (New York: Basic Books, 1999).

Bourke, Joanna, *Wounding the World: How Military Violence and War-Play Invade Our Lives* (London: Virago, 2014).

Brain, C.K., 'New Finds at the Swartkrans Australopithecine Site', *Nature*, 225, 1970, pp. 1112–19.

Brock, Peter, *Pacifism in Europe to 1914* (Princeton, NJ: Princeton University Press, 1972).

Brodie, Bernard (ed.), *The Absolute Weapon: Atomic Power and World Order* (New York: Harcourt, 1946).

Brooks, Deborah Jordan and Benjamin A. Valentino, 'A War of One's Own: Understanding the Gender Gap in Support for War', *Public Opinion Quarterly*, 75 (2) 2011, pp. 270–86.

Brooks, Stephen, *Producing Security: Multinational Corporations, Globalization, and the Changing Calculus of Combat* (Princeton, NJ: Princeton University Press, 2005).

Browning, Christopher, *Ordinary Men: Reserve Battalion 101 and the Final Solution in Poland* (New York: Harper Collins, 1992).

Bull, Hedley, 'Disarmament and the International System', *Australian Journal of Politics and History*, 5 (1) 1959, pp. 41–50.

Bull, Hedley, 'The Great Irresponsibles? The United States, the Soviet Union and World Order', *International Journal*, 35 (3) 1980, pp. 437–47.

Bull, Hedley and Adam Watson (eds.), *The Expansion of International Society* (Oxford: Oxford University Press, 1984).

Butler, Judith, *Frames of War: When Is Life Grievable?* (London: Verso, 2009).

Caprioli, Mary, 'Gender Equality and State Aggression: The Impact of Domestic Gender Equality on State First Use of Force', *International Interactions*, 29 (3) 2003, pp. 195–214.

Carnegie Commission on Preventing Deadly Conflict, *Preventing Deadly Conflict* (New York: Carnegie Corporation, 1997).

Carr, E.H., *The Twenty Years' Crisis 1919–1939: An Introduction to the Study of International Relations* (London: Palgrave, 2016 [1939]).

Castleden, Rodney, *Minoans: Life in Bronze Age Crete* (London: Routledge, 1994).

Cavanagh, William T., *The Myth of Religious Violence: Secular Ideology and the Roots of Modern Conflict* (Oxford: Oxford University Press, 2009).

Ceadel, Martin, *Thinking about Peace and War* (Oxford: Oxford University Press, 1989).

Ceadel, Martin, *The Origins of War Prevention: The British Peace Movement and International Relations, 1730–1854* (Oxford: Clarendon Press, 1996).

Ceadel, Martin, *Semi-Detached Idealists: The British Peace Movement and International Relations, 1854–1945* (Oxford: Oxford University Press, 2000).

Chagnon, Napoleon, *Yanomamo: The Fierce People*, 3rd edition (New York: Holt, Rinehart and Winston, 1983).

Chenoweth, Erica, *Why Civil Resistance Works: The Strategic Logic of Nonviolent Conflict* (New York: Columbia University Press, 2011).

Chirot, Daniel and Clark McCauley, *Why Not Kill Them All? The Logic and Prevention of Political Mass Murder* (Princeton, NJ: Princeton University Press, 2006).

Choucri, Nazli and Robert North, *Nations in Conflict: National Growth and International Violence* (New York: Freeman, 1975).

Churchill, Winston, *The World Crisis Volume V: The Unknown War: The Eastern Front* (London: Bloomsbury, 1931).

Clark, Christopher, *The Sleepwalkers: How Europe Went to War in 2014* (London: Penguin, 2014).

Clausewitz, Carl von, *On War*, trans. Michael Howard and Peter Paret (Princeton, NJ: Princeton University Press, 1976).

Cohn, Carol and Sara Ruddick, 'A Feminist Ethical Perspective on Weapons of Mass Destruction', in Sohail H. Hashmi and Steven Lee (eds.), *Ethics and Weapons of*

Mass Destruction: Religious and Secular Perspectives (Cambridge: Cambridge University Press, 2004).

Coker, Christopher, *Barbarous Philosophers: Reflections on the Nature of War from Heraclitus to Heisenberg* (London: Hurst and Co., 2010).

Coker, Christopher, *Can War Be Eliminated?* (Cambridge: Polity, 2014).

Coker, Christopher, '(Ir)rational Actors: Why Great Powers Can Still Go to War', in Andreas Herberg-Rothe (ed.), *Lessons from World War I for the Rise of Asia* (Stuttgart: Idiben, 2015).

Collier, Paul, *The Bottom Billion: Why the Poorest Countries Are Failing and What Can Be Done About It* (Oxford: Oxford University Press, 2007).

Collier, Paul, V.L. Elliott, Håvard Hegre, Anke Hoeffler, Marta Reynal-Queral, and Nicholas Sambanis, *Breaking the Conflict Trap: Civil War and Development Policy* (Oxford: Oxford University Press, 2003).

Cortright, David, Conor Seyle, and Kristen Wall, *Governance for Peace: How Inclusive, Participatory and Accountable Institutions Promote Peace and Prosperity* (Cambridge: Cambridge University Press, 2017).

Dallmayr, Fred R., 'A War Against the Turks? Erasmus on War and Peace', *Asian Journal of Social Science*, 34 (1) 2006, pp. 67–85.

Dart, Raymond, 'The Predatory Implemental Technique of Australopithecines', *American Journal of Physical Anthropology*, 7, 1949, pp. 1–38.

Dart, Raymond, 'The Predatory Transition from Ape to Man', *International Anthropological and Linguistic Review*, 1, 1953, pp. 201–17.

Dart, Raymond, *Adventures with the Missing Link* (New York: Harper, 1959).

Darwin, Charles, *The Descent of Man* (London: John Murray, 1871).

Davie, Maurice R., *The Evolution of War: A Study of Its Role in Early Societies* (New Haven, CT: Yale University Press, 1929).

Dawkins, Richard, *An Appetite for Wonder: The Makings of a Scientist* (London: Transworld, 2014).

Dentan, Robert K., *The Semai: A Nonviolent People of Malaysia*, 2nd edition (New York: Holt, Rinehart and Winston, 1979).

Deutsch, Karl W., Sidney A. Burrell, Robert A. Kann, and Maurice Lee Jr., *Political Community and the North Atlantic Area: International Organizations in the Light of Historical Experiences* (Princeton, NJ: Princeton University Press, 1957).

de Waal, Frans, *Our Inner Ape: A Leading Primatologist Explains Why We Are Who We Are* (New York: Penguin, 2005).

de Waal, Frans, *Primates and Philosophers: How Morality Evolved* (Princeton, NJ: Princeton University Press, 2006).

Dewey, John, *Human Nature and Conduct: An Introduction to Social Psychology* (New York: Cosimo, 2007 [1922]).

Diamond, Jared, *Collapse: How Societies Choose to Fail or Succeed* (New York: Viking Press, 2005).

Dixon, Jeffrey, 'What Causes Civil Wars? Integrating Quantitative Research Findings', *International Studies Review*, 11 (4) 2009, pp. 707–35.

Dreger, Alice, *Galileo's Middle Finger: Heretics, Activists and the Search for Justice in Science* (New York: Penguin, 2015).

Dunant, Henry, *A Memory of Solferino* (Geneva: International Committee of the Red Cross, 1939 [1862]).

Dunne, Tim and Christian Reus-Smit (eds.), *The Globalization of International Society* (Oxford: Oxford University Press, 2016).

Ehrenreich, Barbara, *Blood Rites: Origins and History of the Passions of War* (London: Granta, 2011).

Elias, Norbert, *The Civilizing Process*, trans. Edmund Jephcott (Oxford: Blackwell, 1982 [1939]).

Elshtain, Jean Bethke, *Jane Addams and the Dream of American Democracy: A Life* (New York: Basic Books, 2002).

Ember, Carol and Mervin Ember, 'Resource Unpredictability, Mistrust and War', *Journal of Conflict Resolution*, 36 (2) 1992, pp. 242–62.

Ember, Carol and Mervin Ember, 'Warfare, Aggression and Recourse Problems: Cross-Cultural Codes', *Behaviour Science Research*, 26, 1992, pp. 169–226.

Ember, Carol and Mervin Ember, 'War, Socialization and Interpersonal Violence: A Cross-Cultural Study', *Journal of Conflict Resolution*, 38 (4) 1994, pp. 620–46.

Fanon, Frantz, *Wretched of the Earth* (London: Penguin, 2014 [1961]).

Farrell, Theo, *Unwinnable: Britain's War in Afghanistan: 2001–2014* (London: Bodley Head, 2017).

Fazal, Tanisha, *State Death: The Politics and Geography of Conquest, Occupation and Annexation* (Princeton, NJ: Princeton University Press, 2007).

Fazal, Tanisha and Ryan Griffiths, 'Membership Has Its Privileges: The Changing Benefits of Statehood', *International Studies Review*, 16 (1) 2014, pp. 79–106.

Fein, Helen, *Accounting for Genocide: National Response and Jewish Victimization During the Holocaust* (New York: Free Press).

Ferejohn, John and Frances McCall Rosenbluth, *Forged Through Fire: War, Peace and the Democratic Bargain* (New York: W. W. Norton, 2017).

Ferguson, Niall, *The Pity of War 1914–1918* (London: Penguin, 1998).

Ferrill, Arthur, *The Origins of War: From the Stone Age to Alexander the Great* (New York: Thames and Hudson, 1985).

Fichte, J.G., *The Science of Rights*, trans. A.E. Kroeger (London: Trubnor and Co., 1889).

Flint, Julie and Alex de Waal, *Darfur: A New History of a Long War* (London and New York: Zed Books, 2008).

Foot, Rosemary, 'Social Boundaries in Flux: Secondary Regional Organizations as a Reflection of Regional International Society', in Barry Buzan and Yongjin Zhang (eds.), *Contesting International Society in East Asia* (Cambridge: Cambridge University Press, 2014).

Fortna, Virginia Page, *Does Peacekeeping Work? Shaping Belligerents' Choices After Civil War* (Princeton, NJ: Princeton University Press, 2008).

Frankopan, Peter, *Silk Roads: A New History of the World* (London: Bloomsbury, 2015).

Freedman, Lawrence, *The Future of War: A History* (London: Allen Lane, 2017).

Freeman, Derek, *Margaret Mead and Samoa* (Cambridge, MA: Harvard University Press, 1983).

Freud, Sigmund, *Civilization and Its Discontents* (London: Hogarth Press, 1930).

Freud, Sigmund, 'Why War?', in Leon Bramson and George W. Goethals (eds.), *War: Studies from Psychology, Sociology, Anthropology* (New York: Basic Books, 1968).

Friedman, Thomas L., *The Lexus and the Olive Tree: Understanding Globalization* (New York: Farrar, Straus & Giroux, 1999).

Fry, Douglas P., *Beyond War: The Human Potential for Peace* (Oxford: Oxford University Press, 2006).

Fry, Douglas P. (ed.), *War, Peace, and Human Nature: The Convergence of Evolutionary and Cultural Views* (Oxford: Oxford University Press, 2013).

Fukuyama, Francis, 'Women and the Evolution of World Politics', *Foreign Affairs*, September/October 1998.

Gallie, W.B., *Philosophers of Peace and War: Kant, Clausewitz, Marx, Engels and Tolstoy* (Cambridge: Cambridge University Press, 1978).

Galtung, Johan, 'Violence, Peace, and Peace Research', *Journal of Peace Research*, 6 (3) 1974, pp. 167–91.

Galtung, Johan, 'Security and Positive Peace', in Furio Cerrutti and Rodolfo Ragionieri (eds.), *Rethinking European Security* (London: Crane Russak, 1990).

Galtung, Johan, 'Peace: Negative and Positive', in Nigel Young (ed.), *The Oxford International Encyclopedia of Peace* (Oxford: Oxford University Press, 2010).

Galtung, Johan and Dietrich Fischer, *Galtung: Pioneer of Peace Studies*, Springer Briefs Vol. 5, 2013.

Gartzke, Erik, 'The Capitalist Peace', *American Journal of Political Science*, 51, 2007, pp. 66–191.

Gat, Azar, *Military Thought in the Nineteenth Century* (Oxford: Oxford University Press, 1992).

Gat, Azar, *War in Human Civilization* (Oxford: Oxford University Press, 2006).

Gat, Azar, *The Causes of War and the Spread of Peace* (Oxford: Oxford University Press, 2017).

Gentry, Caron E. and Laura Sjoberg, *Beyond Mothers, Monsters, Whores: Thinking About Women's Violence in Global Politics* (London: Zed Books, 2016).

Gerwith, Alan, *Marsilius of Padua: The Defender of Peace* (New York: Columbia University Press, 1956), vol. 1.

Ghiglieri, Michael, *The Dark Side of Man: Tracing the Origins of Male Violence* (Reading, MA: Perseus, 1999).

Gibson, Ralph and Paul Oldfield, *Sheffield City Battalion* (Barnsley: Pen and Sword Books, 2009).

Gittens, John, *The Glorious Art of Peace* (Oxford: Oxford University Press, 2012).

Glanville, Luke, *Sovereignty and the Responsibility to Protect: A New History* (Chicago, IL: University of Chicago Press, 2013).

Gledhill, John, 'Assessing (In)security After the Arab Spring', *PS: Political Science and Politics*, 46 (4) 2013, pp. 709–15.

Gledhill, John, 'Conclusion: Managing (In)security in Post-Arab Spring Transitions', *PS: Political Science and Politics*, 46 (4) 2013, pp. 736–9.

Glover, Jonathan, *Humanity: A Moral History of the 20th Century* (New Haven, CT: Yale University Press, 1999).

Goertz, Gary, Paul F. Diehl, and Alexandru Balas, *The Puzzle of Peace: The Evolution of Peace in the International System* (Oxford: Oxford University Press, 2016).

Goldstein, Joshua S., *War and Gender: How Gender Shapes the War System and Vice-Versa* (Cambridge: Cambridge University Press, 2003).

Goldstein, Joshua S., *Winning the War on War: The Decline of Armed Conflict Worldwide* (New York: Dutton, 2011).

Goldsworthy, Adrian, *Pax Romana: War, Peace and Conquest in the Roman World* (London: Weidenfeld & Nicolson, 2017).

Goodall, Jane, *The Chimpanzees of Gombe: Patterns of Behavior* (Cambridge, MA: Harvard University Press, 1986).

Goodall, Jane, *Through a Window: My Thirty Years with the Chimpanzees of Gombe* (London: Houghton Mifflin, 2010).

Gopin, Marc, *Between Eden and Armageddon: The Future of World Religions, Violence and Peacemaking* (Oxford: Oxford University Press, 2002).

Gray, John, *Heresies: Against Progress and Other Illusions* (London: Granta, 2005).

Grayling, A.C., *War: An Enquiry* (New Haven, CT: Yale University Press, 2017).

Greenwood, Christopher, 'The Concept of War in Modern International Law', *International and Comparative Law Quarterly*, 36 (2) 1987, pp. 283–306.

Grey, Edward, *Twenty-Five Years, 1892–1916* (London: Frederick A. Stokes, 1922).

Grossman, Dave, *On Killing: The Psychological Cost of Learning to Kill in War and Society*, revised and updated edition (New York: Back Bay Books, 2009).

Gurr, Ted Robert, 'Historical Trends in Violent Crime: A Critical Review of the Evidence', in Michael Tonry and Norval Morris (eds.), *Crime and Justice: An Annual Review of Research*, vol. 3 (Chicago, IL: University of Chicago Press, 1981).

Haas, Richard, *World in Disarray: American Foreign Policy and the Crisis of the Old Order* (New York: Penguin, 2017).

Hadingham, Evan, *Secrets of the Ice Age: The World of the Cave Artists* (New York: Walker, 1979).

Harari, Yuval Noah, *Sapiens: A Brief History of Humankind* (New York: Harper, 2014).

Harari, Yuval Noah, *Homo Deus: A Brief History of Tomorrow* (London: Vintage, 2015).

Harrer, G.A., 'Cicero on Peace and War', *The Classical Journal*, 14 (1) 1918, pp. 26–38.

Harris, Marvin, *Our Kind: Who We Are, Where We Came From, Where We Are Going* (New York: Harper, 1990).

Hassner, Pierre, 'Beyond the Three Traditions: The Philosophy of War and Peace in Historical Perspective', *International Affairs*, 70 (4) 1994, pp. 737–56.

Hathaway, Oona and Scott J. Shapiro, *The Internationalists: And Their Plan to Outlaw War* (London: Penguin, 2017).

Hedges, Chris, *War Is a Force That Gives Us Meaning* (London: Anchor, 2002).

Hegel, G.W.F., *Elements of the Philosophy of Right*, trans. H.B. Nisbet (Cambridge: Cambridge University Press, 1991).

Hinsley, F.H., *Power and the Pursuit of Peace: Theory and Practice in the History of Relations Between States* (Cambridge: Cambridge University Press, 1962).

Hippler, Thomas, *Governing From the Skies: A Global History of Aerial Bombing* (London: Verso, 2017).

Hobbes, Thomas, *Leviathan*, trans. C.B. Macpherson (London: Penguin, 1982).

Hochschild, Adam, *To End All Wars: A Story of Protest and Patriotism in the First World War* (London: Macmillan, 2011).

Hollander, Neil, *Elusive Dove: The Search for Peace in World War I* (Jefferson, NC: McFarland and Co., 2013).

Holmes, Richard, *Acts of War: The Behaviour of Men in Battle* (New York: Simon & Schuster, 1989).

Holsti, Ole R. and James Rosenau, 'Gender and the Political Beliefs of American Opinion Leaders', *Journal of Conflict Resolution*, 32 (2) 1988, pp. 248–94.

Hook, Sidney, *The Hero in History: A Study in Limitation and Possibility* (New York: John Day, 1943).

Horgan, John, *The End of War* (San Francisco, CA: McSweeney's, 2012).

Howard, Michael, *War and the Liberal Conscience* (London: Temple Smith, 1978).

Howard, Michael, *The Causes of War* (Cambridge, MA: Harvard University Press, 1983).

Howard, Michael, *The Invention of Peace* (New Haven, CT: Yale University Press, 2000).

Howard, Michael, *War in European History*, updated edition (Oxford: Oxford University Press, 2009).

Howell, Signe and Roy G. Willis, 'Introduction', in Signe Howell and Roy G. Willis (eds.), *Societies at Peace: Anthropological Perspectives* (New York: Routledge, 1989).

Hudson, Valerie, Bonnie Ballif-Spanvill, Mary Caprioli, and Chad F. Emmett, *Sex and World Peace* (New York: Columbia University Press, 2014).

Hultman, Lisa, 'UN Peace Operations and Protection of Civilians: Cheap Talk or Norm Implementation?', *Journal of Peace Research*, 50 (1) 2013, pp. 59–73.

Hume, David, *An Enquiry Concerning the Principle of Morals* (Cambridge, MA: Hackett Publishing, 1983 [1751]).

Hume, David, 'Of National Characters', in Eugene F. Miller (ed.), *Essays Moral, Political and Literary* (Indianapolis, IN: Liberty Fund, 1985).

Hume, David, *A Treatise on Human Nature*, edited by Ernest Mossner (London: Penguin, 1986 [1740]).

Hunt, Lynn T., *Inventing Human Rights: A History* (London: W. W. Norton and Co., 2007).

Hunt, Terry and Carl Lippo, *The Statues That Walked: Unravelling the Mystery of Easter Island* (New York: Counterpoint, 2012).

Hutchinson, John, *Nationalism and War* (Oxford: Oxford University Press, 2017).

Huxley, Thomas Henry, 'The Struggle for Existence: A Programme', *Popular Science Monthly*, 32, April 1888.

Ignatieff, Michael, *The Ordinary Virtues: Moral Order in a Divided World* (Cambridge, MA: Harvard University Press, 2017).

Jacoby, Russell, *Bloodlust: On the Roots of Violence from Cain and Abel to the Present* (New York: Free Press, 2011).

James, William, 'The Moral Equivalent of War [1910]', in Leon Branson and George W. Goethals (eds.), *War: Studies from Psychology, Sociology, Anthropology* (New York: Basic Books, 1964).

Jenkins, K. Neil, Nick Megoran, Rachel Woodward, and Daniel Bos, 'Wootton Bassett and the Political Spaces of Remembrance and Mourning', *Areas*, 44 (3) 2012, pp. 356–63.

Johnson, Emily Cooper (ed.), *Jane Addams: A Centennial Reader* (New York: Macmillan, 1960).

Johnson, James Turner, *The Quest for Peace: Three Moral Traditions in Western Cultural History* (Princeton, NJ: Princeton University Press, 1987).

Joll, James and Gordon Martell, *Origins of the First World War* (London: Routledge, 2006).

Jones, Adam, *Genocide: A Comprehensive Introduction* (London: Routledge, 2017).

Junger, Ernst, *Storm of Steel* (London: Penguin, 2004).

Kagan, Donald, *On the Origins of War and the Preservation of Peace* (New York: Anchor, 1995).

Kaldor, Mary, *Global Civil Society: An Answer to War* (Cambridge: Polity, 2003).

Kant, Immanuel, *Perpetual Peace* (Cambridge, MA: Hackett, 1983).

Kapossy, Bela, Isaac Nakhimovsky, and Richard Whatmore, *Commerce and Peace in the Enlightenment* (Cambridge: Cambridge University Press, 2017).

Kathman, Jacob D., 'Civil War Contagion and Neighboring Intervention', *International Studies Quarterly*, 54 (4) 2010, pp. 989–1012.

Kaysen, Carl, 'Is War Obsolete?', *International Security*, 14 (4) 1990, pp. 42–64.

Keegan, John, *A History of Warfare* (New York: Vintage, 1994).

Keegan, John, *War and Our World* (London: Pimlico, 1999).

Keeley, Lawrence H., *War Before Civilization: The Myth of the Peaceful Savage* (New York: Oxford University Press, 1997).

Keeley, Lawrence, 'Giving War a Chance', in S. Rice and S. LeBlanc (eds.), *Deadly Landscapes: Case Studies in Prehistoric Southwestern Warfare* (Salt Lake City, UT: University of Utah Press, 2001).

Kelly, Raymond C., *Warless Societies and the Origin of War* (Ann Arbor, MI: University of Michigan Press, 2000).

Kelly, Robert C., 'From the Peaceful to the Warlike: Ethnographic and Archaeological Insights into Hunter-Gatherer Warfare and Homicide', in Douglas P. Fry, *Beyond War: The Human Potential for Peace* (Oxford: Oxford University Press, 2006).

Kennedy, John F., 'Commencement Address at the American University', 10 June 1963, John F. Kennedy Presidential Library and Museum, accession no. TNC: 319.

Kiernan, Ben, *Blood and Soil: A World History of Genocide and Extermination From Sparta to Darfur* (New Haven, CT: Yale University Press, 2007).

Knauft, Bruce M., 'Culture and Cooperation in Human Evolution', in Leslie E. Sponsel and Thomas Gregor (eds.), *The Anthropology of Peace and Nonviolence* (Boulder, CO: Lynne Rienner, 1994).

Kropotkin, Peter, *Mutual Aid: A Factor of Evolution* (New York: Dover, 2009 [1902]).

Kupchan, Charles A., *How Enemies Become Friends: The Sources of Stable Peace* (Princeton, NJ: Princeton University Press, 2010).

Kuper, Leo, *Genocide: Its Political Use in the Twentieth Century* (New Haven, CT: Yale University Press, 1982).

Leader Maynard, John, 'Rethinking the Role of Ideology in Mass Atrocities', *Terrorism and Political Violence*, 26 (5) 2014, pp. 821–41.

Lemke, Douglas, *Regions of War and Peace* (Cambridge: Cambridge University Press, 2002).

Leroi-Gourhan, A., *Le Geste et la Parole, Vol. 2: La Mémoire et les Rythmes* (Paris: Albin Michel, 1965).

Levene, Mark, *Genocide in the Age of the Nation State, Vol. 2—The Rise of the West and the Coming of Genocide* (London: I. B. Tauris, 2005).

Lévi-Strauss, Claude, *Structural Anthropology* (New York: Doubleday, 1963).

Locke, John, *Two Treatises on Government* (1690), reproduced in Michael L. Morgan (ed.), *Classics of Moral and Political Theory* (Indianapolis, IN: Hackett, 2011, fifth edition), pp. 705–69.

Loescher, Gil, Alexander Betts, and James Milner, *The United Nations High Commissioner for Refugees (UNHCR): The Politics and Practice of Refugee Protection into the Twenty-First Century* (London: Routledge, 2008).

Lorenz, Konrad, *On Aggression*, trans. M. Wilson (London: Methuen and Co., 1966).

Lounsbery, Marie Olsen and Frederic Pearson, *Civil Wars: Internal Struggles, Global Consequences* (Toronto: University of Toronto Press, 2009).

Lowe, Vaughn, Adam Roberts, Jennifer Welsh, and Dominik Zaum, 'Introduction', in Vaughn Lowe, Adam Roberts, Jennifer Welsh, and Dominik Zaum (eds.), *The United Nations Security Council and War: The Evolution of Thought and Practice since 1945* (Oxford: Oxford University Press, 2008).

Luck, Edward C., *United Nations Security Council: Practice and Promise* (London: Routledge, 2008).

Mac Ginty, Roger, 'Everyday Peace: Bottom-Up and Local Agency in Conflict-Affected Societies', *Security Dialogue*, 45 (6) 2014, pp. 548–64.

Mac Ginty, Roger and Pamina Firchow, 'Top-Down and Bottom-Up Narratives of Peace and Conflict', *Politics*, 36 (3) 2016, pp. 308–23.

MacMillan, Margaret, *The War That Ended Peace: How Europe Abandoned Peace for the First World War* (London: Profile Books, 2013).

MacMillan, Margaret, '1914 and 2014: Should We Be Worried?', *International Affairs*, 90 (1) 2014, pp. 59–70.

MacMillan, Margaret, 'It Would Be Stupid to Think We Have Moved on From War: Look Around', *The Guardian*, 24 June 2018.

Malesevic, Sinisa, *The Rise of Organized Brutality: A Historical Sociology of Violence* (Cambridge: Cambridge University Press, 2017).

Mandelbaum, Michael, *The Rise and Fall of Peace on Earth* (Oxford: Oxford University Press, 2019).

Mann, Michael, *The Sources of Social Power: Volume 1* (Cambridge: Cambridge University Press, 1986).

Mann, Michael, *The Dark Side of Democracy: Explaining Ethnic Cleansing* (Cambridge: Cambridge University Press, 2009).

Mansfield, Nick, *Theorizing War: From Hobbes to Badiou* (London: Palgrave, 2008).

Marshall, Monty G. and Benjamin R. Cole, *Global Report 2014: Conflict, Governance and State Fragility* (Vienna, VA: Center for Systemic Peace, 2014).

Marshall, Tim, *Worth Dying For: The Power and Politics of Flags* (London: Elliott and Thompson, 2016).

Martin, Mike, *Why We Fight* (London: Hurst, 2018).

May, Larry, *Contingent Pacifism: Revisiting Just War Theory* (Cambridge: Cambridge University Press, 2015).

Mazower, Mark, *Governing the World: The History of an Idea* (New York: Allen Lane, 2012).

McDonald, Patrick J., *The Invisible Hand of Peace: Capitalism, the War Machine and International Relations Theory* (Cambridge: Cambridge University Press, 2009).

McIntosh, Jane R., *A Peaceful Realm: The Rise and Fall of the Indus Civilization* (Boulder, CO: Westview, 2002).

Mead, Margaret, *Coming of Age in Samoa* (New York: William Morrow and Co., 1928).

Mead, Margaret, 'War Is Only an Invention—Not a Biological Necessity', in Richard K. Betts (ed.), *Conflict after the Cold War: Arguments on the Causes of War and Peace* (Boston, MA: Pearson, 4th edition, 2013).

Meggitt, Mervyn, *Desert People: A Study of the Walbiri Aboriginals of Central Australia* (Chicago, IL: University of Chicago Press, 1965).

Melander, Erik, 'Gender Equality and Intrastate Armed Conflict', *International Studies Quarterly*, 49 (4) 2005, pp. 695–714.

Melander, Erik, Therese Pettersson, and Lotta Themner, 'Organised Violence, 1989–2015', *Journal of Peace Research*, 53 (5) 2016, pp. 727–42.

Mishra, Pankaj, *Age of Anger: A History of the Present* (New York: Farrar, Straus & Giroux, 2017).

Mitrany, David, *A Working Peace System* (New York: Quadrangle, 1966 [1943]).

Montagu, Ashley (ed.), *Men and Aggression* (New York: Oxford University Press, 1973).

Morgenthau, Hans J., *Peace, Security, and the United Nations* (Chicago, IL: University of Chicago Press, 1946).

Morgenthau, Hans J., *Politics Among Nations: The Struggle for Power and Peace* (New York: Knopf, 1985 [first published 1948]).

Morris, Ian, *War: What Is It Good For? The Role of Conflict in Civilization from Primates to Robots* (London: Profile Books, 2014).

Mosse, George, *Fallen Soldiers: Shaping the Memory of the World Wars* (Oxford: Oxford University Press, 1990).

Mowat, R.C., *Creating the European Community* (New York: Barnes and Noble, 1973).

Muchembled, Robert, *A History of Violence* (Oxford: Polity, 2012).

Mueller, John, *The Remnants of War* (Ithaca, NY: Cornell University Press, 2007).

Mueller, John, *Atomic Obsession: Nuclear Alarmism from Hiroshima to Al Qaeda* (Oxford: Oxford University Press, 2010).

Mulligan, William, *The Great War for Peace* (New Haven, CT: Yale University Press, 2014).

Nabulsi, Karma, *Traditions of War: Occupation, Resistance, and the Law* (Oxford: Oxford University Press, 1999).

Nagel, Thomas, 'The Problem of Global Justice', *Philosophy and Public Affairs*, 33 (2) 2005, pp. 113–47.

Neal, Toby, 'Seasons Over the Decades, 1914', *Shropshire Star*, 26 December 2014.

Nietzsche, Friedrich, *On the Genealogy of Morals*, Keith Ansell-Pearson (ed.), Carol Diethe (trans.) (Cambridge: Cambridge University Press, 1997 [1887]).

Nolan, Cathal J., *The Allure of Battle: A History of How Wars Have Been Won and Lost* (Oxford: Oxford University Press, 2017).

Obama, Barack, 'A Just and Lasting Peace', Nobel Lecture delivered by President Barack Obama, Oslo, 10 December 2009.

OCHA, *Global Humanitarian Overview 2016* (Geneva: OCHA, 2016).

O'Connell, Robert L., *Ride of the Second Horseman: The Birth and Death of War* (Oxford: Oxford University Press, 1999).

O'Hanlon, Michael and Peter W. Singer, 'The Humanitarian Transformation: Expanding Global Intervention Capacity', *Survival*, 46 (1) 2004, pp. 77–100.

Oppenheim, Lassa, *International Law: A Treatise*, Vol. 2, *War and Neutrality* (London: Longmans, Green and Co., 1906).

Orwell, George, *Homage to Catalonia* (London: Penguin, 1962 [1938]).

Orwell, George, *The Lion and the Unicorn: Socialism and the English Genius* (London: Penguin, 1970 [1941]).

Otterbein, Keith and Charlotte Otterbein, 'An Eye for an Eye, a Tooth for a Tooth: A Cross-Cultural Study of Feuding', *American Anthropologist*, 70, 1968, pp. 277–89.

Pagden, Anthony, *The Enlightenment and Why It Still Matters* (Oxford: Oxford University Press, 2015).

Paine, Thomas, 'Rights of Man', in Philip S. Foner (ed.), *Complete Writings of Thomas Paine* (New York: Citadel Press, 1945), vol. 1.

Pankhurst, Christabel, 'No Compromise Peace', *Britannia*, 3 August 1917, p. 72.

Pascoe, Bruce, *Dark Emu: Aboriginal Australia and the Birth of Agriculture* (Melbourne: Scribe, 2018).

Pim, Joam Evans, 'Man the Singer: Song Duels as an Aggression Restraint Mechanism for Nonkilling Conflict Management', in Douglas P. Fry (ed.), *War, Peace, and Human Nature: The Convergence of Evolutionary and Cultural Views* (Oxford: Oxford University Press, 2013).

Pinker, Stephen, *The Better Angels of Our Nature: A History of Violence and Humanity* (London: Penguin, 2012).

Proudhon, Jean-Pierre, *La Guerre et la Paix: Recherches sur la principe et la constitution du droit des gens* (Paris: Hachette Livre, 2016 [1861]).

Prunier, Gerard, *Darfur: The Ambiguous Genocide* (London: Hirst, 2005).

Purvis, June, *Emmeline Pankhurst: A Biography* (London: Routledge, 2002).

Raaflaub, Kurt A., 'Introduction: Searching for Peace in the Ancient World', in Kurt A. Raaflaub (ed.), *War and Peace in the Ancient World* (Oxford: Blackwell, 2007).

Raaflaub, Kurt A., 'Greek Concepts and Theories of Peace', in Kurt A. Raaflaub (ed.), *Peace in the Ancient World: Concepts and Theories* (Oxford: John Wiley, 2016).

Ravenhill, John, 'Production Networks in Asia', in Saadia Pekkanen, John Ravenhill, and Rosemary Foot (eds.), *The Oxford Handbook of the International Relations of Asia* (Oxford: Oxford University Press, 2014).

Reardon, Betty A., *Sexism and the War System* (Syracuse, NY: Syracuse University Press, 1996).

Regehr, Ernie, *Disarming Conflict* (London: Zed, 2015).

Reiss, H.S. (ed.), *Kant: Political Writings* (Cambridge: Cambridge University Press, 1970).

Richmond, Oliver P., *Peace: A Very Short Introduction* (Oxford: Oxford University Press, 2014).

Ridley, Matt, *The Origins of Virtue* (London: Viking, 1996).

Rieff, David, *In Praise of Forgetting: Historical Memory and Its Ironies* (New Haven, CT: Yale University Press, 2017).

Robinson, Annabel, *The Life and Work of Jane Ellen Harrison* (Oxford: Oxford University Press, 2002).

Rosecrance, Richard, *The Rise of the Trading State: Commerce and Conquest in the Modern World* (New York: Basic Books, 1986).

Rossiter, Mike, *Sink the Belgrano* (London: Corgi, 2008).

Rummel, R.J., 'Is Collective Violence Correlated with Social Pluralism?', *Journal of Peace Research*, 34 (1) 1997, pp. 163–75.

Russell, Bertrand, 'Has Religion Made Useful Contributions to Civilization?', 1930, available at http://www.update.uu.se/~fbendz/library/has_reli.htm.

Russell, Bertrand, 'Some Psychological Difficulties of Pacifism in Wartime', in Julian Bell (ed.), *We Did Not Fight: 1914–1918 Experiences of War Resisters* (London: Cobden-Sanderson, 1935).

Schabas, William, *Unimaginable Atrocities: Justice, Politics and Rights at the War Crimes Tribunals* (Oxford: Oxford University Press, 2012).

Scheidel, Walter, *The Great Leveler: Violence and the History of Inequality from the Stone Age to the Twenty-First Century* (Princeton, NJ: Princeton University Press, 2017).

Scott, James C., *Against the Grain: A Deep History of the Earliest States* (New Haven, CT: Yale University Press, 2017).

Scott Appleby, R., *The Ambivalence of the Sacred: Religion, Violence and Reconciliation* (Lanham, MD: Rowman & Littlefield, 1999).

Scott Bennett, D. and Allan C. Stam, *The Behavioural Origins of War* (Ann Arbor, MI: University of Michigan Press, 2004).

Sellars, Kirsten, *'Crimes Against Peace' and International Law* (Cambridge: Cambridge University Press, 2013).

Sen, Amartya, *Identity and Violence: The Illusion of Destiny* (London: Penguin, 2006).

Sen, Amartya, *The Idea of Justice* (New York: Allen Lane, 2009).

Shankman, Paul, *The Trashing of Margaret Mead: Anatomy of an Anthropological Controversy* (Madison, WI: University of Wisconsin Press, 2009).

Sharman, J.C., *A Global Military Revolution? War, European Expansion and the Making of the Modern International System* (Cambridge: Cambridge University Press, 2018).

Shaw, R.P. and Yuwa Wong, *Genetic Seeds of Warfare: Evolution, Nationalism and Patriotism* (Boston, MA: Unwin Hyman, 1989).

Sheffield, Gary, *Douglas Haig: From the Somme to Victory* (London: Aurum Press, 2016).

Shue, Henry, *Basic Rights: Subsistence, Affluence and US Foreign Policy*, 2nd edition (Princeton, NJ: Princeton University Press, 1996).

Shute, John, 'The Forgotten Christmas Truce the British Tried to Suppress', *The Telegraph*, 26 December 2016.

Siedentop, Larry, *Inventing the Individual: The Origins of Western Liberalism* (London: Penguin, 2014).

Slessor, John, *The Central Blue: Recollections and Reflections* (London: Cassell, 1956).

Sloan-Wilson, David, *Darwin's Cathedral: Evolution, Religion and the Nature of Society* (Chicago, IL: University of Chicago Press, 2007).

Smith, Adam, *The Theory of Moral Sentiments* (London: Penguin, 2010 [1759]).

Smith, John Maynard, *The Theory of Evolution*, 3rd edition (London: Penguin, 1975).

Smith, Rupert, *The Utility of Force: The Art of War in the Modern World* (London: Penguin, 2006).

Solingen, Etel, *Regional Orders: At Century's Dawn: Global and Domestic Influences on Grand Strategy* (Princeton, NJ: Princeton University Press, 1998).

Solingen, Etel, 'Internationalization, Coalitions and Regional Conflict and Cooperation', in Edward D. Mansfield and Brian M. Pollins (eds.), *Economic Interdependence and International Conflict: New Perspectives on an Enduring Debate* (Ann Arbor, MI: University of Michigan Press, 2003).

Solingen, Etel, 'Pax Asiatica versus Belli Levantina: The Foundations of War and Peace in East Asia and the Middle East', *American Political Science Review*, 101 (4) 2007, pp. 757–80.

Sontag, Susan, *Regarding the Pain of Others* (London: Picador, 2004).

Sontag, Susan, *At the Same Time* (London: Penguin, 2007).

Spector, Céline, 'Who Is the Author of the Abstract of Monsieur l'Abbé de Saint-Pierre's "Plan for Perpetual Peace"? From Saint-Pierre to Rousseau', *History of European Ideas*, 39 (3) 2013, pp. 371–93.

Spence, Jonathan D., *The Memory Palace of Matteo Ricci* (New York: Penguin, 1985).

Stagneth, Bettina, *Eichmann Before Jerusalem* (New York: Alfred Knopf, 2014).

Stearns, Peter N., *Peace in World History* (London: Routledge, 2014).

Stewart, Frances (ed.), *Horizontal Inequalities and Conflict: Understanding Group Violence in Multiethnic Societies* (London: Palgrave, 2008).

Stoessinger, John, *Why Nations Go to War* (New York: St. Martin's Press, 1997).

Strachan, Hew, *The Direction of War: Contemporary Strategy in Historical Perspective* (Cambridge: Cambridge University Press, 2013).

Stromberg, Roland, *Redemption by War: The Intellectuals and 1914* (Lawrence, KS: University of Kansas Press, 1982).

Stuurman, Siep, *The Invention of Humanity: Equality and Cultural Difference in World History* (Cambridge, MA: Harvard University Press, 2017).

Sumner, William, *Folkways: A Study of the Sociological Importance of Usages, Manners, Customs, Mores, and Morals* (Boston, MA: Gin and Co., 1906).

Sumner, William Graham, 'War' [1903], in *War and Other Essays* (New Haven, CT: Yale University Press, 1919).

Supino, Phillip, 'The Norman Angell Peace Campaign in Germany', *Journal of Peace Research*, 9 (9) 1972, pp. 161–4.

Swain, Tony, *A Place for Strangers* (New York: Cambridge University Press, 1993).

Thapar, Romila, *Asoka and the Decline of the Mauryas* (Oxford: Oxford University Press, 1961).

Tharoor, Shashi, *Inglorious Empire: What the British Did to India* (London: C. Hurst and Co., 2017).

'The Peace Endowment of Mr Carnegie', *American Journal of International Law*, 5 (1) 1911, pp. 210–14.

Thucydides, *History of the Peloponnesian War*, trans. Rex Warner (London: Penguin, 1974).

Tilly, Charles, *The Formation of National States in Western Europe* (Princeton, NJ: Princeton University Press, 1975).

Tilly, Charles, 'War Making and State Making as Organized Crime', in Peter Evans, Dietrich Reuschemeyer, and Theda Skocpol (eds.), *Bringing the State Back In* (Cambridge: Cambridge University Press, 1985).

Tilly, Charles, *Coercion, Capital and European States, AD 990–1990* (Oxford: Blackwell, 1992).

Tolstoy, Leo, *The Kingdom of God Is Within You* (London: Dover, 2006 [1894]).

Tolstoy, Leo, *War and Peace* (London: Penguin, 2008 [1869]).

Tomlinson, Robert, 'Social Control and Conflict Management Among Australian Aboriginal Desert People Before and After the Advent of Alcohol', in Douglas P. Fry (ed.), *War, Peace, and Human Nature: The Convergence of Evolutionary and Cultural Views* (Oxford: Oxford University Press, 2013).

Tuchman, Barbara W., *The Guns of August* (New York: Ballentine, 1962).

Tuchman, Barbara W., *The Proud Tower: A Portrait of the World Before the War: 1890–1914* (New York: Macmillan, 1966).

UNHCR, *Global Trends: Forced Displacement in 2014* (Geneva: UNHCR, 2016).

Van Creveld, Martin, *The Transformation of War* (New York: Free Press, 1991).

Van Creveld, Martin, *More on War* (Oxford: Oxford University Press, 2017).

Vico, Giambattista, 'New Science', in Giambattista Vico, *Vico: Selected Writings*, edited and trans. Leon Pompa (Cambridge: Cambridge University Press, 1982).

Vitoria, Francisco de, 'On the Law of War', in Anthony Pagden and Jeremy Lawrence (eds.), *Vitoria: Political Writings* (Cambridge: Cambridge University Press, 1991).

Von Bernhardi, Friedreich, *Germany and the Next War* (London: Edward Arnold, 1912).

Von Einseidel, Sebastian, 'Civil War Trends and the Changing Nature of Armed Conflict', United Nations University Centre for Policy Research, Occasional Paper No. 10, March 2017.

Von Pufendorf, Samuel, *Of the Law of Nature and Nations*, trans. Basil Kennet (London: Carew, 1729).

Wæver, Ole, 'Insecurity, Security and Asecurity in the West European Non-War Community', in Emanuel Adler and Michael Barnett (eds.), *Security Communities* (Cambridge: Cambridge University Press, 1998).

Wallensteen, Peter, *Quality Peace: Peacebuilding, Victory and World Order* (Oxford: Oxford University Press, 2015).

Walzer, Michael, *Just and Unjust Wars: A Moral Argument with Historical Illustrations* (New York: Basic Books, 1977).

Watts, Steven, *The People's Tycoon: Henry Ford and the American Century* (New York: Alfred Knopf, 2014).

Weaver, John, *A Sadly Troubled History: The Meanings of Suicide in the Modern Age* (Montreal-Kingston: McGill-Queen's University Press, 2009).

Weber, Max, 'Politics as a Vocation', lecture given in Munich, 28 January 1919, available at http://anthropos-lab.net/wp/wp-content/uploads/2011/12/Weber-Politics-as-a-Vocation.pdf.

Weintraub, Stanley, *Silent Night: The Remarkable Christmas Truce of 1914* (London: Simon & Schuster, 2001).

Weiss, Thomas G., *What's Wrong with the UN and How to Fix It?* (Cambridge: Polity, 2013).

Wells, H.G., *Anticipations of the Reaction of Mechanical and Scientific Progress upon Human Life and Thought* (London: Chapman and Hall, 1902).

Welsh, Jennifer, *The Return of History: Conflict, Migration and Geopolitics in the Twenty-First Century* (Toronto: House of Anansi Press, 2017).

Wendorf, Fred, *The Prehistory of Nubia* (Dallas, TX: Southern Methodist University Press, 1968).

Wheeler, Gerald, *The Tribe, and Intertribal Relations in Australia* (London: John Murray, 1910).

Wilkinson, Glenn R., *Depictions and Images of War in Edwardian Newspapers, 1899–1914* (London: Palgrave, 2003).

Williams, Paul D., *War and Conflict in Africa*, 2nd edition (Cambridge: Polity, 2017).

Winter, Jay, *Dreams of Peace and Freedom: Utopian Moments in the 20th Century* (New Haven, CT: Yale University Press, 2006).

Winter, Jay M., 'Notes on the Memory Boom: War Remembrance and the Use of the Past', in Duncan Bell (ed.), *Memory, Trauma and World Politics: Reflections on the Relationship Between Past and Present* (London: Palgrave, 2006).

Wistrich, Ernest, *After 1992: The United States of Europe* (London: Routledge, 1991).

Woolf, Virginia, *Three Guineas* (San Diego, CA: Mariner, 1963 [1938]).

Wrangham, Richard and Dale Peterson, *Demonic Males: Apes and the Origin of Human Violence* (Boston, MA: Houghton Mifflin, 1996).

Wright, Quincy, *Study of War* (Chicago, IL: University of Chicago Press, 1964).

Zakaria, Fareed and Niall Ferguson, *The End of the Liberal Order?* (London: Oneworld, 2017).

Zampaglione, Gerardo, *The Idea of Peace in Antiquity*, trans. Richard Dunne (Notre Dame, IN: University of Notre Dame Press, 1967).

Zegveld, Liesbeth and Frits Kalshoven, *Constraints on the Waging of War: An Introduction to International Humanitarian Law*, 4th edition (Cambridge: Cambridge University Press, 2015).

Zimbardo, Philip, *The Lucifer Effect: How Good People Turn Evil* (London: Rider, 2007).

Zimmern, Alfred, 'Organize the Peace World!', *The Political Quarterly*, 5 (2) 1934, pp. 153–66.

Zweig, Stefan, *The World of Yesterday* (Lincoln, NE: University of Nebraska Press, 1964).

INDEX